OLD SOUTH, NEW SOUTH, NO SOUTH

A COLLECTION OF SHORT PLAYS

David J. Holcombe

authorHOUSE®

AuthorHouse™
1663 Liberty Drive
Bloomington, IN 47403
www.authorhouse.com
Phone: 1-800-839-8640

Published by AuthorHouse   01/18/2013

ISBN: 978-1-4817-0470-0 (sc)
ISBN: 978-1-4817-0469-4 (e)

ACKNOWLEDGEMENT & DISCLAIMER

"Old South, New South, No South" expands on material presented in *"Beauty and the Botox,"* published in 2011. The play format allows the development of characters and dramatic situations without indulging in the necessity of expository writing. The characters literally speak for themselves, in voices as diverse as their backgrounds and origins.

Some of these plays follow the traditional ten-minute structure, but others are combinations of short plays and still others are much longer multiple-scene works. The subject matter varies from race relations, to gay marriage, to the complexities of end of life issues in the medical setting. Although several plays have medical characters and deal with medical subject matter, most of the works are non-medical and all are very accessible to the layperson.

These plays have been the product of a long period of thought and writing, extending back almost twenty years. Spectral Sisters Productions, one of our local theater groups, has been instrumental in organizing a Ten Minute Play Festival. That Festival stimulates local authors, including myself, and provides an opportunity for growth and professional enhancement. Contributing play writing workshop instructors have included Doug Rand, Rosary O'Neill, Rachel Ladutke, Diane Glancey, Colin Denby Swanson, Steve Barton, William Griffin and others. The Writers Guild of Central Louisiana has also provided a venue to read and discuss works in progress. Many helpful suggestions have come from the participants of that group, some of whom are professional writers, including Emilie Griffin.

Although these plays might never attain the perfection and longevity of those of Dr. Anton Chekhov, his works nonetheless remain a constant inspiration to any physician writer. His profound knowledge of human nature, psychology and the art of theater all combine to make him unparalleled among anyone interested in the stage, especially any doctor-writer.

As with all previous works, the characters and events portrayed here may bear a vague resemblance to real people and circumstances. Any such resemblance is strictly accidental. I would like to thank, however, anyone who has unintentionally provided inspiration for these plays. And, of course, none of this could have been accomplished without the constant vigilant support and organizational skills of my lovely wife, Nicole. Only a saint could have put up with my literary aspirations and Renaissance pretensions.

David J. Holcombe, MD, MSA
September 2012

Contents

BURYING BARBIE

CAST OF CHARACTERS

HEATHER: Daniel's older sister, perhaps 16 or so. (This character can be played by an adult who acts in a child-like fashion.)

DANIEL: Heather's younger brother, a boy around 13 years old. (This character can also be played by an adult. The actor would simply make it clear he is playing a young adolescent.)

SETTING

The set is stark. Daniel has made a sarcophagus of wood about the size of a fruit crate. It can be simple wood, or decorated with various symbols: Egyptian, Mayan, Christian or others. The box is sitting on the stage and is brightly illuminated. There is also a piece of brown cloth that represents dirt. It is used to cover the box at the end of the play.

(*DANIEL is holding a Barbie doll, which he is wrapping in strips of cloth, either gauze or plain cotton. A shovel is sitting on the ground next to him. HEATHER sneaks up from behind and surprises DANIEL.*)

HEATHER: (*Yelling.*) What are you doing?

DANIEL: (*Stops and tries to hide the partially wrapped Barbie doll behind his back.*) Nothing!

HEATHER: That's not true. I can see you're doing something. (*Tries to yank the doll away from DANIEL.*)

DANIEL: NO!

(*DANIEL and HEATHER struggle until she finally succeeds in snatching the doll from behind his back.*)

HEATHER: (*Holds the doll up in triumph.*) Got it! (*Partially unwraps the doll.*) It's my Barbie.

DANIEL: No it's not.

HEATHER: Of course it is. (*Unwraps the doll, which is now naked.*) It's naked! (*Turns to DANIEL.*) What were you doing, you little pervert?

DANIEL: Nothing. (*Tries to hide the sarcophagus.*)

HEATHER: (*Pushes him aside and looks at the box.*) It's a coffin.

DANIEL: No, it's not. It's a sarcophagus.

HEATHER: (*Looks at the shovel lying nearby.*) You were going to bury Barbie, weren't you? You are a pervert!

DANIEL: (*Quietly.*) Yes, I was. But I'm not a pervert.

HEATHER: Yes you are! You're thirteen years old and you still play with dolls with the girls instead of football with the boys. And now this! What on earth were you trying to accomplish?

DANIEL: Nothing. It was just an experiment. I wanted to bury Barbie and then dig her up in a few years when I was older and see what happened to her.

HEATHER: (*Laughs.*) What do you think is going to happen? She's made out of plastic. She'll be here in a thousand years when all of us are dead and gone. (*Pauses.*) You're ridiculous!

DANIEL: No more ridiculous than you dressing in boy's clothing.

HEATHER: That's crazy. What are you talking about, anyway?

DANIEL: I've seen you. Not just in jeans and that sort of thing, but in this, too! (*Reaches in the box and pulls out a jock strap.*) What does

3

a normal sixteen year old girl need with a jock strap? Tell me that if you're so smart!

HEATHER: You're lying. You have never seen me put that thing on.

DANIEL: (*Waving the jock strap around.*) Oh yes I have! And that's not all. (*Pulls a football jersey out of the box.*) What about this thing? A guy's football jersey. (*Pauses.*) A week ago when you thought I was asleep, I came downstairs and saw you parading around in your jock strap and your football jersey. That's all. Nothing else. Just those two things. (*Pauses.*) Oh yes, and a banana in the jock strap, of course. (*Pulls a plastic banana from the box.*) Mustn't forget the crowning touch, the plastic banana.

HEATHER: You're lying, you perverted little creep. (*Knocks the objects out of DANIEL's hands. Lunges at him and starts to strangle him.*)

DANIEL: (*Choking but still talking.*) It's true and you know it.

> (*DANIEL Struggles with her and manages to break free. HEATHER chases DANIEL around the box a few times before HEATHER stops and sits down next to the box.*)

HEATHER: (*Starts to whimper.*) Don't tell anyone, please don't tell anyone. The girls at school would destroy me. It could be on Facebook in a matter ten minutes.

DANIEL: That long? I'd say more like three.

HEATHER: Please don't tell anyone, I beg you!

DANIEL: Why should I? Unless, of course, you tell anyone about me burying Barbie. The guys at school might find it a bit bizarre, too. (*Sits down next to HEATHER.*) That's okay. I'm not going to tell anyone about you and the jock strap. You're my sister after all and I don't want to hurt you, at least not on purpose.

HEATHER: Thank you. (*Pauses.*) I won't say anything about Barbie. (*Hands him back the doll.*) Here, do what you want with her.

DANIEL: (*Takes Barbie.*) Don't you want her back?

HEATHER: No. I don't play with dolls much anymore. Go ahead and bury her if you want. (*Pauses.*) But it won't work.

DANIEL: What do you mean?

HEATHER: It's just like that jock strap and jersey. I could bury them, too, but it won't make any difference.

DANIEL: Difference to what?

HEATHER: (*Points to her head.*) These thoughts. (*Points to her heart.*) These feelings.

DANIEL: What feelings?

HEATHER: (*Looks at DANIEL.*) I like girls.

DANIEL: So?

HEATHER: I mean more than just as friends. (*Pauses.*) I want to kiss them and play with their private parts.

DANIEL: Really? And you're calling me a pervert?

HEATHER: (*Sighs.*) Life's full of contradictions. (*Pauses.*) And you? What's up with Barbie? You don't want to play with dolls anymore, do you? Even Ken? Although it doesn't look like you're burying Ken. And there's plenty of room in that box for two.

DANIEL: What's that supposed to mean?

HEATHER: I mean don't you sometimes want to kiss boys and play with their dicks? (*Pauses.*) Don't you sometimes think about their private parts all stiff and pulsating and imagine them deep inside you? (*Looks at DANIEL.*) You're young, but thirteen isn't that young.

DANIEL: NO! I don't want to do any of that! I've never thought about any of that.

HEATHER: Have you ever noticed Rob Grossman's big penis when he wears those tight gym short? His hairy armpits? His facial hair? Have you ever noticed that little tuff of black hair on his chest?

DANIEL: (*Shrugs his shoulders.*) Sure, so what?

HEATHER: Have you ever dreamed of him naked? Kissing him?

DANIEL: No. That's sick.

HEATHER: Maybe. But I see how you look at him and he even sometimes looks at you in a strange way. I bet he'd like to play with your little weenie and you would even like that a lot, wouldn't you?

DANIEL: (*Stands up.*) Stop it! Shut up! You are perverted!

HEATHER: (*Picks up the jock strap and swings it around.*) I bet Rob fills this up and when his dick gets all stiff and hard, I bet it jumps right out of the top. (*Hands DANIEL the jock strap.*) Here! It's yours. Put it on and rub it against your little weenie and think of Rob.

DANIEL: (*Throws it back into the box.*) No! This is wrong. This is sick. You're just talking filth.

HEATHER: (*Confronts DANIEL.*) Am I? Tell me I'm lying. Tell me you've never had those thoughts!

DANIEL: I haven't.

HEATHER: Liar! Liar! LIAR!

DANIEL: (*Sits down. Quietly.*) Yes. I have had those thoughts sometimes.

HEATHER: (*Puts her arm around DANIEL.*) It's okay. Everyone does, I think, it's just that some people have stronger thoughts than others.

DANIEL: (*Pushes her arm away.*) You don't know what you're talking about. You're no psychiatrist.

HEATHER: No. I'm not.

DANIEL: (*Jumps up.*) Let's bury it all: Barbie, the jockstrap, the jersey. We need to bury it all now.

HEATHER: Okay, if you want to.

(*DANIEL takes the shovel and begins to mimic frantically digging a hole. HEATHER holds the box and watches him dig.*)

HEATHER: It won't help. You can bury everything, but Barbie will take on a life of her own. And all the pushing and shoving and denying will be like trying to hold back the tide. (*Looks at DANIEL.*) You can't hold back the tide. Trust me, I've tried. It won't work. I even tried to will my periods to stop so I wouldn't grow up. But it didn't work for me and burying Barbie won't work for you either.

DANIEL: Yes it will! I can bury Barbie and all those ideas and feelings will die and shrivel up until nothing is left. It's got to work.

HEATHER: (*Calmly.*) No, it won't. Barbie and everything she means in your little mind will kick and scream in your head until she bursts out like the Second Coming of Christ.

DANIEL: That's blasphemy.

HEATHER: No, it's not. It's true. Barbie will twist and turn and grow and grow in your mind. (*Takes the doll and waves it around DANIEL.*) She's never going to die and she'll never leave you!

DANIEL: Give her to me! (*Grabs the doll and shoves it into the box and closes the top.*) There! She's gone! And all those evil thoughts are gone with her.

7

HEATHER: I wish you were right, little brother. (*Makes the sign of the cross and begins to pray.*) Oh Barbie, blessed are thou among dolls. May your soul rest in peace. May your body wait in anticipation of the Second Coming of Christ when your flesh shall be made incorruptible and you shall rise from the dead. (*Pauses.*) And give peace to your faithful servant, Daniel. May his days and nights be spared from the misery of temptation and may his soul know peace from all anxiety. (*Throws an imaginary clot of earth on the box.*) In the name of the Father, the Son and the Holy Spirit. (*Makes the sign of the cross again.*) Amen.

DANIEL: Rest in peace. (*Covers the box with a piece of brown cloth. Mimics shoveling. Finishes shoveling and shoulders the shovel. Makes the sign of the cross.*)

HEATHER: (*Laughs loudly.*) Let me know when you're ready to let Barbie out. I'll talk to you then, little brother.

(*HEATHER takes DANIEL's free hand and leads him offstage. Lights dim to dark.*)

THE END

ONLY OUR GENES

CAST OF CHARACTERS

CHRIS (OR CHRISTINE): One of the two brothers or sisters. No particular characteristics. He (or she) can be white, black or yellow. If Chris is a girl (Christine), then Aaron needs to be a girl, too, (Andrea). He or she should be casually dressed in jeans.

AARON (OR ANDREA): The other brother (or sister). He or she should be more cocky and self-assured. He or she should be casually dressed in jeans.

SETTING

The set is simple. There should be a table with a big cooking pot in the middle. There are two chairs, one on each side. The brothers (or sisters) are cutting up things to put in the large gumbo pot. Chris has the vegetables and Aaron has the meat. The both have knives (not real ones, please, because they fight with one another.) There should also be a couple of large wooden spoons for stirring. They make references to their brother (or sister) and script changes should reflect that choice.

AARON: No! You can't leave him out of the preparations for the party.

CHRIS: Why not?

AARON: Because he's part of the family. He's our brother, for heaven's sake. And this party is for Dad from his children, all of them.

CHRIS: Well, if he were really part of the family then he would contribute to it.

AARON: Everyone contributes what they can. He just doesn't have the same resources.

CHRIS: Not the same resources! He's squandered everything he's ever gotten by making stupid decisions. Asking him to pitch in anything to this party is useless. Besides, it would be awkward for him.

AARON: Isn't it more awkward leaving him out entirely?

CHRIS: We're not leaving him out. When the gumbo's done and the party's ready, he can come and eat with us like all the other guests.

AARON: That's the point. It's a party for Dad and he's father to all of us, not just you and me. He's our brother, not just another guest.

CHRIS: He can't bring anything! He doesn't have anything to offer. Don't you get it? He just lives off Dad's charity and he squanders that, too. He's worse than a guest, he's a parasite.

AARON: He could cut up vegetables and meat. He could stir the pot. He could send out the invitations. He could set the table. There's a lot he could contribute without buying anything.

CHRIS: Don't be a fool. He has so many problems; he doesn't have the time, the money, or the inclination to add anything to this party.

AARON: Why don't you let him decide?

CHRIS: (*Turns toward AARON in anger.*) Do you really want to sabotage this event? We can do this just fine together, just the two of us. In fact, I could do it myself if I wanted to, and you know that as well as I do. Why transform things into a three ring circus by including our dear loser brother?

AARON: Because the preparations are just as important as the final product. We're the ones who are squandering an opportunity to create some brotherly memories.

CHRIS: For God's sake, stop it with the touchie-feely crap!

AARON: It's not crap! (*Stands up and walks around.*) Bringing people together is essentially moral. Tearing them apart, or keeping them apart (*Points his knife at CHRIS.*) is immoral. (*Pauses.*) We have an opportunity to create some bonding time together. In fact, it's important because we would be joining together people who don't think alike.

CHRIS: (*Interrupting his brother.*) That's sure the truth. Or act alike for that matter.

AARON: (*Continues.*) But that's what's important. If we thought alike, then coming together would just be like bringing together people who belong to the same church or the Klu Klux Klan, for that matter. That's just not as important or as significant as bringing together people who really don't even like each other, especially brothers.

CHRIS: (*Throws down his knife and stands up.*) Would you please spare me your pontification? I get your point. (*Pauses.*) I can already see it. This is supposed to be Dad's party and you somehow manage to monopolize all the attention by giving a speech about the importance of the family. Yes, it's interesting. Yes, it's important. But this party is not about you. It's about Dad. (*Swings his arms around.*) When I talk to Dad, he's already always talking about you. Aaron this, Aaron, that. Don't you think I get tired of hearing all that shit?

AARON: You're jealous, aren't you?

CHRIS: No! I'm disgusted. What do you think it feels like just sitting there and listening to Dad extol your virtues, your accomplishments, your contributions to the world? (*Pauses.*) It's boring! It's frustrating! It's painful!

AARON: (*Walks over to CHRIS.*) We both have the same father. We both have the same needs. We are really both very much alike. (*Reaches out to touch CHRIS.*)

CHRIS: (*Pulls away.*) No! We are not alike. We don't share anything but our genes!

AARON: Jeans? (*Points to his pants.*)

CHRIS: No! Not your pants, our genetic material.

AARON: Oh, those genes. (*Shrugs and moves away.*) Nothing but our genes, eh? That's already a lot. Add to that our similar childhood experiences and we share both nature and nurture. That's an awful lot to share, in my humble opinion.

CHRIS: (*Advances toward AARON.*) Humble! Humble! There's not a humble bone in your body and you know it! You take over everything. You're like some sort of black hole that extracts all the energy. You even suck in the light so that there is nothing else left, no warmth, no oxygen, and no life expect yours.

AARON: (*Speaks in a very soothing voice.*) I sense anger. I sense frustration. Don't you think it's good we're having such a cathartic conversation?

CHRIS: Cathartic! (*Returns and grabs the knife, pointing it in AARON's direction.*) You know what would be cathartic?

AARON: Don't tell me? You want to kill me. You think that if I'm out of the way that everything would be all right. You think you would finally be daddy's favorite because I'd be gone. That's what you're thinking, isn't it?

CHRIS: (*Continues to advance.*) Those thoughts have crossed my mind.

AARON: (*Grabs a large wooden spoon and goes into fencing position.*) Yes. Killing me would certainly solve a lot of your problems. Or so you think. En garde! (*CHRIS advances and they have a choreographed combat, like a fencing match. As they fight, AARON continues to talk.*) You would go to prison. You would break Dad's heart. You would go to the electric chair and cause more pain. (*Continues to fight.*) And then, our brother, the one you despise so much, would be the only one left to inherit all of Dad's wealth. He would dance on both of our graves. Did you think about that?

CHRIS: (*Steps away and lowers his knife.*) Touché!

(*AARON and CHRIS return to the table and resume cutting vegetables and meat and putting it into the gumbo pot.*)

AARON: (*Looks into the pot.*) It looks pretty good.

CHRIS: You always win, don't you? One way or another, you always win.

AARON: It's not a contest. Dad loves all of us the same way.

CHRIS: (*Sarcastically*) Right.

AARON: (*Laughs and then pauses.*) He just loves some of us more than others. (*Leans toward CHRIS.*) You know what Dad calls me sometimes?

CHRIS: No.

AARON: His favorite son.

CHRIS: You're lying!

AARON: No, I'm not. As God is my witness.

CHRIS: I don't believe you. Besides, why are you telling me this?

AARON: Because it's the truth, and the truth shall set you free.

CHRIS: I don't believe you!

AARON: (*Stands up, drops his knife and crosses his heart.*) Cross my heart and hope to die.

(CHRIS jumps up and stabs AARON in the chest. AARON, with a surprised look on his face, falls to the ground and dies. CHRIS looks at AARON and goes back to his chair, where he sits down.)

CHRIS: *(Pulls out a cell phone and dials.)* Hello, 911? Yes, there's been an accident. *(Pauses.)* Yes, someone is hurt. Well, actually he's dead. *(Pauses.)* It's my brother. I just killed him. *(Pauses.)* Yes, this is 1914 Harmony Lane, Paradise, Louisiana. I'll be waiting for you. *(CHRIS closes the phone and sits down. Takes AARON'S knife and continues to cut up vegetables, which he drops in the gumbo pot. Lights dim to dark.)*

THE END

A CLEAR CASE OF NEGLIGENCE

CAST OF CHARACTERS

DR. PASAGOULI: Greek descent by birth, but raised in the U.S. He has no foreign accent.

MR. SANSAME: Plaintiff attorney. Very well dressed and speaks with a slightly nasal voice.

MR. DROITIER: Defense attorney. Also well-dressed, but a bit more casual.

SETTING

There is a very simple set with only three chairs. The witness stand is just the middle chair which is raised on a platform upstage. Dr. Pasagouli is seated in the upstage center chair. The other two chairs are arranged as the points of a triangle downstage. Mr. Sansame is stage left and Mr. Droitier is stage right. There is no judge and the audience is the jury.

SANSAME: Dr. Pasagouli, you killed Mr. White just as surely as if you had driven a scalpel into his heart!

DROITIER: Objection! This is not a question, it is a baseless accusation.

SANSAME: Withdrawn. I'm sorry, doctor, I just get carried away in the pursuit of justice. Now, you said that Mr. White would NOT have benefitted from cardiac bypass surgery, yet you testified that he suffered from serious multiple blockages in the arteries to his heart and that he suffered almost constant anginal pain. Is that correct?

PASAGOULI: No, it is not correct.

SANSAME: Then what exactly did you say?

PASAGOULI: I said that Mr. White would have benefitted from heart surgery.

SANSAME: (*Interrupts.*) Then why did you deprive Mr. White of the privilege of life saving surgery and condemn him to death?

DROITIER: Objection! Mr. Sansame is badgering the witness who never even had the chance to finish his sentence.

SANSAME: Excuse me, doctor. I do get carried away. Please continue.

PASAGOULI: As I was saying, Mr. White would have benefitted from heart surgery, but he was 75 years old and he suffered from kidney failure, emphysema, and severe diabetes with eye and nerve damage. I think he would have died during surgery or from complications after surgery.

SANSAME: You think?

PASAGOULI: Yes, I think he would have died. He was an unacceptably high surgical risk. That is my professional opinion.

SANSAME: Are you aware that Mr. White's three loving daughters did NOT agree with you?

PASAGOULI: Yes, but Mr. White's three daughters all lived out of state.

SANSAME: (*Paces around.*) Yes, doctor, but they all came to be at their father's bedside during his hospitalization and they all interacted with you during that time, isn't that true?

PASAGOULI: Yes, they all came.

SANSAME: Mr. White died in the ICU, did he not?

PASAGOULI: Yes, he did.

SANSAME: And is it true that he did not receive any cardiopulmonary resuscitation prior to his death?

PASAGOULI: No, he did not.

SANSAME: And yet the hospital record clearly states that there was NO living will on Mr. White's chart, just a vague note by you about Mr. White not wanting extraordinary measures in case of death, is that accurate?

PASAGOULI: Yes, that is true.

SANSAME: And is it true, doctor, that you knew that all three of Mr. White's daughters wanted everything done to their father, including intubation and cardiac massage if necessary?

PASAGOULI: Yes, I was aware of that.

SANSAME: Then, if I understand correctly, you chose to ignore the wishes of the family and deny the patient cardiopulmonary resuscitation that may have saved his life, and you did that even in the absence of any written, signed document to that effect on the chart?

PASAGOULI: Yes.

SANSAME: Why would anyone not consider that negligence, doctor? In fact, why would anyone not consider that non-assistance to a person in danger? In fact, why would any reasonable person not consider that cold-blooded murder?

DROITIER: Objection! This is outrageous! These are not questions, they are slanderous accusations!

SANSAME: I withdraw the question. That is all, doctor.

DROITIER: Dr. Pasagouli, how long did you know Mr. White?

PASAGOULI: About eight years or more.

DROITIER: Did you have a good relationship with him?

PASAGOULI: I think so. Mr. White came to the office about every four months. He had a good sense of humor. I liked and respected him and I think he liked and respected me.

DROITIER: How would you describe Mr. White's general health?

PASAGOULI: He was in extremely bad health. As I mentioned earlier, he had congestive heart failure, kidney disease, bad diabetes, emphysema and other medical problems.

DROITIER: Did he have a close relationship with his daughters?

PASAGOULI: They visited off and on. They all lived out of state, but they seemed to care about their father.

DROITIER: Did they call your office for information?

PASAGOULI: Yes, they would call me after his visits to find out about him. Sometimes one or the other would come in with him for a visit. They all seemed interested and concerned, but none of them ever agreed to take him home with them.

DROITIER: Had you proposed that?

PASAGOULI: Yes, several times. I recognized that his health was declining and I thought it might be better for him to be nearer to one or other of his daughters.

DROITIER: Why did they refuse?

SANSAME: Objection! My clients are not on trial here. All of this is irrelevant to the case.

DROITIER: I'll withdraw the question. Now, doctor, did you have a good relationship with Mr. White's daughters?

PASAGOULI: I thought so. But I also felt that their level of expectation for his health was unrealistic. They never wanted to discuss end of life issues. In fact, it seemed to me that they might be motivated as much from a sense of personal guilt than of concern for their father's welfare.

SANSAME: Objection! This is all slanderous speculation. I insist those last remarks be stricken from the record.

DROITIER: We can strike the last remarks from the record if you insist. Now, doctor, you said that Mr. White told you he did not want any more suffering and he agreed with you and did not want cardiac surgery or cardiac resuscitation in case of death, is that true?

PASAGOULI: Yes.

DROITIER: Why is there no signed document to that effect on the hospital chart?

PASAGOULI: Mr. White told me before he died that he was tired of tubes and wires and sickness. He did not want any surgery and he did not want any cardiac resuscitation. I offered him a paper to sign, but he did not want to sign it, even though he agreed with the contents.

DROITIER: Why did he not want to sign the document?

PASAGOULI: He told me he did not want to sign anything because he did not want to hurt his daughters' feelings. But he also said he was afraid of what they might make him go through just to placate their own misplaced sense of guilt.

SANSAME: Objection! This is baseless slander. There is nothing in the chart to substantiate Dr. Pasagouli's remarks. They could all just be speculation and lies for all we know. Mr. White's daughters were concerned and loving and we have no evidence to the contrary. What's more, they are not on trial here, and Dr. Pasagouli is on trial for negligent behavior. And now he adds tasteless insults to his list of errors of judgment. How can anyone trust this man? Everything he says may be lies.

DROITIER: *(Produces a Bible. Presents it to PASAGOULI.)* Perhaps. But Dr. Pasagouli is under oath, and, just in case anyone has forgotten, here is a Bible. Dr. Pasagouli, do you swear you are telling the truth, the whole truth, and nothing but the truth, so help you God?

PASAGOULI: *(Takes the Bible.)* I swear and I kiss the Holy Book. *(Returns the Bible to DROITIER.)*

SANSAME: Bravo! What a show! This isn't a courtroom, it's a theater. And at least I know good acting when I see it. I also know when I'm defeated. Let's call a brief recess. I'd like to meet with counsel for the defense in about a half hour, if that's okay with you Mr. Droitier.

DROITIER: Of course, Mr. Sansame. Always willing to oblige an honored colleague.

(SANSAME stomps off the stage, shaking his head in disappointment and disgust. PASAGOULI steps off the witness stand and approaches DROITIER. The two shake hands.)

DROITIER: That was a brilliant gesture, doctor. Kissing the Bible. How inspirational and convincing. Congratulations! There is no way this case will go forward. Sansame will probably just want a symbolic settlement to cover his expenses or even drop the whole case.

PASAGOULI: Thank you for your help, Mr. Droitier. Can I tell you a little secret? *(Pulls DROITER a bit closer and both move downstage.)* My name is Greek in origin, but my ancestors lived in Thrace for generations under the Ottomans. They converted to Islam generations ago.

DROITIER: Why are you telling me this, doctor?

PASAGOULI: Muslims are required to honor Christians and Jews as people of the book, your Holy Bible. But they are not obliged to honor the book itself. The Muslim holy book is the Koran, as you know.

DROITIER: Why are you telling me this? You didn't lie, did you?

PASAGOULI: As Muslims say, there is no God but Allah and Mohamed is his prophet. He is the judge and the jury. And to him alone we must answer. Besides, I might even be an atheist. Only God knows for sure. *(Pats DROITIER on the back and hands him back his Bible.)* This is yours, I believe.

(Lights dim to dark.)

THE END

THROWING OUT TRASH

CAST OF CHARACTERS

SALLY: Older woman very disheveled. A chronic hoarder.

CLAIRE: Sally's daughter. Neat, but not fancy.

SETTING

The stage has a couple of chairs and a coffee table and couch. There is garbage, clothes, and papers strewn everywhere.

(*SALLY rummages through a pile of dirty clothes. CLAIRE stands by and watches. She is holding a binder.*)

SALLY: (*To CLAIRE.*) Well at least you could help me find it.

CLAIRE: I don't care if you find it or not.

SALLY: If we don't pay the property tax, then they will evict me, and then what would you do? I doubt whether you'll take me in. (*Looks at the binder.*) What is that? I don't think it's mine. I know everything around here. (*Waves around the cluttered stage.*)

CLAIRE: It's not yours, but it's about you. I wrote a book about living with a mother who was a compulsive hoarder.

SALLY: (*Grabs the binder and begins to read.*) "She was so possessive that she could not throw anything away. Every room was stacked to the ceiling with trash of all sorts. Not an empty can or newspaper or grocery bag could be thrown away because, as she said, 'it might come in handy some day.'" (*Pauses and looks at CLAIRE.*) This really is about me. And it isn't nice at all. What are you going to do with it?

CLAIRE: I'm going to publish it and sell it to anyone willing to buy it.

SALLY: You can't do that!

CLAIRE: Why?

SALLY: Because that's a violation of my privacy. It's a breach of a trust between mother and daughter. (*Pauses.*) Besides, it's just mean spirited!

CLAIRE: (*Takes the book back.*) I have been working very hard on this book. It's taken a huge amount of physical and psychological energy. It was the only way to cast out my personal inner demons and get on with my life. And now I'm going to share it with the world whether you like it or not!

SALLY: Why? Why do you have to share it with the world? If you're just expiating your inner childhood demons by writing this thing, then why should it matter if the world sees it? (*Pauses.*) Just let it be. Write it. Read it yourself. And leave me in peace.

CLAIRE: It's a story that needs to be told.

SALLY: It's just washing our dirty laundry in public, that's what it is. (*Scoops up a bunch of dirty clothes and throws them in the room.*)

CLAIRE: I think the expressions is airing our dirty laundry, not washing it.

SALLY: Airing, washing, it doesn't make any difference. Your book is nothing but voyeurism disguised as literature. You think I'm sick and crazy? What do you think you are if you exploit me, a harmless and defenseless invalid, for your own selfish ends? You're just like everyone else who uses me to get ahead. You're exploiting me. It's elder abuse. It's exploitation of the infirm. That's what it is! (*Grabs the book.*) Give it here!

CLAIRE: What are going to do with it? Throw it away? Now that's a laugh. (*Motions around the cluttered stage.*) You haven't thrown a thing away in years. Are you going to start now with my book? That's ridiculous.

SALLY: (*Opens the book and reads.*) "We ate week old bread after we cut off the mold. Papa pleaded with Mama to clean up the house, but she refused over and over again. There wasn't a chair we could sit on or a bed we could sleep in. We slept on the floor on piles of laundry, sometimes clean and sometimes not. Only one toilet worked and that one had to be cleaned out almost weekly because rubbish fell in and clogged it when we stood up after using it." (*Screaming at CLAIRE.*) How could you! Do you hate me so much? Do you want to humiliate me even more than I am already? What good will that do for anyone?

CLAIRE: I don't hate you. I want to see you well and happy and trash free. (*Makes a sweeping gesture.*) Maybe we can read the book together and you can get some professional help if you want to. Or maybe we can start by renting a dumpster?

SALLY: (*Clutches the book.*) I don't need professional help! And I don't need a dumpster. I need you to stop attacking me! (*Holds up the binder.*) This is an attack on me, nothing more or less. You are killing me with your words.

SALLY: Maybe you just want to kill me so you can have father all to yourself? Maybe that's what you want to do?

CLAIRE: That's a ridiculous idea.

SALLY: Is it? You do something like this. (*Holds up the binder.*) Your cruelty breaks my heart and I die from grief or shame or some combination of both and *voilà*! Papa is all yours to have and hold forever more. Everyone is happy because your mentally ill mother is out of the picture.

CLAIRE: That's sick!

SALLY: Is it? (*Pauses.*) I'm going to hide this book. (*Glances around the room.*) There are so many places here to hide something. You'll never find it. (*Starts rummaging around in the piles of clothing and trash. Pulls out a paper.*) Well, I'll be darned. Here's the property tax bill.

CLAIRE: (*Grabs the binder while SALLY is distracted.*) Give it to me! It's mine!

(SALLY swings around and tries to get the binder back. SALLY and CLAIRE struggle with the book. They pull it back and forth violently until SALLY yanks it away from CLAIRE.)

CLAIRE: I wrote it and I'm going to publish it. I'm going to sell it all over town and go to every book club with rich old ladies and talk about you and Papa and this landfill you call home! *(Makes a gesture around the room.)*

SALLY: Just what I thought! This isn't about me at all, is it? It's all about you. Poor little girl, trapped with a sicko mother who abused her emotionally. That's it, isn't it? *(Pauses.)* Do you really think that this will heal you? Do you really think it will be some sort of cathartic narrative that will free you from the misery you carry around in your mind? Do you really think that?

CLAIRE: Yes, I do! The more I can spread this book around the world, the smaller and smaller this hell hole will become in my mind until one day all this delusional misery will just disappear.

SALLY: You're delusional, not me! This book is just your own mental masturbation. It's rumination of the worst sort, like a cow with its cud. Over and over, up and down, back and forth. And instead of getting smaller, the problem will get bigger and bigger as it takes on a life of its own. *(Gestures around the room.)* Do you think it makes me happy to live like this? Do you think I'm happy? Do you think that this your book will make me or you happy?

CLAIRE: *(Looks at the binder.)* I don't know.

SALLY: *(Slumps down on the cluttered chair.)* I thought you came over to have lunch.

CLAIRE: I'm not hungry.

SALLY: *(Finds some food under some clothing.)* Here. Here are some mini-pretzels. Would you like a pretzel? *(Makes a space on the table and pours out some pretzels. Tries one.)* Try one. They're still good. *(Pauses and chews.*) Maybe a little stale. Come on, have one, on me. It makes me think I'm giving you something instead of stealing your happy childhood and adolescence.

CLAIRE: Mama, I'm not hungry.

SALLY: (*Pulls CLAIRE next to her.*) Sit down. Here. (*Sits CLAIRE down.*) There, just like the good old days when you came home from school, so bright and fresh and full of ideas. (*Holds out a pretzel.*) Come on, open up. This will feed your body and soul. It's my gift to you.

CLAIRE: (*Opens her mouth and takes the pretzel like a communion wafer. Chews and swallows with difficulty.*) It's stale.

SALLY: (*Takes her hand.*) Now, let's start over. Let's forget about that binder and all that meanness and be like we used to be. (*Hugs CLAIRE.*)

CLAIRE: (*Starts to cry.*) Mama, what can I do for you? How can I help you?

SALLY: (*Strokes CLAIRE's hair.*) There, there, little girl. Mama's going to make everything better. We will start fresh and you can take that book and hide it somewhere where no one will every find it. (*Continues to stroke CLAIRE's hair.*) That's a good girl. Now promise me you'll hide your book and never let it see the light of day.

CLAIRE: (*Imploringly.*) Mama.

SALLY: Promise me. Promise me you'll destroy it, or at least keep it hidden until I'm dead. Have that decency, won't you? Once I'm dead, it won't be able to hurt me anymore.

CLAIRE: (*Pauses.*) Mama, I can't. I've got to publish this book. (*Clutches the binder.*) I just can't keep it inside any more. It's got to come out so I can be free at last.

SALLY: (*Stands up and pushes CLAIRE away.*) Free! Free at my expense while I live a prisoner in hell. (*Gestures around the room.*) Then get out! Get out of my house and never come back! You're no daughter of mine, you're a vain, selfish bitch, a stranger. (*Points to the door.*) You said I can't throw anything away. Well, you're wrong! Wrong about writing this book and wrong that I can't throw anything away! You're trash to me and I want you out of my house right now. Get out! (*Points to the door.*) Get out! GET OUT!

(*CLAIRE takes her binder and gives SALLY a last look. CLAIRE reaches out to SALLY, but she turns her back. CLAIRE walks off stage. SALLY remains among the trash. SALLY turns to face where CLAIRE walked away.*)

SALLY: (*Yelling.*) You can't say I never threw out any trash! You can just re-write that damn book and say whatever you want, but you can't say that about me any more. I threw you out. Trash! Trash! Trash! (*Collapses on the couch and sobs.*)

(*Lights dim to dark.*)

THE END

THE PROM DRESS/
AFTER THE PROM

ACT I: THE PROM DRESS

CAST OF CHARACTERS

DONNA: Teenage daughter getting ready to go to the prom.

CAROL: Donna's mother. She is in her mid-thirties or a bit older.

SETTING

Donna is in a room with a table and a couple of chairs, a coat rack and nothing more. Donna is trying on a pair of shoes as Carol enters. Music is "Moon River."

CAROL: (*Walks on stage holding a box.*) Here it is . . . your prom dress! (*Sets the box on the table and opens it, and then hands a long, elegant prom dress to DONNA.*) It's so beautiful. You'll look like a movie star. It'll be the perfect prom dress for the perfect little girl.

DONNA: (*Looks at the dress.*) It's gorgeous. And all the more beautiful because I shed blood, sweat and tears to pay for it. All those hours slaving away for minimal wage at McDonalds, I thought I'd never get enough money.

CAROL: Your father and I volunteered to pay for your dress. So don't blame us for all that after-school work.

DONNA: No, I wanted to buy it with my own money. I wanted it to be a gift to myself, an expression of independence from a grown up woman to herself.

CAROL: That's the nicest part of all. You wanted it to be your dress that you picked out yourself and paid for by yourself. I'm so proud of you. You are certainly a grown up woman, not a little girl anymore. No one can argue with you about that. (*Gives DONNA a big hug and backs away, looking at the shoes.*) And those shoes, they're a perfect match.

DONNA: (*Puts the dress up against her sweat shirt and pants and admires the effect.*) It's beautiful. (*Spins around and lets the dress swirl in front of her.*) Great dress, great shoes, but I'm just missing one thing to make it a truly perfect evening.

CAROL: I know, you must be talking about jewelry. I have Grandma's pearls, or maybe my amber necklace that you admire so much?

DONNA: (*Taking on a serious tone.*) No, Mama, I'm missing my pills. What did you do with them?

CAROL: What pills?

DONNA: My birth control pills, of course. The ones you undoubtedly took out of my dresser when you were snooping around in my room.

CAROL: I . . . . (*Does not finish.*)

DONNA: I need those pills. And I need them today.

CAROL: Why? Why will you need them? Where did they come from? Who gave you such a thing?

DONNA: Ah, so you admit you took them. Well, first, I need to take them everyday so I won't get pregnant. That seems pretty obvious, doesn't it? Second, if you must know, I got them from the nurse practitioner at the health unit and she was glad to do it.

CAROL: Why didn't I know about this?

DONNA: Because I'm a grown woman, like you said yourself, and because the health unit is confidential. They do family planning, you know. And they don't have to tell parents about anything if you're older than twelve.

CAROL: Twelve! You can get pills without your parent's knowledge at twelve! That's an outrage!

DONNA: Yeah, and it's pretty outrageous that half the senior class is pregnant before they graduate. Or that they pop out deformed little premies like Melissa Hargrove's baby that get stuck on ventilators for weeks before they die anyway. That's pretty shocking, too, isn't it?

CAROL: We're not discussing other people's health, we're talking about you. And that still doesn't answer my question of why you need those pills now, just for the prom.

DONNA: Because I plan on having the perfect prom. That seems pretty obvious, too, doesn't it?

CAROL: Are you going to have sex with Greg?

DONNA: (*Pulls off the sweat shirt and pants and tries on the dress.*) Help me with this, please.

> (DONNA pulls on the dress and CAROL zips it up in the back and helps adjusts it.)

DONNA: Wow! It looks great! And the answer to your question about having sex with Greg is yes, I do plan on it. We are going to have real sex, just like grown-up people.

CAROL: Where?

DONNA: Where? You mean vaginal or anal, or in whose bed?

CAROL: Don't be disgusting! How can you talk about such things?

DONNA: Well, it is an interesting question. (*Adjusts the shoes.*) Anyway, Greg doesn't like condoms. So if I don't have my pills back, I sure won't be able to do vaginal sex, will I? And frankly, I don't like anal sex at all.

CAROL: Stop this! You don't have to have sex anywhere with anyone. You're a young girl, a beautiful young girl. You can wait. There's no rush. There's no obligation to have sex after the prom. You cherish your independence, so don't be like the other girls, and don't give in to peer pressure.

DONNA: You certainly don't know much about boys nowadays, do you? I suppose when you went to the prom, you thought a first kiss was a big deal. (*Tries on some earrings.*) It's not like that anymore. Most girls at school are already experts at hand and blow jobs. If you're not doing at least that, then you're just not cool.

CAROL: You don't have to be cool! You need to be smart and well-educated and successful, not some sort of low-life high school whore.

DONNA: Give me back my pills! You just don't understand. I want the perfect prom, with a long romantic evening, ending with fulfilling sex with my boyfriend, who happens to love me.

CAROL: Love? What do you know about love?

DONNA: I'm 18 years old, not eight. I've had periods since I was 12 and have done things you probably never dreamed of (*Pauses*) and certainly wouldn't approve of. I want a real prom to remember my whole life, not some fairy tale, hand-holding fantasy like you had.

CAROL: (*Sits down.*) Back then I wanted the same thing that you want now. I wanted a romantic evening with the love of my life, just like you do. We're not as different as you might think.

DONNA: So, did you have sex after the prom, like I want to?

CAROL: Yes.

DONNA: With Dad?

CAROL: No.

DONNA: Then with who?

CAROL: With whom.

DONNA: Oh Mama, you're ridiculous. Just answer the question.

CAROL: It doesn't matter, but it wasn't your father. And three months later I had an abortion. (*Pauses.*) I don't remember too much about the prom because we got kind of drunk. I do remember the abortion. We went to a sleazy place, with a horrible smell of alcohol or Lysol or something. There was a garbage can filled with bloody gauze in the so-called operating room, at least that's what was written on the door. The doctor was so matter of fact, if he even was a real doctor. Back then, it wasn't legal yet, you know. All hush, hush and dangerous. (*Pauses.*) I still think about it all the time. And I think about that fancy blue dress I wore to my prom. Your grandma picked it out for me. It was blue like the Virgin's veil. I still can't see that blue to this day without thinking about that abortion. Every time I look at a statue of the Virgin Mary, I think about that horrible day and the garbage cans full of bloody gauze.

DONNA: (*Long pause.*) An abortion! You had an abortion! That's horrible! (*Spins around.*) You killed one of my brothers or sisters and you worry about me taking the pill? I don't want to go ever go through that sort of thing, even if it is legal. I want happy memories, a beautiful night of young love. I'm sorry for you. I'm sorry for your experience. But I'm not a baby-killer. Now, give me my pills back, for heaven's sake. (*Extends out her hand.*)

CAROL: Is it too much to expect that you be beautiful, pure and virginal until you get married?

DONNA: Yes, it is!

CAROL: (*Pauses.*) You know, back in my high school days, all of the dances, including the prom, always ended with "Moon River." (*Holds out her arms and beckons DONNA.*) Come on, take my arms.

DONNA: What on earth are you doing?

CAROL: I want to teach you how to dance the waltz. Everyone needs to know how to do it. That's what "Moon River" was, you know, a waltz. It was the romantic end to every romantic evening at our high school dances.

DONNA: Mama, this is stupid.

CAROL: No it's not. I'll be the man and you'll be my partner. Now take my arms.

(*DONNA takes CAROL's arm and they assume dance position.*)

CAROL: That's right. Now it's very easy. You go backwards and I go forward. One-two-three, two-two-three, three-two-three, four-to-three. That's right.

(*"Moon River" begins to play and the two women dance the waltz with increasing elegance. They dance for several seconds before the music fades. DONNA turns under CAROL's arms and bows. As DONNA straightens up, CAROL hands her the package of birth control pills.*)

DONNA: Thank you. (*Clutches the pills.*) I doubt whether we will be doing any waltzing at our prom, but I'm still looking forward to dancing with my Prince Charming.

CAROL: I suppose you think doing the waltz is so 70's.

DONNA: Right! 1870!

CAROL: (*Laughs.*) Here, let me help you out of that dress. You don't want to mess it up before the prom.

(*CAROL helps DONNA take off the dress. DONNA removes the shoes and is left in her underclothes. They are putting the dress on a hanger and the shoes in a box. DONNA puts back on her shirt and pants.*)

CAROL: And I think you will still need these. (*Hands her a small bag.*)

DONNA: I hope it's not Grandma's pearls. They looked good on her, but I'm not wearing any vintage jewelry. (*Looks in the bag.*) What is it?

CAROL: Condoms.

DONNA: You're worried about me taking birth control pills and you're giving me condoms?

CAROL: Birth control pills don't prevent sexually transmitted diseases. You might not get pregnant, but you can still get herpes or HIV. Better safe than sorry.

DONNA: You're so full of surprises. Perhaps I can educate Greg about these things. He can be so stubborn. (*Looks in the bag.*) Are these flavored condoms?

CAROL: No! I do have my limits. (*Embraces DONNA.*) Have a wonderful prom. And be safe.

(*Lights dim to dark.*)

ACT II: AFTER THE PROM

CAST OF CHARACTERS

DONNA: Teenage girl, dressed in her flashy prom dress. A bit disheveled.

CAROL: Donna's mother. She is in her mid-thirties and dressed in a robe and slippers.

SETTING

The den or living room of a home. There are a couple of chairs, perhaps a couch and lamp with a table. It does not need to be a complex or realistic set. Music can be "After the Ball is Over" by Charles K. Harris.

(*CAROL is sitting in a chair and is doing some sort of handwork. DONNA, dressed in her prom dress and a bit disheveled, comes in on tip toe. She is carrying her shoes in her hand.*)

CAROL: Back so early?

DONNA: Mama, what are doing up at this hour? (*Looks at her watch.*) And it's certainly not early, it's almost two a.m.

CAROL: You said you were going to dance all prom night long with Prince Charming. I just wanted to make sure you got home safely. There's a lot of drinking and driving that goes one out there. I don't want you to be some sort of statistic.

DONNA: Help me out of this dress, please.

(*CAROL gets up and begins to help DONNA out of her dress. DONNA is wearing a simple slip so she is not just in a bra and underwear on stage. CAROL holds up the dress with admiration and DONNA snatches it away.*)

41

DONNA: Give me that piece of crap! I'm going to burn it out in the yard along with the shoes and the purse.

CAROL: Burn it?

CAROL: (*Pulls the dress back.*) No! You worked and saved for this dress and you are not going to destroy it. You told me yourself that it was a symbol of your personal independence. Why would you want to destroy that?

DONNA: (*Grabs for the dress.*) Give it back! It's a symbol alright, but not of independence.

CAROL: (*Clutches the dress and looks at DONNA.*) I guess it's not appropriate to ask if you had a good time.

DONNA: Good time?

CAROL: Yes, with Prince Charming.

DONNA: Prince Charming is a crap head. His name is Greg Hillstrom, by the way, and he's a rotten good-for-nothing asshole.

CAROL: I thought you said you loved him and he loved you. And he's always been a polite, respectful young man with me. Besides, his parents are God-fearing, church-going community members and they happen to own the Ford dealership. That's not a bad combination in this day and age.

DONNA: I don't care if his parents are deacons or saints or whatever they are, but their cute little boy raped me!

CAROL: Raped you? How could he rape you?

DONNA: The usual way, by over-powering me and forcing me to have sex when I didn't want to. What do you think?

CAROL: You told me yourself that you were planning on having sex with him tonight to consummate the perfect prom night. So how exactly could he rape you if you wanted to have sex?

DONNA: Yes, I did want to have sex with him, but not in the back of his crummy pickup truck on a filthy mattress. (*Pauses.*) He said he wanted to rent a nice hotel room, but that it was just too expensive and that he didn't have the money at the time. Too expensive! He even asked me if I had cash or a credit card. Can you imagine?

CAROL: Oh dear.

> (*CAROL tries to go and comfort DONNA, but she pushes CAROL away.*)

DONNA: I already told him I was on the pill and that was a big mistake. So he thinks everything's cool. He just assumed that any girl would want to have sex on a mattress in his truck. I told him to stop groping and he just wouldn't. And, of course, he wouldn't even think about using a condom. Not him. It's not natural, he says. And when I told him that condoms protect from other diseases, he tells me that I'm insulting him. He says he's doesn't have anything dirty like that and he just keeps pawing me.

CAROL: So he forced you to have sex?

DONNA: He tried. But I told him he could take his cheap dick and shove it anywhere he wanted, but not in me.

CAROL: So he left you alone? He didn't rape you.

DONNA: NO! He grabbed my face and forced it down into his crotch until I was just over his stiff penis. (*Shudders.*) I can't stand that! I can't stand doing what he forced me to do. I wanted to bite his dick off. I swear I did. Then it was in my mouth and then his sperm was in my mouth. (*Screws up her face and wipes her lips.*) Yuk! It's disgusting. (*Pauses.*) Then you know what he does?

CAROL: No.

DONNA: He offers me a swallow of warm beer to get the taste of his sperm out of my mouth. (*Shakes her head in disgust.*) That was Prince Charming's token gesture. Ugh!

CAROL: (*Pauses.*) What kind of beer?

DONNA: Mama! What the hell difference does that make?

CAROL: None, I suppose. It's just that some European beers are meant to be drunk at room temperature. (*Sits down in a chair. Pauses as she fingers the dress.*) I told you not to take birth control pills. I told you not to have sex or even think about it or talk about it. I'm sorry for you, but at least you only got a mouthful of sperm instead of a one night stand in some cheap hotel and maybe an STD and bed bugs to boot. It's all too disgusting, but if you have to choose, at least what you did was over in a minute.

DONNA: I didn't choose! Don't you get it! I didn't choose, but he did. That's rape, non-consensual sex of any kind. (*Reaches for the dress.*) Give it to me! I'm going to burn this dress. I don't want to see a scrap of cloth to remind me of this night. All I want to see is a pile of black ashes and a shoe buckle. That's it. So give it to me!

CAROL: No!

> (*DONNA and CAROL struggle with the dress. The battle can be violent, with slapping and grabbing to increase the intensity. Eventually CAROL gives up and DONNA yanks the dress away and clutches it tightly.*)

CAROL: That dress is yours. You bought and paid for it. I guess you can do what you want with it. (*Backs away.*) Is this really the way you imagined the end of your perfect romantic prom night?

DONNA: (*Still holding the prom dress.*) Fighting with my mother over a stupid prom dress? Heck no!

CAROL: Maybe you can give the dress to your cousin, Judy. She's about your size and she would never be able to afford such a nice dress. Transform tragedy into a gesture of hope and good will. I would have given my right boob for a dress like that at my prom, not that virgin blue thing your Grandma picked out for me.

DONNA: Yeah, and you would have looked great with one breast. (*Shakes her head.*) No! I can't. It makes me sick to think about it. Greg's tie was the same color as my dress. He picked it out on purpose. Now I'll never be able to look at that color again.

(*DONNA puts the dress on the table between them.*)

CAROL: Shouldn't we call the police if it was rape?

DONNA: The police? Who would believe me? I was on the pill by my own choice. I had condoms that I brought myself. I told you I wanted to have sex with him. Who would ever believe me? Every girl in high school wants Greg any way they can get him. (*Pauses.*) I got him all right, a whole mouthful. Now he can just move on to Cindy or Roberta or Cathy. (*Starts to cry.*) He even told me that he was leaving me because I was such a prude. (*Pauses.*) I'm a fool, not a prude.

CAROL: We can all be foolish. I just hate to see you suffer. You wanted a prom to remember your whole life through, a wonderful romantic evening.

DONNA: Ending in a forced blow job? Oh, I'll remember this prom my whole life, that's for sure.

CAROL: (*Takes DONNA in her arms and rocks her.*) Think about the future: college, the right young man, the right time, the right place. You are still in one piece. You aren't pregnant. We can fix the dress and . . . (*Stops.*)

DONNA: No! It's mine and I really want to burn it. I want to see the fire and smoke and think about Greg, burning in hell. And maybe some of my foolish adolescent notions will go up in flames, too.

CAROL: Just like your innocence?

DONNA: Yes, just like my innocence. (*Looks up and takes on a religious tone and look.*) And the smoke will rise up from the altar of my innocence to the high heavens, a signal to all those stupid teenage girls who think that a fancy dress and their scumbag boyfriend will make for the perfect prom.

CAROL: Go get yourself cleaned up. Let's get you to bed. Get some sleep and tomorrow the sun will come up, and the world will look so various, so beautiful, so new.

DONNA: (*Continues slowly.*) But hath really neither joy, nor love, nor light, nor certitude, nor peace, nor help for pain. (*Pauses.*)

CAROL: So let us be true to one another. (*Takes DONNA's hands.*) Let me kiss you before you go off to bed. (*Bends to kiss her on the lips.*)

DONNA: Not on the lips, please! Not after what they've been through tonight.

CAROL: Your lips will be sweeter than honey, wherever they have been. (*Kisses her on the lips.*) Now off to bed with you. I'll clean up here.

DONNA: (*Gets up to leave and turns.*) Go ahead and give the dress to Judy. She's a nice girl, even if she's about a homely as they come. (*Pauses.*) And that so-called boyfriend of hers, what a nut case.

CAROL: No worse than your Prince Charming?

DONNA: You've got a point there. I'm going to take a shower and go to bed.

CAROL: Don't forget the mouth wash!

DONNA: Thanks, Mama.

(DONNA gets up and leaves. CAROL picks up the dress and shoes and clutches them to herself. CAROL puts the dress to herself and begins to waltz to the melody "After the Ball if Over," as lights dim to dark.)

THE END

STAYING ALIVE

CAST OF CHARACTERS

SISTER T.: Nun from an order suggestive of Mother Theresa's. She is dressed in a white gown with linear color markings. She may have an ill-defined foreign accent.

MAN: A homeless man, down in his luck. He is shabbily dressed and has a large draining wound on his arm.

ATTORNEY: Dressed in a very tasteful and expensive looking suit.

SETTING

A street scene. There is a sturdy bench and the man is on the ground, leaning his back against the bench with a garbage can next to it.

(*SISTER is applying ointment to the MAN's wound and placing a bandage. The ATTORNEY comes up and watches a few seconds before speaking.*)

ATTORNEY: What do you think you're doing, young lady?

SISTER: (*Looks up.*) I'm applying an antibiotic ointment to this man's infected arm and then covering it with a bandage.

ATTORNEY: Do you have a license to practice medicine in this state?

SISTER: No, I'm not a doctor.

ATTORNEY: Are you a physician's assistant?

SISTER: No.

ATTORNEY: Are you a nurse?

SISTER: No.

ATTORNEY: Then I must ask you to cease and desist this illegal practice of medicine.

MAN: Bug off, dude! She's helping me.

SISTER: (*To ATTORNEY.*) I think this man may have MERSA.

ATTRONEY: Mercy?

SISTER: No, M-R-S-A, that's an antibiotic resistant Staph infection and he might develop sepsis or even die if we don't help him now. He's homeless and doesn't have any means of transportation to a medical center.

ATTORNEY: (*To MAN.*) Listen to me. This lady here is practicing medicine. She even talks like a nurse or a doctor. That's illegal in this state without a license. (*To SISTER.*) You'd better stop right now or I'll sue the socks of you.

SISTER: (*Stands to face ATTORNEY.*) I'm not asking for any money. If I'm not mistaken, I'm considered a Good Samaritan. (*Turns to MAN.*) I'm not asking to be paid, am I?

MAN: No ma'am. (*To ATTORNEY.*) She ain't never asked a dime for any of the help she's given me. Not a penny. Why, if it weren't for her, I wouldn't be able to get no help at all. Where would I go, anyway?

ATTORNEY: You need to go to the public hospital and be treated by licensed professionals. That's what it's there for and that's why we pay taxes, well at least I do.

MAN: At the public hospital you have to wait six hours or more to git seen. And half the time it ain't even a doctor. It's some nurse or somethin'. I been up their lots of times and they are just too busy. It's a cryin' shame. Besides, Sister here comes to me where I am, right here in the street. I don't have to worry about no transportation or anythin'. There's no way for me to git out to the public hospital even if I wanted to. Like the lady said, I ain't got no transportation. (*Points to SISTER.*)

She comes here regular like and has seen me and a lot of other hard-luck folks. She's been doin' it for years, too. She's practically a saint.

ATTORNEY: (*To SISTER.*) So, you've been doing this for some time, eh? (*To MAN.*) This lady's bound to have some assets. A home? A car? A 401K? She might even own some sort of nice convent or other. (*Helps MAN up and both sit on the bench.*) Think about it! You could be the proud owner of a whole convent. You'd never be homeless again. In fact, you could have a whole bunch of rooms to rent to your homeless buddies. And you could all do whatever you wanted. (*To SISTER.*) You do own property, don't you? (*Does not wait for a reply. To MAN.*) You'd even get a portion of any financial assets they might have and get spending money for yourself. How does that sound?

SISTER: Our group home belongs to the sisters. And I believe we really can be considered as Good Samaritans. That sort of thing is covered by special laws in this state, if I'm not mistaken. (*Continues wrapping the wound.*)

ATTORNEY: Good Samaritan laws only cover true medical emergencies in life and death circumstances, and in bona fide registered free clinics, not street medicine or whatever you call what you're doing now. (*To MAN.*) For a third of all money recovered through award or settlement, I can almost guarantee you would get a roof of your own over your head and we would get this charlatan, the medical impostor, off the streets. She's a menace to society!

MAN: (*To ATTORNEY.*) What's it gonna cost me?

ATTORNEY: Nothing, absolutely nothing. If we don't recover any money, you haven't lost a thing. (*Bends closer to MAN and shows his profile.*) Surely you've seen my ads on television?

MAN: (*Examines the ATTORNEY.*) Yeah, you do look kinda familiar. From television and those giant billboards all over town.

ATTORNEY: Yes, indeed. And from my cash-mobile. You've got to have seen that around town, haven't you?

MAN: Yeah, that van with the money plastered all over it. Who coulda missed that?

ATTORNEY: (*Straightens up.*) Of course you know it's not about the money.

SISTER: (*To ATTORNEY.*) Lying is a sin!

ATTORNEY: (To SISTER.) Cool it, Sister! (*Turns back to MAN.*) It's about getting illegal medical practitioners off the street. (*Pulls out a paper from his pocket.*) Just sign here and we can get this show on the road. (*To MAN.*) Just think of it, a new life with a home to call your own, a bed with clean sheets, showers, and a kitchen with a working stove and refrigerator. (*To SISTER.*) You do have working showers and toilets in that place of yours, don't you?

SISTER: (*Irritated.*) Of course, and we have a fully equipped kitchen. (*To Attorney.*) Would you please let me finish taking care of this man's wound?

ATTORNEY: (*Screams at SISTER.*) You don't get it, do you! I want you to stop right now! You are breaking the law and this fine gentleman and I are going to take away anything and everything you and your band of charlatans possess. You'll be the homeless one and it's what you deserve. You may hide behind a façade of charity, but you're nothing but a bunch of criminal do-gooders and, trust me, you are not above the law.

SISTER: (*To MAN.*) Surely you're not going to help this man dispossess my sisters and me? We have sacrificed our lives in the service of the poor and down-trodden.

MAN: (*Hesitates.*) Well, I have always wanted to live in a place of my own. You can't blame me, can you? It's only human nature to want some security. Sister, you know, the flesh is weak and it is a very temptin' offer, even if this guy is a heartless, greedy sleaze. (*Looks at the paper.*) One signature and I might be set for life.

SISTER: At the Lord's expense, I might add. (*Looks heavenward.*) Father, forgive them for they know not what they do. (*Looks at ATTORNEY.*) And deliver us from evil for yours is the kingdom, the power and the glory now and forever. Amen.

ATTORNEY: (*Laughs.*) Oh, stop your sniveling. God is not going to save you from the American legal system, pray as you might. This is the real world. Not some fantasyland. (*Pauses. Clutches his chest.*) No! (*Staggers around.*) I feel like there's an elephant sitting on my chest. (*Gasps.*) This can't be happening. Oh, my God, it's the big one. I'm having a heart attack. (*Stares at SISTER.*) You've giving me a heart attack, you bitch! (*Spins and falls to the ground.*)

(*SISTER and MAN look down in amazement.*)

MAN: What do we do now?

SISTER: (*Bends down to check the pulse. To MAN.*) No pulse. Quick! Call 911 and see if there's an AED around here! (*Opens the MAN's jacket and rips up the shirt.*)

MAN: (*Bewildered.*) A what?

SISTER: An A-E-D, a defibrillator. (*Waves her hand.*) Just go on and call 911!

(*MAN runs off stage.*)

SISTER: (*Starts CPR.*) 1-2-3-4, staying alive, staying alive, 5-6-7-8, staying alive, staying alive. (*Continues pumping and counting in rhythm.*)

MAN: (*Returns to SISTER.*) They're goin' call 911 down at the liquor store. No one knows what an A-E-D is. (*Looks on and listens.*) That's the Bee Jees, isn't it?

SISTER: Yes, it's the Bee Jees. (*In rhythm.*) Staying alive, staying alive, 27-28-29-30. Staying alive, staying alive. (*Stops cardiac compressions.*) Now, kneel down and give two mouth-to-mouth breaths.

MAN: What you are talkin' about?

SISTER: Mouth-to-mouth breathing. Come on, quick! We can't interrupt compressions.

MAN: No way! I ain't touchin' this dude's lips to mine and I'm pretty darn sure he doesn't want my lips on his. Besides, if he dies, why would you care? He wants to sue you.

SISTER: (*Goes to ATTORNEY's head and bends down.*) Okay! You give the cardiac compressions. Get going! (*Gives two breaths to the ATTORNEY.*)

MAN: (*Continues CPR.*) 1-2-3-4.

MAN and SISTER: Staying alive! Staying alive!

MAN: (*Continues CPR.*) 5-6-7-8.

MAN and SISTER: Staying alive! Staying alive!

ATTORNEY: (*Gasps and chokes. Sits up and looks around. Speech remains slightly slurred in the beginning.*) Wha's goin' on here? (*Wipes his mouth. To SISTER. Speech is a bit slurred in the beginning.*) Did ya just kiss me? (*Turns to MAN.*) Did ya see her do that?

SISTER: Well, technically I just gave you mouth-to-mouth resuscitation.

MAN: (*To ATTORNEY.*) Sure enough. (*Points to SISTER.*) This lady just saved your life. Cross my heart and hope to die. (*Crosses his heart.*)

ATTORNEY: (*Clutches his chest.*) My chest hurts. You broke my ribs!

SISTER: I did CPR, Cardio-Pulmonary Resuscitation. Sometimes there are fractures.

ATTORNEY: (*Rubbing his chest.*) You broke my ribs! (*Screams.*) Illegal practice of medicine! Sexual harassment! Assault and battery! (*To SISTER.*) Lady, you're going to jail and this man and I are going to make sure you stay in a long, long time. And when you get out, if you ever do, you wouldn't have a sheet to wrap yourself in.

MAN: She saved your life, dude. You understand? You should be kissin' the hem of her holy shawl and givin' a fat donation to her sisters and her. What kind of a shit are you?

ATTORNEY: The only thing I'm going to give this impostor is a summons! (*To MAN.*) And you'll get one, too, if you don't straighten up and cooperate. You'll be an accessory to the crime. Think about it. You won't be homeless anymore because you'll be in jail.

MAN: (*To ATTORNEY.*) I don't wanna go to jail again. (*To SISTER.*) Do you think I ought to let him sue you?

SISTER: (*To ATTORNEY.*) Gandhi said that wealth without work and business without ethics were two of the great moral evils of the world, and you seem to be indulging in both. (*Turns to the MAN. Indicates the bench.*) Please sit down. I need to finish the dressing.

ATTORNEY: Gandhi! Now you're quoting some foreign radical terrorist. I bet you're not even a red-blooded American. Look at your get-up. You're probably an illegal alien, some agent in an Al Qaeda sleeper cell. (*To MAN.*) Just another reason to get this woman off the streets. She's a threat to the American way of life. You've got to agree with me.

MAN: Dude, you're a bigger threat to national security than she is by far. (*Turns his back on the ATTORNEY. Sits down. To SISTER.*) I got a bad spot over here. (*Points to his arm.*) Can you put some cream on and somethin' over that? It really hurts when I brush it up against anythin'.

SISTER: Of course. (*Continues to treat the arm.*) Now, it's very important to keep this clean and please do not share towels or personal items. Staph infections are very common among the homeless and it spreads easily from person to person, especially in less than sanitary conditions.

MAN: I understand, Sister. I'll do the best I can.

ATTORNEY: (*Takes a few pictures with his cell phone. Hands his card to the MAN.*) Here's my card. I'll expect you to come by my office if you want to get out of your current condition and into a far more favorable one. You have my word that we will make a killing. This bitch is going to rue the day she every crossed my path. (*Looks disdainfully at SISTER and walks off.*)

SISTER: (*To MAN.*) The Lord is your shepherd, you shall not want. He leads you in paths of righteousness for his name's sake.

MAN: (*Puts the card in the garbage can.*) Amen.

(*Lights dim to a single spot light on SISTER and fade to black.*)

THE END

SORTING FOR THE FOOD BANK

CAST OF CHARACTERS

BROTHER JETHRO: The pastor of a conservative small town Southern church. He is middle aged or older and dressed in working clothes. He speaks without a pronounced Southern accent.

JOSH: Young man in his early twenties, attractive, dressed in clean casual clothes and may be sporting a tattoo. He speaks with a mild Southern accent, tempered by a Northern education.

SETTING

It is a room in a church. There might be a window or the shadow of a window on the ground. There is a table in back of Jethro and Josh that is stacked with various assorted cans and dry goods, which may be in unmarked boxes. On the ground in front of them are a series of boxes marked "FRUIT," "VEGETABLES," "DRY GOODS" and "OTHER" in bold, black lettering.

(JETHRO and JOSH are sorting the cans from the back table into the boxes on the floor in front of them. They work in silence for a few seconds.)

JOSH: *(Holds up a can and examines it.)* Is rhubarb a fruit or a vegetable?

JETHRO: It's a vegetable.

JOSH: My mama used to make cobbler out of it. That was really super sweet. I always thought rhubarb was a fruit.

JETHRO: No, it's a vegetable, a sort of chard. It's usually cooked with a lot of sugar because it's very bitter.

JOSH: (*Continues sorting.*) What about tomatoes? I heard people think it's a vegetable, but it's really a fruit.

JETHRO: (*Points to the "Vegetable" box.*) It's a vegetable. And if you don't hurry up, Josh, you're going make me be late for Bible study. They can't exactly start without their pastor, can they?

JOSH: No. (*Pauses and sorts.*) Brother Jethro, can I ask you somethin'?

JETHRO: (*Looks at the can JOSH is holding.*) Sweet potatoes are a vegetable even if you can make a pie out of them.

JOSH: What if I wanna get married?

JETHRO: (*Stops sorting.*) Why I'll be! I thought you'd never get ready to be married. I've never even seen you do any serious dating. At least not since that Shelby girl in high school anyway, the one that turned out so bad up there in Memphis. (*Grabs JOSH by the shoulders.*) I'd be very honored to marry you. Your parents, bless their souls, would have wanted you to get married right here in the same church where they got married and their folks before them. Hallelujah! Praise the Lord! (*Hugs JOSH.*) I'm so pleased and happy for you. (*Releases JOSH and backs away.*) And who's the lucky gal?

JOSH: That's just it, Brother Jethro. It isn't a girl. It's a guy, someone from around here.

JETHRO: (*Turns back to sorting.*) Why did you get me all excited about marrying you and then tell me something nasty like that? (*Turns to JOSH.*) Is this some sort of bad joke? You think this is funny?

JOSH: No, it's not a joke. It's for real. You know I've been gay for years. I told you myself three years ago. What did you think happened?

JETHRO: I thought you were going through a psychological phase, something transitory. (*Continues sorting.*) I prayed and prayed over you, son. I hoped you'd go away to college and see the error of your ways.

Then I heard you were going to that liberal Ivy League place where you would soak up all sorts of devilry. I warned your parents not to send you there. I had some friends who went there back in my day and they all turned to be radicals and homosexuals. (*Turns to face JOSH.*) And then you came back to town to work at the high school teaching English and history. I thought my prayers had been answered and you were following the straight and narrow path. All those nose rings and green hair you had were finally gone. You looked normal and natural. You even came back to church and became a regular member, tithing and helping with fund raising and everything. (*Turns away.*) And now you tell me you want to marry another man in my church! What do you think you're doing?

JOSH: (*Holds up a can.*) Sortin' canned goods for the homeless pantry, that's what I'm doin' right now.

JETHRO: Yes, that's what you're doing. (*Gestures to the boxes.*) Helping to feed the poor and homeless that never had the social privileges you had. (*Drops the can and grabs JOSH's hands.*) Pray with me, Josh. Let's pray to God to release you from Satan's terrible grip. (*Looks heavenward.*) O Lord, save this lost lamb and bring him back to your light and away from the Evil One's bondage. (*Tries to pull JOSH down to pray.*) Right now, let's pray to God to give up your sinful ways and be saved!

JOSH: (*Yanks his hands away and turns.*) I don't wanna to be saved and certainly not by the likes of you. I'm already saved. I don't believe that God wants me to hide in the closet for the rest of my life. (*Lifts his arms heavenward, a can in each hand.*) I believe in a loving, merciful God that accepts all his children into his forgiving bosom.

JETHRO: God is loving! But he's a righteous God, too, and a man lying with another man is an abomination. It's a sin! It's evil. (*Slams down two cans with a clatter.*) And rhubarb is a vegetable whether you sweeten it or not!

JOSH: (*Calmly.*) So I guess your answer is no?

JETHRO: Don't mock me, boy. (*Puts some more cans in the boxes.*) That's not just no, it's hell no!

JOSH: (*Continues sorting.*) How much money did my parents leave to the church when they died?

JETHRO: They were God-fearing folks who loved the Lord's house and his servants.

JOSH: How much?

JETHRO: Only the Pharisees give in public to impress the people. And your parents gave in humble secrecy.

JOSH: Enough for a new roof?

JETHRO: Yes.

JOSH: And a new parking lot?

JETHRO: Yes.

JOSH: And a new family activity center?

JETHRO: Yes. (*Turns to face JOSH.*) And enough to send you away to a prestigious Eastern university and then set your up for life with a fat trust fund, I suppose.

JOSH: Well, you suppose wrong. (*Puts a few cans in boxes.*) I borrowed money for school and I had an academic scholarship. My folks offered to help, but I refused. And then when they died, they left their money to the church, not a cent to me. I told them I didn't want any.

JETHRO: Bad blood, eh?

JOSH: No. They wanted me to be independent and not be morally polluted by unearned wealth. "Wealth without work," that's what Dad called it, one of Gandhi's evils.

JETHRO: And it didn't have anything to do with your sexual orientation by any chance?

JOSH: No, nothin' at all.

JETHRO: (*Faces JOSH and shakes a can.*) I don't believe you. Lying is a sin, just like fornication with a man.

JOSH: (*Turns away and continues working.*) I'm not lyin'. But you do, Brother Jethro.

JETHRO: Insulting a man of the cloth isn't going to get you married to your boyfriend in my church.

JOSH: And the new roof and the new parking lot and the new activity center won't help change your mind either, I suppose? That won't buy a holy favor or two?

JETHRO: That was your parent's money, freely given as a love offering to God's house. Besides, my soul's not for sale at any price. You aren't going to be married in my church, and certainly not to another man!

JOSH: Yes, I know. My parents always told me "Give freely for to withhold is to perish." I've heard it before. (*Holds up a can.*) Are you sin free Brother Jethro?

JETHRO: No man is without sin. But I have lived a life following the straight and narrow path to salvation. I won't have any fear standing before God and being judged. (*Points to JOSH.*) But you will be sent with the fornicators to burn in eternal hellfire while I go to my heavenly reward.

JOSH: (*Pauses. Sorts a can or two.*) You remember Phillip Parker?

JETHRO: Sure. Hank and Hazel's boy. A very nice young man. Is that the one you want to marry?

JOSH: No, but he is the one who told me how you molested him and the other boys at summer church camp for years.

JETHRO: (*Turns and faces JOSH.*) That's a lie! That's a mean-spirited, God-hating lie!

JOSH: Is it? The way he tells it, you worked him over right nicely for at a couple of summers. (*Turns to face JETHRO.*) He says you were pretty good at givin' pleasure to a young man, whether he wanted it or not.

JETHRO: Stop it! (*Covers his ears.*) It's not true!

JOSH: No? (*Moves closer to JETHRO.*) It kind of made me jealous to hear him talk about it. (*Sets down his cans.*) I might have liked to get to know you better. Maybe you can give me some pleasure now, you know what I mean?

JETHRO: (*Backs up. Drops his cans.*) No! You get away from me with your lies and your evil thoughts.

JOSH: (*Grabs JETHRO.*) And evil deeds. What about those? (*Pulls JETHRO closer.*) Give me a big kiss with those rugged, manly lips, Brother Jethro.

JETHRO: (*Falls to his knees. Clutches his hands in prayer.*) No! God have mercy. Protect me from evil.

JOSH: Oh, you wanna do it that way. I'm sure you're right good at it from what I heard.

JETHRO: (*Pushes JOSH away.*) Get away from me!

JOSH: Lost your taste for it? That's not what Phillip told me. He said you couldn't get enough. Two, three times a night. It's true isn't it, you perverted old man!

JETHRO: (*Covers his face, and then looks up at JOSH.*) What do you want? Money? I haven't got any money. You want to humiliate me in front of the whole congregation, the whole town, and destroy everything I built up here? Is that what you want?

JOSH: (*Turns away and picks up some cans.*) I already told you what I wanted. I wanna get married right in the church with flowers and organ music and a big reception in the activity center, followed by a wild night of dancing and drinking.

JETHRO: I can't. I can't do it.

JOSH: Really?

JETHRO: I swear I've been leading a clean life for years and years. No boys, no men, no porn. The devil had me for awhile, but now I'm free. I'm a changed man.

JOSH: Your wife know about what you did?

JETHRO: No! My wife's a Godly woman, a saintly woman. Don't you dare hurt her!

JOSH: A bit too saintly, eh? Maybe that's why you went for the boys instead?

JETHRO: I've been good, I swear. I never wanted to hurt anyone. It was stronger than me. Something about those young boys, so innocent, so beautiful, so pure . . . .

JOSH: So tasty?

JETHRO: (*Shakes his head and holds up two cans.*) Kill me! Just bash in my brains and be done with it. I'd rather die.

JOSH: Killing's a sin. (*Takes the cans and puts them in boxes.*) No, we're going to announce my marriage and do it right. You're going to tell your congregation that you had a change of heart about same-sex marriage and homosexuality in general. And now you believe in a loving God that accepts all of his children, gay, straight, black, white, all the same, even in holy matrimony. Okay?

JETHRO: (*Mumbles.*) Yes.

JOSH: I didn't hear that, Brother Jethro.

JETHRO: (*Nods his head.*) Yes, I'll do it!

JOSH: And when the deacons want to say no, you'll hold your ground and tell everyone that you know every dirty secret in town and would just hate to be spoutin' all of those ugly stories to the whole congregation from the pulpit. Okay?

JETHRO: (*Nods and hangs his head.*) Yes.

JOSH: You swear?

JETHRO: As God is my witness.

JOSH: (*Pauses. Calmly continues to sort cans.*) Is couscous a vegetable or a dry good?

JETHRO: Cous-cous? I don't even know what that is.

JOSH: I guess it depends on whether it's cooked or not. (*Puts it in the dry goods. Looks down at JETHRO.*) Come on, Brother Jethro. Get up and let's finish up the work. Those homeless people don't want to wait for their food any more than that Bible study group wants to wait for their pastor.

JETHRO: (*Stands up and takes a can and mechanically sorts.*) Yes.

JOSH: By the way, aren't you even interested in knowing who the lucky man is?

JETHRO: Not really. (*Stops and looks apprehensive.*) I mean, yes, of course, who is the lucky man? Phillip Parker, I suppose?

JOSH: (*Laughs.*) Heck no. Phillip's as straight as an arrow. (*Grabs JETHRO by the shoulders.*) It's your son, Christopher.

(*Lights dim to dark.*)

THE END

PARADISE, LOUISIANA

CAST OF CHARACTERS

JUDGE DEBRUDER: Local elected district judge in Louisiana.

BRIAN FOUTRE: Private attorney.

SETTING

Debruder is sitting at a large desk covered with various neatly stacked piles of papers. Debruder stares at one particular document for some time before laying the pile back on his already cluttered desk. There are a couple of leather office chairs facing the desk. Under them is a tasteful oriental carpet. There can be a wall with the usual diplomas and awards.

SCENE I

VOICE ON THE INTERCOM: Excuse me, Judge Debruder.

DEBRUDER: Yes.

VOICE ON THE INTERCOM: Brian Foutre is here to see you. Can he come in?

DEBRUDER: *(Frowns. Shoves the papers he's been examining into the top drawer of his desk.)* Sure, let him in.

> *(BRIAN strides into the room as if he owns it. DEBRUDER rises to greet him. He extends his hand toward his colleague.)*

DEBRUDER: Brian, what a surprise. Nice to see you again.

BRIAN: *(Glances around the room as if to check and see if no one were hiding in the corners. BRIAN does not take DEBRUDER's hand, but instead plops down into one of the two guest chairs.)* Cut the crap,

Debruder. What was your paralegal doing snooping around in Mrs. Becko's legal papers in the courthouse?

(*There is an uncomfortable pause.*)

DEBRUDER: Brian, I received an anonymous letter the other day accusing you and Mrs. Cruzado of manipulating Mrs. Becko and making yourselves beneficiaries of her estate. (*Pulls a letter out of a file.*) I don't know who wrote this thing or why exactly, but let me read you a bit of it. "Mrs. Becko's attorney, Brian Foutre and her private banker, Mrs. Cruzado, are conspiring to keep this senile old lady, estranged from her family, and then making themselves beneficiaries of her estate, valued at more than five million dollars. They have also given themselves impressive and unreasonable retainers as well making themselves heirs to Mrs. Becko's fortune in case of her death and the subsequent death of the sickly daughter. This behavior is at best, immoral, and probably illegal. In my opinion, this represents flagrant abuse of the infirm elderly and must be stopped by appropriate legal action. This letter, while anonymous, represents the truth. Only fear of subsequent legal reprisals prevents me from revealing my true identity. Signed, a True Friend of Mrs. Becko and her daughter."

(*A long silence ensues.*)

DEBRUDER: Is this true?

(*BRIAN remains silent.*)

DEBRUDER: I am legally and morally obliged to tirelessly defend the public interest as well as assure the integrity of the legal profession in this community. We have to police our own profession. If we can't, then who can?

BRIAN: (*Obviously angry.*) What the hell are you doing sticking your nose into this? Everything's on the up and up. Nobody in the world takes care of that old lady like us. We're all she's got. She and her daughter want for nothing. If it weren't for us they'd both be in some institution.

DEBRUDER: Perhaps, but at what cost? *(Reaches in the desk and pulls out some other documents.)* These are records of notarizations and registrations of various documents including one granting power of attorney to Mrs. Emily Cruzado for both the mother and daughter and establishing Attorney Brian Foutre as the trustee and official attorney for the Becko estate. We do not, of course, have access to the contents of Mrs. Becko's last will and testament, but it can hardly be much of a mystery, can it? This is a very cozy arrangement. Perhaps not illegal, but with a demented old lady and a sickly daughter, it certainly appears immoral to me. *(Pauses.)* I've been told be reliable sources that you have just completed your divorce and that the same is true of Mrs. Cruzado. She quit her job and the bank and now it appears that you have rented an office together. Apparently your entire respective careers are devoted to the sole management of the Becko estate. What exactly are the terms of Mrs. Becko's will? You and Mrs. Cruzado are not, perhaps, the beneficiaries in the case of the death of the demented mother and ill daughter?

BRIAN: That's none of your damn business.

DEBRUDER: How much are your private attorney and private banker fees coming to?

BRIAN: That's none of your damn business, either!

DEBRUDER: You, as an individual, and the legal profession, as a whole, do not need this kind of scandal. Maybe it is all on the up and up as you say. And maybe it is elderly abuse and exploitation as this letter suggests. Under any circumstances, this could be a subject for the State Legal Board of Ethics and you know it as well as I do. If it's all really on the up and up, let me review the documents and then we can drop the whole thing nicely. That's if it's really on the up and up, of course.

BRIAN: Damn you! Get your fucking nose out of this or you'll regret it for the rest of your life.

DEBRUDER: Don't threaten me!

BRIAN: I swear to God, you fuck this up and I'll smear your name through the mud until you couldn't be dog catcher anywhere in this state. *(Storms out of the office, slamming the door behind him.)*

SCENE II

(JUDGE DEBRUDER's office. Again, the desk has an abundance of legal papers.)

DEBRUDER: *(Speaking in the intercom.)* Miss Way?

VOICE ON THE INTERCOME: Yes, Judge.

DEBRUDER: Did you finish that letter to the Ethics Board of the Louisiana Bar Association?

VOICE ON THE INTERCOM: Yes, Sir. It's on your desk in the manila envelope.

DEBRUDER: Thank you. *(Picks up an envelope which he turns over and over before finally putting it back in his desk drawer. Stares out the imaginary window.)*

VOICE ON THE INTERCOM: Attorney Foutre here to see you, Judge. May he come in now?

DEBRUDER: Yes, of course. Tell him to come in.

(BRIAN betrays no sense of anger or impatience. On the contrary, BRIAN extends hishand to the startled DEBRUDER who shakes it limply before both of the men sat down.)

BRIAN: You look tired, Judge. Not sleeping well?

DEBRUDER: I am a bit tired. A lot of work. A lot of responsibilities. And a lot of re-election effort. You know how that goes.

BRIAN: Of course. You should slow down. Take it easy. Maybe take a vacation. *(Pauses.)* I hope you haven't done anything foolhardy about the subject we discussed the other day.

DEBRUDER: You mean the case of Mrs. Becko.

BRIAN: Yes, Mrs. Becko, of course.

DEBRUDER: In fact, I have been working on that case. I'm preparing a letter for the Ethics Review Board of the Louisiana Bar Association outlining the possible problems in your relationship with a demented client. Even though I do not have all the information, it appears that there may even be reason to suspect abuse and exploitation of the elderly infirm. I'm sure you're familiar with the statutes.

BRIAN: *(Flushs visible, his face muscles tighten.)* You haven't sent it, I hope?

DEBRUDER: No, I haven't. I was hoping we might work together to insure that nothing questionable is going on. The letter is still in my desk.

BRIAN: Good! And in case you get any stupid ideas about sending it, I thought I'd let you see something I dug up. *(Hands DEBRUDER a paper.)* It's just a copy, of course. I have access to the original and multiple copies in safe places, of course.

DEBRUDER: *(Looks at the paper with astonishment.)* What is this?

BRIAN: Why, it's your selective service file report for 1971. Don't you recognize it?

(DEBRUDER studies the document in silence.)

BRIAN: Let me explain it. You seem to be having a lapse in memory. This is your 4-F classification. That's "Mentally Unsuitable for the Military" in case you've forgotten. But I think the notes under the comments section are more interesting. *(Takes his copy and reads.)* These are notes from an army psychiatrist if I'm not mistaken and they read "mentally unsuitable for the military due to pronounced homosexual attitudes incompatible with military discipline and order." Interesting comments aren't they, Judge.

DEBRUDER: *(Stares at the paper. Pauses.)* Brian, may I use your first name?

BRIAN: Sure, Judge.

DEBRUDER: I can remember that awful day at the New Orleans Induction Center as if it were yesterday. It was 1971 and the Vietnam War was raging. Thousands of young, healthy Louisiana men left. Hundreds, even thousands came back home dead or mutilated or psychological cripples. I knew some of these young men. Up until then, we all got University deferments. Then they ran out of volunteers. *(Pauses.)* You were too young for all this, weren't you?

BRIAN: Yes, Judge. I was a way too young at the time.

DEBRUDER: I hated that futile war and knew then that I could never serve. I got inducted and waited until the intelligence test. Then, as a trembling twenty-one year old, I faced the entire military establishment and just said "no." I refused to take the intelligence test. I refused to participate in that war.

BRIAN: I admire your conviction, Judge.

DEBRUDER: They warned me that I would be going to prison and finally they took me to see that military psychiatrist. *(Continues the narrative in the air, as if to himself and the audience.)* I just told him that I had dedicated myself to loving my fellow man both mentally and physically, and that I couldn't join the army. I suppose that didn't leave too much up to the imagination, did it?

BRIAN: No, Judge. That sure as hell didn't leave too much up to the imagination. In fact, it still doesn't.

DEBRUDER: You know what he asked me?

BRIAN: No.

DEBRUDER: He asked me whether I really wanted to go into the military. And I just said, no. That was it. I just said no. *(Pauses. Looks up at BRIAN with pained surprise.)* Where did you get this? I understood that all the old selective service records had been destroyed in a warehouse fire in St. Louis.

BRIAN: Sorry, Judge, you're not so lucky this time. I got my friends too, you know. Somebody told me you had gotten out of the draft, but I never knew why, and never really cared until now. But you always did seem a little fruity to me, wife and kids notwithstanding. *(Pauses a few seconds.)* What do you think your election opponent will do with this information in the upcoming elections? Do you think our patriotic, God-fearing people of Central Louisiana will want a draft-dodging, queer judge for their husbands and sons? Do you? *(Pauses.)* I think not. Can't you just see the billboards now? Say "No" to the queer, draft-dodging judge. Vote for morality. Vote for LaFaye.

    (DEBRUDER just sits there.)

BRIAN: Then again, who needs to know about this? Maybe I can just forget about this bit of old history, and you can just forget about Mrs. Becko and your letter and your evidence and just about everything to do with me and that old lady. So before you go sending any letters to the Ethics Board, my friend, I'd seriously consider the consequences. *(BRIAN rises and turns to leave.)* Just in case you're wondering, Judge. That's just a copy, of course, and there are plenty more where that came from.

    (Lights dim to dark.)

SCENE III

(DEBRUDER's office. The next day. He is clearing out is desk. There are cardboard boxes here and there with books, papers and memorabilia. The desk is over flowing with letter.)

BRIAN: *(Knocks gently.)* May I come in? I didn't see your secretary.

DEBRUDER: She's taking off, looking for a new job if I'm not mistaken. Come on in. *(Looks at BRIAN.)* I hope you're not here to gloat.

BRIAN: Gloat? On the contrary, I just heard that you were withdrawing from the election and taking early retirement. I just came to tell you that the community will be losing an experienced and impartial judge, loved by the people.

DEBRUDER: *"Tout flatteur vit au dépens de celui qui l'écoute."*

BRIAN: I'm sorry, I don't speak French. You'll have to translate.

DEBRUDER: It's La Fontaine from his fable about the fox and the crow.

BRIAN: *(Looks down at a bunch of letters on the desk.)* A lot of correspondence here.

DEBRUDER: Yes. It's an outpouring of support from the community and pleas for me to change my mind about running for judge again.

BRIAN: Well, they're right. There's nothing to keep you from running again that I know about.

DEBRUDER: I believe it is best I retire at this time.

BRIAN: Why? Even though you could benefit from a cozy retirement, I have salted away that documentation about your youthful indiscretions. No need to worry about that as long as you don't lose your head and do something stupid.

DEBRUDER: *(Sits down and indicates a chair to BRIAN.)* I parked my car four blocks from the courthouse today, down on Washington Street. I know that I would have to cross the National Veteran's Cemetery to come here. You know the one, don't you?

BRIAN: Of course. My father's buried there.

DEBRUDER: I'm sorry. I didn't know.

BRIAN: No need to be sorry. He survived World War II and then worked for the post office until a few years ago. Then he died of lung cancer from smoking. Not too glorious, but respectable.

DEBRUDER: I walked through there. It's an immaculate cemetery with row upon row of crosses, mostly World War II veterans, but a few from Korea and the Vietnam. I wandered through the crosses until I stopped in front of one marked 1948-1971. That was the year, 1971, the year I had gotten my 4-F status and was deferred from the military. I reached out and touched that cross. It was cold, moist marble. "Born 1949, died 1971." That poor guy had been twenty-two years old, just the same age as I had been at the time. That poor, young man was dead while I was alive, breathing, eating, sleeping, going home each night to my wife and kids. Is there any justice in that at all?

BRIAN: Judge, you have worked hard. You have helped hold together the justice system of this area. You have done good work and honorable work.

DEBRUDER: Thank you, but perhaps what's happening now is just retribution for past sins? Perhaps it is my time to pay a long overdue debt to justice, divine justice, and you are the dark angel of that retribution?

BRIAN: Angelic? I don't think so. At least my first wife never thought so. *(Looks down at a sealed manila envelope on the desk.)* To the State Board of Ethics. Nothing stupid in here, I hope?

DEBRUDER: Yes, it outlines your role in the fleecing of Mrs. Becko and dispossession of her daughter in collusion with Mrs. Cruzado. I'm sure the board will find it of great interest.

BRIAN: (*Slams down his first on the table.*) Just because you're retiring, it doesn't mean you can escape! You may retire to the county, or leave the area or the state for all I care, but I will make sure that no one is unaware of your dirty past. (*Pauses. Takes the envelope.*) You will be branded a faggot, yellow-bellied, draft dodging coward and you won't find a hole big enough to hide in if you send this.

DEBRUDER: Give me the envelope. I'll drop it off at the post office on my way out. (*Takes the envelope. Looks back at BRIAN.*) And by the way, you won't have to look far. I'm retiring to our camp in Grant Parish.

BRIAN: Where? Okay, make my day! I'll have signs put up so you won't be able to live anywhere up there, you sanctimonious old fool. I'll have a full length ad printed in the Colfax Chronicle.

DEBRUDER: I won't be hiding. Our camp's up in Paradise, Louisiana, population 545.

BRIAN: Paradise, eh? Well get ready because I will make it a living hell. Don't you dare mail that letter!

DEBRUDER: It's a done deal. It's going to the mail.

BRIAN: (*Snatches the envelope away.*) Give me that thing! (*Tears it up.*)

DEBRUDER: (*Shakes his head.*) It's already gone as an e-mail attachment. You're too late.

BRIAN: (*Seething.*) I'll kill you, you son of a bitch! (*Lunges toward DEBRUBER.*)

DEBRUDER: Try it! (*Points to a camera in the corner.*) And the video of your performance will go viral before you can hit the door. My secretary has been watching and recording everything.

BRIAN: Damn you! Damn you to hell! You think you're going to Paradise, eh. Well get ready for living hell. (*Looks around and lowers his voice.*) I've got news for you, the Board of Ethics is going to uphold the validity of Mrs. Becko's will, whatever you do or say. None of this sanctimonious grand standing and righteousness is going to matter at all. I know every man on that board and there's not a one who will upset my applecart for a place in some hypothetical paradise, in heaven or in Grant Parish. (*Laughs.*) Grant Parish, there's not even a stop light in Grant Parish. You're just a fool, Debruder. You're a fool and you'll learn a bitter less. Nice guys don't finish first, people like me do. Now go on to paradise and tell me what you find there, you old fool!

(*BRIAN turns to walk away. He flips the bird to the presumed camera. DEBRUDER shakes his head. Lights dim to dark.*)

THE END

OLD SOUTH,
NEW SOUTH, NO SOUTH

(A TRAGEDY IN THREE ACTS)

This is a tragedy in three acts. The same characters play different roles in the three acts, the first act represents the Antebellum OLD SOUTH, the second depicts the Jim Crow so-called NEW SOUTH and the third shows the NO SOUTH or the South after the Civil Rights Act and integration. The four characters, two white men and a black man and black woman, may be reversed and the white characters played by blacks and vice versa. It will certainly heighten the audience interest and should be left to the discretion of the director.

ACT I: THE OLD SOUTH

CAST OF CHARACTERS

MASTER BAILEY: Plantation owner. He is dressed in a stereotypical white suit with a hat and cane. He looks like Colonel Sanders.

OVERSEER O'NEILL: Plantation overseer. He is dressed in a dirty shirt and pants. He is obviously not of the same social or educational class as Mr. Bailey.

BETSY: Attractive young slave girl. She is beautiful, but dressed in rags and barefoot.

GEORGE: Young man, handsome and well-built, but also dressed in rags and barefoot.

SETTING

There is a suggestion of a cotton field in the Antebellum South.

(GEORGE and BETSY are mimicking cotton picking. They may have cotton bags or not, depending on the available props. Nothing is really required. MASTER BAILY and OVERSEER O'NEILL come on stage and watch the two slaves working.)

OVERSEER: Mister Bailey, there they be. The buck is as hard a worker as you could want, a real good boy and very obedient.

BAILEY: And that woman?

OVERSEER: That be Betsy. She's a real looker and she and George be married in their own way.

BAILEY: Jumping the broom?

OVERSEER: Yep. That be the case. Not in church like or anything formal.

BAILEY: Any children?

OVERSEER: None that I knows of. Good thing, too. When them women starts havin' babies, they get so flat and flabby it looks like they been deflated. Their tits just hangs down to their belly buttons. It's a damn shame, too.

BAILEY: Watch your tongue, Mr. O'Neill. None of that vulgar barnyard language around me or my family if you please.

OVERSEER: Sorry, Mr. Bailey. It won't never happen again. And I don't never talk like that in front of the ladies. I weren't raised like that.

BAILEY: Fetch the woman, please.

OVERSEER: (*Grabs BETSY by the arm and pulls her over to BAILEY.*) Look right smart, woman. Master Bailey wants to see you up close.

BAILEY: How old are you?

BETSY: Right near sixteen, I thinks. Not sure at all, Massa.

BAILEY: You know how to cook?

BETSY: Yes, sir. My mama taught me how to cook at the plantation where we was before here.

BAILEY: And where was that?

BETSY: Up near Natchitoches, with Madame Claire Prudhomme.

OVERSEER: Mr. Prudhomme died of the fever a few months back. We picked up George and Betsy there in a lot when they sold the hands at an auction. Got a right good deal for them, too. Only $500 for Betsy here and $700 for George, he bein' a strappin' buck and all.

BAILEY: Yes, of course. Please spare me the details of the transactions. It's much too mercantile for my liking. (*To BETSY.*) How would you like to come up and live near the big house in that little cottage with the other cook?

BETSY: That'd be real nice, but I prefers to come up and cook during the day and stay with my husband down in the slave houses at night, if that be all right?

OVERSEER: You don't have any say in the matter, missy! This is the master and he can do whatever he pleases with you whenever he wants, you understand that?

BAILEY: Now, now, Mr. O'Neill. Perhaps Betsy doesn't understand the situation. (*To BETSY.*) This is a full time job and you live up there in the cottage next to the big house. You will have your own room with a separate entrance in the back and another one in the front.

BETSY: My own private door?

BAILEY: Yes, Betsy, for you to go in and out and for visitors to go in and out.

BETSY: You mean my husband?

OVERSEER: You ignorant bitch! Mr. Bailey means for himself when he wants to come and visit you private like for his own pleasure.

BAILEY: Mr. O'Neill, let me remind you about the profanity. I will not tolerate profanity in my presence. It offends me and it offends God.

OVERSEER: Sorry, sir.

BETSY: (*Begins to understand.*) Oh no, Massa. I ain't interested in that kind a job at all. I's just fine here with George and we be just fine in our little cabin . . . .

BAILEY: (*Touches BETSY's arm.*) Betsy, you don't understand.

OVERSEER: You ain't got not choice!

BAILEY: Be nice to her, O'Neill. A little kindness goes a lot further than a lot of abuse. (*To BETSY.*) Mrs. Bailey is often ill and she visits her family in New Orleans for months at a stretch in the winter. Our children have gone away to France to school and it gets mighty lonely up there in that big house. It would be a big comfort to me to have someone to give me some companionship, someone like yourself who has been raised by gentile folks up river.

BETSY: Please, Massa Bailey. I ain't that kinda woman. I love George. He loves me. We be happy together. Aint got no children but it won't be much longer. I knows it. (*Falls on her knees and clutches BAILEY's legs.*) I wanna stay here and just be a field hand with George. I'll work hard. I promise I won't make no trouble and we have lots of babies to grow up and work with us. Please.

OVERSEER: (*Pulls BETSY away and knocks her down.*) Don't touch Mr. Bailey with your grubby hands.

GEORGE: (*Watches the unfolding drama. Rushes over to pick BETSY up.*) Betsy!

OVERSEER: (*Lashes out at GEORGE with a whip and beats him off.*) Get outta this, you dog. You got nuttin' to say.

GEORGE: Please, Massa Bailey. We be happy together. We gonna work harder dan any other hands. I swear. Betsy be a good girl. She got religion from Madame Prudhomme. She been baptized in the Catholic church and all.

OVERSEER: Shut up, I tell you. (*Strikes GEORGE again.*)

BAILEY: (*Stops O'NEILL's hand.*) That's enough. There won't be any more arguing. (*To GEORGE.*) Betsy will be coming up to the big house and I will treat her very nicely. She will get good food, clean clothes, and a nice bed with a real mattress. She may even be allowed to participate in some religious instruction if she is so inclined.

GEORGE: Please, Massa Bailey.

OVERSEER: (*Raises his whip.*) You cheeky fool!

BAILEY: (*Holds O'NEILL's hand.*) I want none of that. We can be persuasive in other ways. (*To BETSY.*) Miss Betsy, I think you know that a buyer from New Orleans has just been up here looking for hands for down South. George here is a good, strong buck and he would fetch a handsome price. You know that when folks get sold down further South or in Mississippi or even Texas, there is almost no chance of ever seeing them again. (*Pauses.*) You want to see George again?

BETSY: (*Nods.*) Yes, Massa, I wants to see him everyday of my life.

BAILEY: I'm an older man, Betsy. There may be a day not too far off that I would no longer need your companionship. And you might be able to go back to George here.

BETSY: Please, Massa Bailey, that ain't no life, waitin' for a day that might never come.

BAILEY: Or we can just tell that buyer from New Orleans that we have some extra hands for sale. Do you want that for George?

BETSY: No, Massa. I wants him near to me. We be married.

BAILEY: Not legally. That broom ceremony doesn't mean a thing. Besides, you are my property. As Mr. O'Neill has so crudely suggested, I can do what I please with my hands the same as if they were swine or cattle.

BETSY: I ain't no animal, Massa Bailey. I's a woman with a heart and soul and this is breakin' my heart and killin' my soul. (*Begins to whimper.*)

BAILEY: (*Touches BETSY on the arm.*) Now, now. It will be hard in the beginning, but with the soft work at the house and the good food and clothes, this field work will just be like a distant nightmare. (*To O'NEILL.*) You take her up to the house for Mrs. Carter to clean up and dress properly. I want her to be presentable by tomorrow evening. Do you understand? And no rough stuff either.

OVERSEER: Of course, sir. And what about tonight? Do they get to spend the night together.

BAILEY: Heaven's no! I want you to take her to Mrs. Carter tonight with strict instructions. No more hanky-panky with George.

BETSY: Oh please, Massa Bailey, can I have a last night with George? He be my husband and the only man I ever known.

BAILEY: And have you run away or kill yourself together or some other foolish scheme? No! The decision's been made. You can say your goodbyes to George now and Mr. O'Neill will be bringing you up to the house directly. Good day. (*Leaves the stage.*)

BETSY: (*Rushes over to GEORGE and embraces him. Weeps bitterly.*) Oh George. I can't leave you. Don't let 'em take me away. I don't wanna be at the big house. I don't wanna make love to the Massa. I don't care if I dies. (*Begins to sob.*)

OVERSEER: Come on, bitch! No weepy farewells.

BETSY: (*Clutches GEORGE.*) No, no, no!

OVERSEER: (*Grabs BETSY and yanks her away.*) You comin' with me you little she-devil.

GEORGE: (*Lunges after BETSY.*) Betsy!

OVERSEER: (*Takes his whip and brutally beats GEORGE to the ground.*) What do ya think you're doin' you crazy cur.

BETSY: (*Throws herself over GEORGE to protect him.*) No, leave him alone. Beat me instead.

OVERSEER: (*Drags BETSY off.*) Can't beat you, missy. No scars or bruises or Master Bailey goin' have my hide. (*Kicks GEORGE away.*) Enough! Get back to work and don't let me see you hangin' around that big house. Never! You hear me, boy! Never! And if you tries to get up there and see Betsy, you'll be hangin' from that tree with your privates cut off. You hear that! (*To BETSY.*) You hear that you little she-devil!

(*The OVERSEER drags BETSY offstage as GEORGE lies on the ground, convulsed with tears.*)

GEORGE: Oh lawdy, oh lawdy. Lets me die. Lets me die here and now. Oh lawdy.

(*Lights dim to dark.*)

ACT II: NEW SOUTH

CAST OF CHARACTERS

JUDGE CARTER: A well-dressed older gentleman.

SHERIFF MCCOY: A typical sheriff in khaki uniform. He has a night stick and a service revolver (imitation) if available.

DORIS: A young, attractive woman, simply dressed, but clean and stylish. She wears simple shoes.

JOHN: A young man in laborer's clothing, perhaps overalls and a plaid shirt. He is clean shaven, with short, neatly trimmed hair. He wears boots.

SETTING

Street in Southern town, circa 1930's to 1950's, the Jim Crow era.

(*SHERIFF MCCOY are walking in the other. DORIS and JOHN move to one side to let the JUDGE and SHERIFF walk by. The JUDGE and SHERIFF do not seem to even notice the couple, who continues. JOHN laughs at something DORIS says and both the JUDGE and SHERIFF turn around to confront them.*)

SHERIFF: (*Confronts JOHN.*) You laughin' at us, boy?

JOHN: (*Turns around.*) No, sir. I ain't laughin' at you, Sheriff McCoy.

JUDGE: (*Moves closer.*) What's this all about, Sheriff?

SHERIFF: I do believe this young buck be mockin' us, Judge.

JUDGE: Really? (*To JOHN.*) That so, boy?

89

JOHN: No, Judge. I ain't be laughin' at you. No way. (*Points to DORIS.*) Doris here be tellin' me a funny story bout folks we knows up in Natchitoches.

JUDGE: (*Examines JOHN.*) You working or are you just loitering around here?

JOHN: I works down at Mr. Bentley's Lumber Mill. Today be a day off for me.

SHERIFF: You say "sir" or "judge" when you be talking to this man. None of this low-life sassin' around here.

DORIS: John's not sassin' anybody, Sheriff. He's as good as good can be and he's one of the best workers Mr. Bentley ever seen.

SHERIFF: (*To DORIS.*) You shut your mouth, young lady. No one asked 'bout your opinion on nuttin'. Who you work for?

DORIS: I works as a domestic for Miss Gauthier, down on Fourth Street.

SHERIFF: Ain't you supposed to be workin' today?

DORIS: No, sir. I got the day off and jus came to town to be with John here.

JUDGE: (*To DORIS.*) You two married?

JOHN: No, sir. We is jus fiancéd.

JUDGE: (*Uses a mocking tone.*) Fiancéd, eh. (*Pause. To DORIS.*) So you are walking the streets with an unmarried single man with no (*exaggerates the word*) chaperone?

DORIS: We be both adults and he's my fiancé, Judge Carter. There's no law against that.

SHERIFF: (*To DORIS.*) You shut up, missy. You hear! You speaks when you spoken to and not one second before. (*Screams.*) You got no business tellin' the Judge what's the law and what ain't! You understand!

JOHN: Sheriff McCoy, Doris don't mean any harm. She's just tryin' to explain.

SHERIFF: (*Backhands JOHN.*) Shut your mouth, too, boy.

JUDGE: (*Eyeing DORIS more closely.*) You are a pretty young thing. What's your name, Miss?

DORIS: Doris. Doris Metoyer.

JUDGE: (*To SHERIFF.*) That's why she looks so pretty, she's one of those Creole women from up there around Natchitoches.

SHERIFF: She's got so much white blood in her she can most almost pass if she wanted to. At least up North.

JUDGE: (*To DORIS.*) Why would you be fiancéd with a man like this (*Points to JOHN.*) when you can have most any man you please. Even I'd be right honored to entertain you on a regular basis at the Martin Hotel down the street if you're in the mood.

JOHN: She's not interested.

SHERIFF: (*Hits JOHN.*) Shut your mouth! The Judge ain't be talking to you.

DORIS: Judge, I'm not interested. I'm pleased to be fiancéd with John and we be gettin' married in the next couple of months.

JUDGE: (*Takes out his wallet.*) I can make it worth your while, Miss Doris. We might be able to make this a long term sort of relationship. (*Show DORIS the money.*) It could be worth a lot more than what Old Miss Gauthier is paying you and the work would be so much easier. You could make enough money to buy a little house somewhere. (*Pauses.*)

Who knows? When you and I get a bit older, you might just be able to retire and then you can get married to John here. (*Points to JOHN.*)

JOHN: Don't do it, baby. I can work for two. We can get plenty to live on from my job at da mill.

SHERIFF: (*Slaps JOHN.*) You shut up, you good for nuthin' rascal! The Judge is talkin' to the young lady.

JUDGE: (*Caresses DORIS's arm.*) It could be very worth your while, missy. Nice clothing, a steady income, easy work.

DORIS: No, sir. I ain't interested. John and me, we be gettin' married and if we be poor, so be it. I's a Christian woman and Jesus can forgive, but he gives us free will to decide.

JUDGE: (*Irritated.*) I know Robert Bentley very well. He's married to my cousin and my aunt is related to him by marriage as well. A phone call to him and John here would be fired in a minute with no chance of getting hired in any of the mills around here.

JOHN: That ain't true, Judge. There be lots of places to work all over this parish.

JUDGE: You don't think I know people all over this parish? You wouldn't get a job in hundred miles around here in any direction.

DORIS: That's threatenin' and you can't be doin' that, Judge. You been elected by the people and you supposed to serve 'em all, da rich and da poor, da black folks and da white ones.

JUDGE: (*Laughs.*) The people, eh? Not your folks! We got so many restrictions in place that there aren't ten of your kind who can vote in this parish, or any other in this state for that matter. (*Pauses.*) Besides, don't think you can threaten me. You are here, sauntering up and down the street in full daylight with an unmarried man. (*Turns to SHERIFF.*) Why, if I'm not mistaken, Miss Doris might be arrested and taken to jail as a common prostitute, soliciting in public. What do you think?

SHERIFF: (*Smiles.*) You are a genius, Judge Carter. A trip to jail and a hefty fine might just change the little lady's mind about a lot of things.

JOHN: She ain't no prostitute. She's a good woman, a Christian woman.

SHERIFF: (*Knocks JOHN down.*) Now you listen to me, boy. We have heard enough of your belly achin'! Miss Doris here is walkin' the streets. If the Judge wants me to take her in for some (*Exaggerates each syllable.*) interrogation, then that's the law.

DORIS: You can't do that. We got our rights, too, Judge.

JUDGE: (*Laughs.*) Yes, Miss Doris. You have the right to be quiet and keep in place and do whatever we tell you to do. (*Strokes her again.*) So you can be nice and come along with the Sheriff or you can be troublesome and resist arrest. Which way do you want it?

DORIS: No! I ain't goin' no way!

SHERIFF: (*Grabs DORIS by the arm and twists it back to restrain her.*) You sure is, missy. Now stop your yakkin' and come on with me.

DORIS: It's against da law! This is a free country! I got my rights!

JUDGE: I am the law! (*Points to the SHERIFF.*) And he is the law. And you are nothing. You are less than nothing. Now let the sheriff take you to jail where we can all do a proper interrogation. (*Caresses DORIS.*)

JOHN: (*Jumps up and tries to drag DORIS away.*) Come on. Run!

SHERIFF: (*Releases DORIS. Pulls out a gun and points it at JOHN.*) You make one more step, boy and your heart is goin' to be scattered all over the sidewalk. You hear me, boy!

DORIS: (*To JOHN.*) Do what he says!

SHERIFF: That's a good girl. You tell your hot-headed young buck here to keep his distance and not do anything stupid. (*To DORIS.*) And you be nice and go along with the judge down to the jailhouse.

JOHN: (*Reaches out to DORIS.*) Please, don't go.

SHERIFF: (*Screaming.*) Shut your mouth, I said. (*Kicks JOHN.*)

JOHN: Shoot me! Shoot me, 'cause my heart be breakin' anyways. You killin' me anyway. (*Goes to his knees and prays.*) Oh, God, help us. Jesus help us. Deliver us from evil, Dear Jesus, deliver us from evil.

SHERIFF: (*Knocks him down completely.*) Stop your blabberin', boy. None of this Jesus talk. Jesus is on our side and has been and always will be. You ain't learned nuttin' in church?

JUDGE: Well, Sheriff, it looks like you have the situation under control here. Let me just escort Miss Doris here back to the jail. (*To DORIS.*) Sheriff McCoy has a nice little room in the back of the jail for more gentle interrogations, if you know what I mean. There's a nice big bed for the Sheriff to relax in after a hard day on the streets. It's got a nice side table and a lamp and there's usually a pitcher of lemonade in the ice box. Doesn't that sound right nice?

(*JUDGE leads DORIS away. DORIS is weeping in her hands. JOHN curls up in a ball and rocks back in forth. The SHERIFF stands triumphant over JOHN. Lights dim to dark.*)

ACT III: NO SOUTH

CAST OF CHARACTERS

JUDGE: Same person who has played Doris and Betsy in the other acts. The Judge wears an official robe and wields a gavel.

BAILIFF: Same person who played Sheriff and overseer. He wears a badge of some sort and carries a canister of mace and/ or a stick.

FRANK: Same person who played Master Bailey and Judge Carter. He is dressed in a prisoner's jumpsuit.

DISTRICT ATTORNEY (D.A.): Same person who played John and George. He is well-dressed and holds himself very erect.

SETTING

There is a stylized courtroom. The Judge is seated at a desk, if one is available. The Judge wears a robe and has a gavel and a desk if possible. The Bailiff stands off to one side and the D.A. and Frank are on the other so the audience can see everything that goes on.

(*The JUDGE, dressed in a black robe, presides over the courtroom, where the BAILIFF, D.A. and FRANK, the defendant, are located.*)

FRANK: I don't want no court-appointed attorney, Your Honoress.

JUDGE: It's Your Honor.

FRANK: But you're a woman. It can't be the same word for women as for men, can it?

95

JUDGE: Yes, it is the same, Mr. Thornton. It's "Your Honor" whether it's a man or a woman.

FRANK: Yes, ma'am.

BAILIFF: (*Starts to move toward FRANK.*) You impudent rascal! This is the judge and you'd better treat her with respect.

JUDGE: Bailiff, please restrain yourself. I won't have any shenanigans from the defendant or anyone else, including you. Ma'am is okay with me if that's what Mr. Thornton prefers.

BAILIFF: (*Backs up.*) Yes, Your Honor. Sorry.

JUDGE: (*To FRANK.*) Even though this is only a preliminary hearing, you realize that your lack of legal knowledge deprives you of a significant advantage in this court of law. You deserve the same chance as anyone else.

FRANK: Chance? That's a good one! What chance do I stand to get in this sort of kangaroo court?

JUDGE: (*Brings down her gavel.*) That's enough! (*To BAILIFF.*) Take this man to his chair. I would like to hear from the District Attorney about this case.

DISTRICT ATTORNEY: Your Honor, the facts of the case are clear. Mr. Frank Thornton here (*Points to FRANK*) doesn't even deny the events. He pursued the victim through the neighborhood, and then confronted him with a gun. And when the victim refused to submit to a strip search, Mr. Thornton here killed him, shot him right through the heart execution style, as if the victim were an animal.

FRANK: (*Yells.*) That ain't true! That guy was threatenin' me. He shouldn't have been there no way. What was a young kid doin' in the dark in a nice neighborhood anyway?

DISTRICT ATTORNEY: Your Honor, it was six in the evening in May. It was well before sunset at that time of year and not at all dark as Mr. Thornton contends.

FRANK: (*To JUDGE.*) That's a lie! That's a goddamn lie and this lyin' bastard knows it!

JUDGE: (*Bangs her gavel.*) Mr. Thornton, I will not accept the use of vulgar language in my courtroom. You will either refrain from swearing or the bailiff will drag you back to your cell.

FRANK: Jus you try! I'll go kickin' and screamin' and bitin' like you ain't never seen.

JUDGE: (*To BAILIFF.*) Bailiff, another outburst from Mr. Thornton and you can use whatever means necessary to remove him from this court and return him to his cell.

FRANK: (*More contrite.*) Yes ma'am. You're right. I done overstepped my bounds. (*Pauses.*) But that was the way I was brung up. We didn't have no kid's books around the house. I didn't even know how to read 'til I was near seven. And my dad beat us kids regular like. (*Pauses.*) How do you think I was goin' turn out with that sort of upbringin'?

DISTRICT ATTRONEY: Your Honor, you see that you might actually use Mr. Thornton's unfortunate childhood as extenuating circumstances. But the fact remains that Mr. Thornton killed an innocent young man in cold blood.

FRANK: (*To the JUDGE.*) I said I felt threatened. I swear I did. How did I know that he didn't have no gun on him? Or a knife? (*Pauses.*) I been beat up and robbed more than once and I didn't ever want that to happen again to me or anyone else. The kid had a black sweatshirt with a hood on it, jus like gang members does. You know the kind.

DISTRICT ATTORNEY: Your Honor, Mr. Thornton killed a 15 year old boy, regardless of how he was dressed. That victim's blood cries out for justice. His family and friends cry out for justice. (*To FRANK.*) This self-proclaimed vigilante cut short a promising life and now all of society cries out for justice. Where are the rights of the victim and his family in this tragedy?

FRANK: I got my rights, too! I had a gun and it was legal, too. I got a permit all legal like and if I feels that someone is goin' do somethin' bad to me, I gotta constitutional right to defend myself.

DISTRICT ATTORNEY: The victim was unarmed! Not only that, but you, Mr. Thornton, pursued the victim through the neighborhood in an aggressive and threatening manner. Who was the threat to whom? Who is dead?

JUDGE: Did you really feel threatened Mr. Thornton?

FRANK: You bet, ma'am. I was afraid for my life.

DISTRICT ATTRONEY: That is clearly an unrealistic perception on the defendant's part. There was no real threat, except that posed by Mr. Thornton to the real victim.

JUDGE: (*To the D.A.*) Sometimes perception is stronger than reality. (*To FRANK.*) Do I threaten you, Mr. Thornton?

FRANK: You bet, ma'am. You can throw me in jail for the rest of my life or send me to the electric chair. (*Pauses.*) You bet you threaten me.

JUDGE: That's the sentencing part of the case. But what about me as a person? Do I frighten you now?

FRANK: I dunno.

JUDGE: I could be hiding a weapon under my robe? Or be convinced you are guilty and want to do you harm from some sense of previous personal injustice. Does that frighten you?

FRANK: Yes, I does, ma'am. And I suspect that you do think I'm guilty and will throw me in jail even though I ain't done nothin' wrong jus to prove a point. You may even recommend that they put me down like a rabid dog: shoot me, or gas me or lectrocute me. (*Pauses.*) And they did the same thing to Jesus, too. They killed him. But he triumphed over death and now His Kingdom won't have no end.

DISTRICT ATTORNEY: Your Honor, do we need to listen to this pseudo-religious diatribe?

(*The JUDGE goes down and stands directly in front of FRANK. The BAILIFF and D.A. move closer in an effort to protect the JUDGE.*)

JUDGE: Here, Mr. Thornton. I'm right in front of you. If you think I threaten you, will you try and kill me now?

FRANK: (*Pauses. Looks around and grabs the JUDGE by the neck and begins to choke her.*) You damn right, you pompous educated man-threatening bitch! Die! Die!

(*The BAILIFF strikes FRANK and tries to pry the JUDGE away. The D.A. pulls at FRANK from behind. FRANK and the JUDGE fall backwards to the ground while the BAILIFF struggles to free the JUDGE.*)

BAILIFF: (*Pulls at FRANK.*) Get off her, you worthless son of a bitch. Give me half an excuse and I'll break your neck. Get off!

DISTRICT ATTORNEY: Guards!

(*The BAILIFF finally manages to free the JUDGE, whom he pulls away while the D.A. pulls FRANK backwards and away. FRANK turns and attacks the D.A. FRANK and the D.A. struggle and fall to the ground.*)

JUDGE: (*Gasping and screaming.*) Help! Help!

(*The BAILIFF attacks FRANK again. The BAILIFF manages to gets FRANK into a back hold. FRANK stops struggling.*)

BAILIFF: Calm down right now! I'll snap both of your arms like match sticks. You want that, tough guy?

DISTRICT ATTORNEY: (*Gets to his feet and struggles toward the JUDGE.*) You okay?

JUDGE: I think so. How about you?

DISTRICT ATTORNEY: I guess so. A bit shook up.

JUDGE: (*To FRANK.*) You are in deep trouble, Mr. Thornton. Murder, attempted murder, resisting arrest, causing a disturbance in court, that's just off the tip of my tongue.

DISTRICT ATTORNEY: (*To FRANK.*) And all that before witnesses.

FRANK: (*Slumps down in a chair.*) I ain't really bad. I jus can't control myself. I never been able to do it. It's jus terrible. I can't control my anger.

JUDGE: Like when you killed that young man? (*To BAILIFF.*) Take him away. He needs a psychiatric evaluation. (*To D.A.*) Do you concur?

DISTRICT ATTORNEY: Absolutely.

BAILIFF: (*Grabs FRANK and begins to escort him out.*) Come on, punk! We goin' take a walk down to meet your new friends in prison. They might be plenty glad to see you.

FRANK: (*Stops and yells at JUDGE.*) I an't no kid! I'm a growed man. My papa used to beat me, you know. I gotta talk to you some more!

JUDGE: Let him talk.

FRANK: Papa loved to drink moonshine. He liked to read strange books with no pictures, too. And he never reads to us or wants us to learn. He was a real peculiar man. He tells me I'm a killer 'cause my dog gits heartworm so bad it can't stand up no mo. Ain't gonna treat no dog for heartworm, he says, just too expensive. So my dog just coughs and wheezes worse and worse and gets all puffy from heart disease and finally dies and Papa calls me a killer. I got so damn angry, I stuck a pitchfork right into papa's right arm. (*Points to a place on his arm.*) Nearly cut it off, too. But they sewed it up and you couldn't hardly tell the right arm from the left after a year or so. (*Trails off.*) What do ya think that does to a kid, things like that.

JUDGE: Please remove the defendant. He will be held without bond and have a court-mandated psychiatric evaluation. (*Bangs the gavel.*) I believe this hearing is over.

BAILIFF: Come on. Enough sob story. We've heard it a hundred times already. Blah, blah, blah. No money, no parents, no school. Blah, blah, blah. A nice shrink is goin' talk to you and make sure you're doin' alright for trial. (*Exits with FRANK.*) Heartworm, eh?

DISTRICT ATTORNEY: That was really foolish, Your Honor, putting yourself in that man's way. It might even be considered recklessly provocative.

JUDGE: Provocative, eh? (*Smoothes out her wrinkled robe.*) Why don't you come back to my chambers? I'll show you provocative. How about it, big boy?

(*The DISTRICT ATTORNEY backs up in apparent shock. The JUDGE pulls him behind her by his tie the DISTRICT ATTORNEY follows, leaning back as he does so. Lights dim to dark.*)

THE END

FOUR SHORT MEDICAL
DIALOGUES

DIALOGUE #1

MR. BOCA'S NEW HEART

CAST OF CHARACTERS

DR. DENISE FAIRCHILD: Middle aged female oncologist

MR. STANLEY FORTIER: Middle aged male lawyer

SETTING

Fortier's office with a big, glass-topped desk and a couple of chairs. There are bookshelves and an oriental carpet on the ground. The wall has framed degrees, awards, commendations, etc. There is a window, out of which the protagonists can look from time to time.

DENISE: Damn that man! (*Throws papers onto FORTIER's desk.*) I treated him with respect and consideration. I stuck with him throughout his whole medical ordeal. I held his hand and prayed with him, for heaven's sake. And this is how he repays me? A lawsuit?

STANLEY: (*Stands up and walks over to DENISE. Puts his hand on DENISE's shoulder.*) Remember, Denise, this isn't about justice. It's about settlement.

DENISE: Settlement? How dare you talk to me about settlement? I don't owe this man a thing even is he is dying. Why is he doing this to me?

STANLEY: (*Shrugs his shoulders.*) Why does anyone sue? For money, of course.

DENISE: And why should I have to pay?

STANLEY: (*Picks a random legal volume off the shelf and wipes away the dust.*) Because he knows you are insured and that you have the money.

And he knows a jury will melt with his tale of deceased wife and three orphaned children, unable to take care of themselves after his tragic and inevitable death.

DENISE: (*Stands up and leans toward STANLEY.*) Who exactly are you working for?

STANLEY: You, of course. (*Replacs the book on the shelf with all the other leather-bound volumes.*) But in these sorts of cases, there are no victors. Mr. Boca will die, just as his wife has tragically died in the past. There is no justice in that, is there?

DENISE: (*Lets out a long, audible sigh.*)

STANLEY: No, it's just bad luck. Mr. Boca's had a run of very bad luck. He's not an evil person. He just wants to take care of his kids the same way you want to take care of yours.

DENISE: I never had to sue anyone to take care of my children.

STANLEY: No. But you're not dying of heart failure, are you?

DENISE: (*Slumps down in her chair.*) I want you to fight. I want you to find the best medical specialists in the state to demonstrate that I was not responsible for that man's dying heart.

STANLEY: Heart. Yes, that's the heart of the matter, isn't it? You should have gotten an echocardiogram, a simple test, to see if her heart was already too weak for such an aggressive cancer treatment.

DENISE: (*Stands up and begins pacing back and forth in front of STANLEY's large desk.*) That was the Oncology Center's responsibility. Mr. Boca was the one who insisted on going to the hot shot cancer center in Dallas and I sent him there. They're the ones who sent him back with chemotherapy and radiation instructions. They were the ones who should have cleared him for the treatment they proposed. As far as I'm concened, nothing could be clearer.

STANLEY: Apparently, nothing was clear at all. They expected you to do the cardiac work-up. You assumed that they had done it. A simple mis-communication with disastrous results. (*Stands up and walks toward the window.*)

DENISE: Of course I assumed they had done the echocardiogram. They're a tertiary center, for God's sake, a world class cancer referral center and if you don't take my work for it, just look at their nightly TV ads. Of course they would do a cardiac work up before recommending giving cardio-toxic chemotherapy. They dropped the ball and I'm paying the consequences.

STANLEY: (*Returns to his desk and sits down. Picks up the papers and flips through the pages.*) But they didn't do the cardiac work up, did they? And Mr. Boca's lawyer says it was your responsibility as the primary oncologist, the one who actually implemented the treatment. (*Picks up a shiny metal letter opener, which he twirls around his finger.*) And why exactly can't he get a new heart?

DENISE: (*Clutches her chest.*) You already know why. Because he's got metastatic lung cancer and no transplant center will waste a valuable donor heart on someone who is going to die anyway. (*Both sit in silence. Looks down at the multi-colored Persian carpet, bends down and picks up a corner.*) It's a fake, Stanley. It's not even a real Persian carpet. Don't you earn enough money for the real thing?

STANLEY: How can you tell it's a fake?

DENISE: (*Lifts up the corner and STANLEY rises from his desk for a better look.*) You see those white lines. Those are only on machine-made carpets. You can't see those lines in a hand knotted carpet. (*Lets the corner drop.*) But it's a good fake. Maybe a fake's even a better idea for an office with such heavy foot traffic. (*Pauses.*) Tell me the truth. Do you think we can win this case?

STANLEY: No.

DENISE: Why?

STANLEY: Because the medical panel said you committed a breach in the standard of care by not getting an echocardiogram. They did say that it had no detrimental effect on Mr. Boca's eventual outcome. He was going to die and they recognized that fact. But you might have never given him his chemotherapy in the first place if you had known his heart was weak to begin with.

DENISE: We didn't know.

STANLEY: That's the problem. You didn't know.

DENISE: But that chemotherapy could have destroyed a healthy heart.

STANLEY: (*Lets the letter opener drop to the floor.*) Could have? Of course. (*Bends down to pick it up.*) This carpet looks pretty good to me. Even if it is a fake.

DENISE: Forget the damn carpet for a minute!

STANLEY: You're the one who brought it up.

DENISE: I know, but now I want to discuss Mr. Boca.

STANLEY: (*Replaces the letter opener on the desk, stands up, and begins walking slowly back and forth behind his desk.*) Just imagine those three little children called to testify about the loss of their dear father, their only source of support. Imagine the tears and the sobs and their pitiful cracked childish voices. Imagine them talking about already losing their beloved mother just a few short years ago. And now, how their dear sweet father has struggled to raise them with only the help of his aging invalid parents. Have you got that mental picture?

DENISE: (*Nods.*) Yes.

STANLEY: Now imagine our oncology expert from St. Elsewhere who defends you by saying that Mr. Boca was going to die anyway. He cites a bunch of statistics and goes on and on about prognosis and longevity, with and without painful and complicated cancer treatments.

(*STANLEY bangs his fist on the table so hard that the letter opener clatters on the glass top. DENISE looks up at him with surprise.*)

STANLEY: (*Raises his voice, speaking in front of an imaginary jury.*) Dr. Faircloth, how could you have possibly neglected to get an echocardiogram on poor Mr. Boca when you knew full well how much was at stake?

DENISE (*Looks up at the STANLEY's face.*) Because it was supposed to have already been done at the Oncology Center in Dallas. (*Jumps to her feet and holds up her hands in supplication.*) God in heaven, damn this man! He's going to get me, isn't she? He's going to get some big cash settlement and I'll get my name in the National Practitioners Data Bank. That's what's going happen, isn't it? (*Moves around the desk and grabs STANLEY by the arms.*) Tell me the truth! You're telling me that's what's going to happen, isn't it.

STANLEY: Yes, Denise. That's what's going to happen, or worse. You could have this thing dragged out in court with nasty experts vilifying you as some sort of incompetent, rich, arrogant, and uncaring monster before a jury made up of some of this town's less than stellar citizens. They would look at you and poor dying Mr. Boca and decide that he, and his children, would benefit from the money and that it was only coming from some wealthy insurance company anyway. No one would really have to pay and there won't be any real consequences to anyone.

DENISE: That's a lie and you know it. My insurance will go up. Their premiums will go up. And I'll be in the National Practitioners Data Base. It's just a lie to believe nothing will happen to anyone.

STANLEY: (*Turns around and walks back toward the window, then turns and points to the empty chairs.*) But will they know it's a lie and that there really will be consequences? Will they even care?

DENISE: Who?

STANLEY: The jury. Don't forget that there will be twelve common, uneducated people sitting there. They are not your peers. Only one in ten people in this area even has a college degree. If you're lucky you will get one educated person. But I doubt whether the plaintiff's attorney will allow that. No, for him, the more ignorant the juror, the better.

DENISE: Only one in twelve with a college education?

STANLEY: Those are the statistics. Most likely they will be poor employees whose average income is $24,000 per year or less, the miserable per capita income in this area. And they know you live in a big house on Westchester Boulevard and that your husband is a rich engineer. And they may even know that your children go to fine private schools in the East. And what do you think will happen when they look at you and then back at poor dying Mr. Boca and his pathetic young children?

DENISE: (*Sits down again in one of the empty chairs.*) I have a headache.

STANLEY: Not half as bad as the one you'll have listening to some high paid medical prostitute, who gets a fortune to come around and tell these twelve simple, uneducated, financially struggling people what a heartless fool you have been.

DENISE: Am I heartless?

STANLEY: No.

DENISE: Am I a fool?

STANLEY: No.

DENISE: What should I do? Give me your advice.

STANLEY: Settle.

DENISE: (*Closes her eyes and puts her head down.*) This isn't going to get Mr. Boca a new heart. And it's tearing mine apart, for what it's worth. I came to this town to help people. I came here to give these people, my patients, my fellow citizens, the benefit of years of study, sleepless nights, and grueling stress. Mr. Boca wants my heart. He's not content with dying with dignity. He wants to poison my heart like . . . ."

STANLEY: Like you poisoned his?

DENISE: Yes, like I poisoned his. But a least I hoped to buy him some additional quality time with his children with the toxins I gave. Has he looked into my heart like I was supposed to have looked into his?

STANLEY: No, he hasn't. And not one of those twelve jurors will have expected him to have done it, or care if he has or not.

DENISE: (*Stands up and goes to the window and looks out.*) What is my pain and suffering worth?

STANLEY: Do you really want me to answer that?

DENISE: No, I don't. (*Looks at STANLEY who again plays with his letter opener.*) What exactly is Mr. Boca's heart worth?

STANLEY: As much as it takes to raise those three children and get them through college.

DENISE: Two hundred thousand dollars?

STANLEY: More like half a million, at least. And that will be a subject of considerable negotiation with his attorney. Remember, Mr. Boca's attorney get's a third of any settlement.

DENISE: A third. Yes, of course. (*Looks out the window.*) It's a beautiful day out there.

STANLEY: (*Returns to his desk, picks up some papers and hands them to DENISE.*) Here's a copy of the lawsuit. Take this home. Read it over again. Nothing surprising. The usual litany of nasty complaints. Then give me a ring when you want to get back in touch. I won't start looking for an expert witness for us until I hear from you. (*Walks over and gives DENISE a pat on the back. DENISE recoils under his touch.*) I'm not the devil, you know, I'm just a lawyer and I happen to be on your side, believe it or not.

DENISE: (*Turns to STANLEY and extends her hand which STANLEY takes.*) Thank you. I know you're just trying to help me. That's what I told Mr. Boca, too. That I was just trying to help him, and look what happened.

STANLEY: (*Again pats DENISE on the shoulder.*) Remember, don't take it personally.

END OF DIALOGUE #1

MEDICAL DIALOGUE #2

GIVE ME BACK MY LICENSE, SON OF SATAN!

CAST OF CHARACTERS

DR. PETER PORTER: Middle aged physician. He is sloppily dressed and is disheveled, with scraggly hair and a blotched shaving job.

DR. ROGER BELLETERRE: President of the Medical Board of Examiners. He is elegantly dressed in a suit and tie.

SETTING

Belleterre's office with a big, glass-topped desk and a couple of chairs. There are bookshelves and an oriental carpet on the ground. The wall has framed diploma, awards, commendations, etc. There is a window, out of which the protagonists look from time to time.

DR. PORTER: (*Speaks as he walks into the room. Wipes the excess saliva of his lower lip and rubs his hand along his soiled pants.*) You've got to give me back my medical license.

DR. BELLETERRE: (*Stands up to greet PORTER.*) Dr. Porter, so nice to see you again.

(*BELLETERRE extends his hand which PORTER takes and shakes.*)

DR. BELLETERRE: (*Indicates a chair.*) Please, sit down and let me know what I can do for you.

DR. PORTER: (*Remains standing.*) Cut the crap, Belleterre! I already told you. I came down here to find out why exactly you haven't given me my license back. I sent you all the papers, including the psychiatrist's

112

reports. I should be able to get something done, even if it's only a restricted license.

DR. BELLETERRE: Please, Dr. Porter. Sit down.

DR. PORTER: No!

DR. BELLETERRE: (*Shrugs his shoulders.*) Suit yourself. (*Unlocks one of the drawers of his desk and pulls out a large file.*) Yes, we did get a letter from your psychiatrist and some others from your medical colleagues up in Fulton.

DR. PORTER: So what is the problem?

DR. BELLETERRE: (*Deposits the folder on his desk and rests his hands on it.*) The problem is that some members of the Board of Examiners feel that you are not yet ready to resume the practice of medicine, even with a restricted license.

DR. PORTER: For God's sake, man! I'm dying. I have no money. I'm sleeping under bridges. I work as a part time gardener for some rich doctor in town. What more do I have to do?

DR. BELLETERRE: Have you considered applying for disability?

DR. PORTER: (*Pulls out one of the high back chairs and plops down.*) If I apply for disability, then I admit that I can no longer practice medicine. I'd be finished as a doctor. I might as well put a bullet through my head.

DR. BELLETERRE: (*Leans forward and half whispers.*) Are you really considering suicide?

DR. PORTER: (*Laughs.*) That's a good one. Now you want me to say that I'm suicidal so you can have me committed and declared completely crazy. Then you can tear up my application for a medical license and kiss me goodbye forever. Is that it?

DR. BELLETERRE: I'm only concerned for your welfare. We have a very good program for impaired physicians.

DR. PORTER: (*Jumps up from his chair and bangs both fists on the desk.*) Impaired! You bet I'm impaired. I'm impaired by you sanctimonious sons of bitches who won't let me get back to doing my medical work. I'm not one of those alcoholic, drug addicted losers. I just had a bout of bad luck. And I'm not asking for the right to prescribe controlled substances. I'm not even asking for any kind of prescription privileges. I'm just asking to be able to do insurance physicals or run EKG's or draw blood, for God's sake. (*Pauses.*) I can't go on like this. Every day, I lose another shred of my self esteem. Every day, I lose some of my medical knowledge. I'm so stiff and tired from cutting branches and pushing a lawn mower around that I can hardly move at night, much less read a medical journal.

DR. BELLETERRE: Are you getting enough to eat?

DR. PORTER: (*Bars his lips to reveal chipped and blackened teeth.*) How can I get enough to eat? Did you see my teeth? (*Pushes himself right up to BELLETERRE's face and opens his mouth as wide as he can.*) Look at my god damned mouth! Half of my teeth are gone and the other half are rotting away. My pyorrhea is so bad that I can't even stand the smell of my own breath. And, but the way, thanks for asking. I wasn't sure you really cared about me. (*Laughs at his own joke and plops back down in the chair.*)

DR. BELLETERRE: (*Leans forward.*) We do care. We care about you and we care about the citizens of this state. We have a responsibility to assure that practitioners achieve and maintain certain standards of professional quality. The Board cannot, in good faith, let you practice medicine in the shape you're in. (*Finishes and leans back in the chair.*)

DR. PORTER: (*Remains slumped down in his chair. Places his hands in a position of prayer.*) I knew your father. He worked as a general practitioner up on Bayou des Glaises, didn't he?

DR. BELLETERRE: Yes, he did.

DR. PORTER: He must have been in his eighties back then.

DR. BELLETERRE: He was eighty-six when he died.

DR. PORTER: I can still visualize your father, with his mane of white hair and his gold-rimmed glasses, the very image of a Norman Rockwell physician. He was a good man. He never turned anyone away. No sir! He would take chickens or sausages or greens or nothing at all for payment. He was a compassionate man, a real gentleman.

DR. BELLETERRE: Porter, I share your great respect for my father. But this isn't about him. It's about you. You are not stable enough to resume the practice of medicine in this state. That's it. You can re-submit your application for next month's Medical Board meeting, but it must contain new elements.

DR. PORTER: I can see by that scar on your neck that you have undergone a carotid endarterectomy on the right side. Are you diabetic or hypertensive? Isn't this high stress job a bit too much for your medical condition.

DR. BELLETERRE: This interview is not about me or my medical condition. It is about your fitness to practice medicine in this state. Can we get back to the subject at hand, please?

DR. PORTER: Of course. Excuse my impertinence, but I couldn't help be see your scar. Now, as far as my application is concerned, I think it did have new elements: the psychiatrist's letter and the two other letters from doctors. That's what you asked for, isn't it? (*Gets up and walks around the desk where he grabs BELLETERRE's hand and goes down on his knees.*) Please, I can't take this anymore. (*His voice is cracking.*) I've gone from having a wife, a family, a profession, to having nothing at all. It's all gone. I don't even know what happened. And you have the key to unlock me from this living hell. Don't send me away empty handed. Don't take away all hope. I'm begging you. (*Heaving with sobs.*) Nothing matters any more. I have no dignity, no honor, no pretense. It's finished isn't it. (*Begins to shake and continues to sob.*)

DR. BELLETERRE: (*Pulls away from PORTER and stands up.*

(*PORTER stops sobbing and starts to tremble uncontrollably, almost like a seizure. BELLETERRE goes over and puts his hand on PORTER's shoulder.*)

DR. BELLETERRE: I don't know what I can give you. But I can't grant you your license, even if I wanted to. Is there something I can do to help you out right now?

DR. PORTER: (*Looks at BELLETERRE imploringly.*) I need forty bucks to get a bus ticket back to Fulton.

DR. BELLETERRE: (*Reaches into his pocked, pulls out his wallet, and removes some bills.*) Here's eighty bucks. Take a taxi to the bus station. Buy something to eat. Get back to Fulton.

DR. PORTER: (*Looks at the money and takes it.*) I'm ashamed. How could I sink so low? Death would be a mercy but not even death's ready to help me out. (*Pauses and looks at the money.*) I knew your mother, too. A strange woman, always mumbling and muttering. It must have been hard on you as a child. (*Looks at BELLETERRE.*)

DR. BELLETERRE: (*Looks taken aback.*) No, it wasn't difficult.

DR. PORTER: I don't believe you. It had to have been hard on you. Everyone thought she was just bizarre in Bordelonville, but I think she was schizophrenic.

DR. BELLETERRE: What are you talking about?

DR. PORTER: (*Fingers the bills as he speaks.*) I saw her when she came to the five-and-dime where I worked in the summers. When no one else was around, she'd tell me about how she heard God talking to her and about you, her son, who was no son at all, but the offspring of Satan. She told me I was a good listener, maybe that's why I went into medicine.

DR. BELLETERRE: Dr. Porter, I think you need to leave right now. (*Returns to his desk.*)

DR. PORTER: She was right, wasn't she? You are that son of Satan, aren't you? (*Looks at BELLETERRE.*) I can't take this money. I really can't. I can't sell my soul to Satan's son for eighty bucks. (*Walks over and deposits the bills on BELLETERRE's desk.*) I don't have anything left but my soul and I can't sell it, not for this paltry sum.

DR. BELLETERRE: (*Scoops up the crumpled bills and stuffs them back into his pocket.*) Suit yourself. Can I at least give you a lift somewhere? It's a long walk back to Fulton.

DR. PORTER: (*Shakes his head.*) It's finished. There's nothing left, is there? There's nothing left to do here but to leave. I know you're never going to give me my license back. I can see it in your eyes. (*Extends his hand to BELLETERRE, who takes it.*) Gosh, your hand is hot. Maybe you are the son of Satan? (*Sniffs.*) It even smells a little like rotten eggs here.

DR. BELLETERE: (*Pulls his hand away.*) Good luck, Dr. Porter.

DR. PORTER: Dr. Porter. Why not Mister Porter? I'll never get my license back.

DR. BELLETERRE: You still have your title. No one is going to take that away.

DR. PORTER: (*Turns to go out the door and turns to face Dr. BELLETERRE.*) God bless you, Dr. Belleterre. And, by the way, I think your mother may have been right, you are Satan's son.

THE END OF DIALOGUE # 2

MEDICAL DIALOGUE #3

CONTROLLED SUBSTANCES

CAST OF CHARACTERS

DR. ROBERT CARTER is a middle aged, good looking young man who is dressed in casual, not medical, attire.

MRS. GERTRUDE CARTER is an older woman who is neatly dressed.

SETTING

The Carter's living room. There is a couch and a couple of chairs as well as a glass topped coffee table and an oriental rug.

(*ROBERT looks at GERTRUDE, who is leafing through a copy of People Magazine.*)

ROBERT: Mother, I tell you I'm depressed.

GERTRUDE: (*Sets down the magazine on the coffee table.*) Stop your nonsense this minute. You have nothing to be depressed about. You earn almost $300,000 a year and you live in a beautiful big house in a wonderful neighborhood with your loving mother who cooks, cleans, and even does the yard work for you.

ROBERT: You're not listening.

GERTRUDE: (*Turns her face toward ROBERT and scowls.*) I am listening. But so far I haven't heard anything to justify your so-called depressed state. (*Grabs her magazine and starts to stand up.*)

ROBERT: (*Grabs GERTRUDE by the shoulders and shoves her back down onto the couch.*) Sit down! Forget your damn magazine, your damn tea time, your damn neighbor's dog in your flower beds and listen to me.

GERTRUDE: All right, but this book is more interesting than anything you have told me so far, dear.

ROBERT: Mother, I'm getting sued again.

GERTRUDE: So?

ROBERT: So! This is the third time this year.

GERTRUDE: So? Everyone sues doctors around here. It's nothing unusual and nothing to be ashamed of.

ROBERT: That's right. Every doctor gets sued. But this case has come to the attention of the hospital Executive Committee. They can suspend my medical privileges if they want. And if they do that, I'm finished. I won't be able to practice here or anyplace else.

GERTRUDE: Let's not be over dramatic. There are other cities and other hospitals. You are a talented, well-trained surgeon. You can find work in lots of places.

ROBERT: Maybe you're right and maybe you're wrong. Under any circumstances, every time anyone makes an application for medical privileges, it is reviewed by the credentials committee of that hospital, then by the executive committee, and then voted on by the medical staff. They get the National Practitioners Data Bank entries about me and pour over every case that was ever settled. Then they get all the specific information about me from all previous hospitals. They must get a letter from the chief of staff of any hospital I've worked in. Just imagine what these guys would say if they find it necessary to suspend any of my privileges? That's the first question they ask in any application, have your privileges ever been partially or completely suspended or revoked by any medical institution at any time? (*Pauses.*) Do you understand what I'm saying?

GERTRUDE: Of course I do. I may be old, but I'm not senile. (*Pauses.*) I still think your overdramatizing the situation. Everyone knows that doctors are just like everyone else, full of imperfections.

ROBERT: I cannot be full of imperfections, as you say, and get hired in another medical group. These guys are like chickens. They see a speck of blood on one of their colleagues and they'll all gang up and peck them to death.

GERTRUDE: (*Shakes her head.*) We are talking about doctors, not chickens. Besides, I think you always go in for theatrics. Your father and I almost thought you might go into acting, not medicine. Thank God you decided on medical school. Who knows where we'd be if you'd gone that other route.

ROBERT: Thank God? (*Sighs and slumps down in one of the matching leather chairs.*) Maybe I would have been happier as an actor? Maybe I wouldn't get up each day with a sense of dread about what catastrophe was going to happen? Is today the day I was going to screw up another case? Is the next patient just waiting for something bad to happen so they can sue me? Are my colleagues just waiting for my next blunder so they can crucify me? Do you think that sounds so nice?

GERTRUDE: (*Gets up from the couch and comes over to him. Perches on the large armrest and gives ROBERT a hug.*) There, there. You need a little dose of maternal kindness. I'm here for that as long and I'm alive.

ROBERT: Are you planning on dying?

GLORIA: (*Caresses his hair.*) Not now. But it worries me to think what will happen to you when I'm gone. You need a good wife to take care of you, like Margaret. She was a nice girl, wasn't she?

ROBERT: Yeah, a real nice girl. That's what I need, a nice gold digging whore with a taste for expensive clothes and liquor. She'd look out for me until the bank account was empty.

GERTRUDE: No woman is perfect. (*Stands up and fishes around in her pocket.*) In fact, no man is perfect either. (*Pulls out an empty medicine bottle.*) Speaking of imperfections, why are you taking OxyContin?

ROBERT: (*Clenches his jaw.*) Have you been rummaging around in the trash can in my office?

GERTRUDE: Yes, and I want to know why you are taking this addictive medication?

ROBERT: I hurt.

GERTRUDE: Where?

ROBERT: All over.

GERTRUDE: (*Hands him the empty bottle.*) You shouldn't take this kind of medicine. It's a controlled substances. It's addictive and it's dangerous.

ROBERT: Dangerous! No more dangerous than those sanctimonious bastards on the Executive Committee. Or those greedy sons of bitches lawyers down at the courthouse. I do have pain. (*Pounds his head.*) Here! (*Strikes his chest.*) And here! (*Indicates his groin. GERTRUDE grimaces and shakes her head.*) I'm suffering and I can't find a way out that makes any sense.

GERTRUDE: For heaven's sake, Robert, get a grip on yourself. You are not a child. And you were not raised to crumble under the slightest adversity. We are Carters, nation builders. As old as the pilgrims. Sons and daughters of the American Revolution, the Civil War, World War I and II. Your father fought in the Pacific and never even mentioned his terrible experiences to you. (*Slaps him across the face.*) Get a grip!

ROBERT: (*Opens his mouth in surprise.*) You hit me.

GERTRUDE: Yes, I did. And I'll do it again if I have to.

ROBERT: Abused by my own mother. (*Begins to tremble.*) I'll kill myself.

GERTRUDE: Ha! That's a good one. You are sniveling about a lawsuit and few unkind colleagues. Really, Robert, your father spent three years in a Japanese prisoner of war camp. Don't you dare talk to me about your pain and suffering. (*Pauses.*) Your father never took a pain pill in his life even when he was eaten up with cancer. Never! Not one! (*Reaches over and tries to grab the empty bottle of OxyContin.*)

(*ROBERT clutches onto the bottle with such force that GERTRUDE cannot even pry it loose even though her nails dug into his flesh.*)

ROBERT: I need these.

GERTRUDE: You don't need them, you want them.

ROBERT: Okay then, I want them. I want them because they make me feel good and I forget all this work and worry about lawsuits and the Executive Committee and the Data Bank. (*Holds up the orange bottle to the ceiling light.*) I can take this stuff and a stiff drink and it all melts away. (*Stands up and approaches GERTRUDE who backs away.*) And for a few blessed moments, it doesn't matter what's out there. I get some relief. I get some peace. Do you even know what that means? You with your busy mind? Your hyperactive social life? Your precious little court of Daughters of the Confederacy bullshit?

GERTRUDE: Shut up! That's enough! (*Raises her hand to slap ROBERT.*)

ROBERT: (*Catches her arm in midair.*) So mother doesn't like to be the object of a little pain and suffering does she?

GERTRUDE: (*Drops her hand and turns to walk out of the room.*) Why don't you go to your room and do whatever you want. Take a whole bottle of those pain killers. You'll see that it won't do anything. You'll just come back to the same reality with your same miserable short-comings and your same pathetic whining. (*Raises her middle finger.*) And if you're going to kill yourself, then just do it. And don't mess up the house in the process.

ROBERT: (*Listens to the clicking of GERTRUDE's high heels on the floor and the slamming of her bedroom door.*) Don't worry! I won't trouble you with any inconveniences. I'll do it at the hospital. How about that? I'll kill myself at the hospital where my loving colleagues will have to clean up the mess.

GERTRUDE: (*The clicking resumes and GERTRUDE returns to poke her head into the livingroom.*) Good! (*Turns and walks away. The door slams loudly again.*)

ROBERT: (*Fumbles with his pocket and pulls out a vial. Speaks to himself.*) Pills are so unreliable. I could inject myself in the doctor's bathroom. (*Looks around.*) I wonder if any of those sons of bitches at the hospital would even notice my dead body. (*Calls down the empty hallway.*) I bet those bastards wouldn't even wonder why I did it! They certainly wouldn't think about what they could have done to prevent it. My death would just be a bother to them. No, maybe it would be a relief. One less problem for them to worry about. They wouldn't even care. (*Yells down the hall.*) And you won't either. (*Sits down in the leather chair and looks around for someone. There is a deathly silence.*) I guess the only one who will be unhappy is my lawyer. He told me once that it was always hard to defend a dead doctor. I wondered what he meant by that. I guess I'll never know. (*Lights dim to dark.*)

THE END OF DIALOGUE # 3

MEDICAL DIALOGUE #4

NO SUCH THING AS A FREE LUNCH

CAST OF CHARACTERS

DR. PETER FRANK: Physician dressed in white coat or sports coat with stethoscope prominently draped around his neck.

DR. DAN DELACROIX: Also a physician with a stethoscope and name badge, perhaps more casually dressed.

SETTING

Doctor's office with a desk and a couple of chairs. There is an oriental carpet on the ground. There are several boxes of medication samples on the desk.

DR. FRANK: We've got to get the pharmaceutical reps out of the clinic.

DR. DELACROIX: Why? They bring samples. (*Picks up a box and shows it to FRANK.*) They bring lunches. They support educational meetings. They take us to fancy dinners and on trips.

DR. FRANK: Sure, they do all that and more. And what do you think they want in return?

DR. DELACROIX: Nothing. I listen to what they have to say and then I use my own clinical judgment.

DR. FRANK: Dan, you're a fool. A smart fool, but a fool nonetheless. Nothing in life is free. Nothing is without cost. That's the first rule of ecology. There's no such thing as a free lunch. (*Takes the box out of DELACROIX's hand and puts it back on the desk.*)

DR. DELACROIX: Oh, you're just a cynical sourpuss.

DR. FRANK: And you're an educated idiot.

DR. DELACROIX: I thought you just said I was a smart fool. Now I'm just an idiot. (*Laughs.*) Anyway, the decision of whether pharmaceutical representatives can come into this clinic is not yours to make. That's a partnership decision. You can't kick them out even if you do think they have a pernicious effect on the choice of which drugs get used.

DR. FRANK: I don't think they're intrinsically evil. They're nice ladies and gentlemen. They are just doing their job and their job is not public health. It's sales, sales, and more sales. (*Knocks DELACROIX on the head.*) Can you get that into your thick head?

DR. DELACROIX: (*Gets up and walks around.*) So you are going to be the valiant doctor, Don Quixote, Man of La Mancha, who goes up against the medico-industrial complex and saves the national debt, one prescription at a time?

DR. FRANK: No, you can't eliminate the national debt at the patient's bedside, but you can be aware of the problem.

DR. DELACROIX: And what if it's not a problem at all? What if their making money and us making money is just a good thing for everyone? It's the American Dream, isn't it? Unbridled capitalism? Getting rich?

DR. FRANK: And what happens when there isn't any more money? Whose health care is going to suffer? Mine? Yours? Or that poor slob with a minimum wage job who can't even afford medical insurance and can't afford the medication he's prescribed by you and me?

DR. DELACROIX: And how does that relate to the question of drug reps inside the clinic?

DR. FRANK: Well, for the cost of a few free notepads, a lunch for the staff, a ticket to the baseball game, a trip as a consultant to Florida, plus some golf tournaments thrown in on the side, do you really thing that nothing is expected in return? Do you really think that's not going to influence you when you take out your prescription pad? (*Pauses. Mimics taking out his prescription pad and thinking about what he's going to write.*) Should I prescribe that old cheap generic drug, or that new expensive medication that patients keep asking for because they are bombarded with publicity on the television? (*Picks up a box and shows it to DELACROIX.*) Look at this one, a new biological drug, genetically engineered and ten times as pricy as the old one. Which one should I prescribe? And besides, that drug rep is so nice and gives me such nice free things and we had such a nice dinner down at the Courtableau Café.

DR. DELACROIX: I retain complete freedom and objectivity in my prescribing. Surely you don't think I can be influenced by a few baubles or a nice dinner?

DR. FRANK: (*Laughs.*) You're lying to yourself. You're lying to me. And you're lying to our patients. (*Drops the box down on the desk.*) Drug reps know they can buy a doctor with a free pen.

DR. DELACROIX: (*Jumps out and shoves DR. FRANK.*) Peter, that's an insult! I'm a good doctor, a caring doctor, a concerned doctor.

DR. FRANK: (*Puts his hand on DELACROIX's shoulders.*) I know. But you're not opening your eyes. Do you really think you can resist that pharmaceutical steamroller? Have your seen those women reps they send. They're beautiful, young, and voluptuous. They hang over your desk with their cleavage inches from your face. (*Imitates a woman's voice. Picks up a couple of boxes and swings them around in a voluptuous way, often circling around the breasts.*) Oh, Dr. Delacroix, I admire you so much for all the things you do for the community. You are a really role model for us all. Is there anything I can do to make you prescribe more of my product? What can I do to really help you out? What about that favorite charity of yours? What if I give a $1,000 to the museum or maybe Duck's Unlimited, or maybe the community theater, the one you like so much? Of course, I don't expect anything in return, especially from such a popular and well-connected physician with such an enormous clientele. (*Holds the boxes over each breast and hangs them down into DELACROIX's face.*) And you are such a good man and a wonderful doctor and your patients love you so. (*Reverts to his regular voice.*) Sound familiar.

DR. DELACROIX: You really do that well. If I didn't know you better, I'd say you'd had some serious practice. (*Laughs.*)

DR. FRANK: Sorry to disappoint you, but that's an amateur performance. But seriously, will you help me to get the drug reps out of the office? Men and women?

DR. DELACROIX: But those lunches? Those treats? The free medical samples? (*Takes a sample box.*) And the heartfelt interest in me and my family?

DR. FRANK: You know very well that those reps only sample the newest, costliest medications until we start prescribing them and then all those free samples suddenly disappear. And no one even remembers that great drug went generic last year and costs a few pennies a pill. (*Picks up a box.*) Look at this! They put two medications in the same pill together that are about to go off patent and voilà! It suddenly becomes a new miracle pill that just happens to cost five times as much as the cheap generic components separately. And it just happens to be patented for another 20 years. True or not true?

DR. DELACROIX: True.

DR. FRANK: So, what do you say? Will you help me or not? Just think of the good you'll be doing to your patients, to society, and to yourself.

DR. DELACROIX: But . . . .

DR. FRANK: No buts. You can be part of the problem or part of the solution. Which would you rather be?

DR. DELACROIX: Didn't Jimi Hendrix say that back in the sixties?

DR. FRANK: No, Malcolm X said it and it was true back then and it's still true now. (*Pushes the boxes of samples into the garbage can.*)

(*A gigantic black "X" is projected over the stage. Lights dim to dark.*)

THE END

TOM'S PERFECT BODY

CAST OF CHARACTERS

TOM: Cindy's husband, a very skinny man in his mid forties.

CINDY: Tom's wife, a very attractive and stylish woman in her late thirties.

MR. (OR MRS.) BASTROP: Human Resources Director at Castor Industries.

DR. FOREST: Physician. A well-dressed doctor in his mid-fifties.

SETTING

The scene is very stark. Stage right has a porcelain toilet. The toilet is separated from the bedroom by a bathroom door. The bed is stage center and it can be in a bedroom or a hospital as the scene dictates. On stage left is a desk with two chairs in front and a larger, executive chair in back. Lighting changes with the scenes and illuminates that part of the stage which is being used.

SCENE I

(TOM hangs over the toilet and retching violently. CINDY is lying in bed. CINDY is dressed in pajamas or in a robe.)

CINDY: Tom! Tom!

TOM: *(Straightens up and wipes his mouth with his sleeve. Brushes his hair back in place.)* Yes, dear.

CINDY: What's taking you so long?

TOM: Nothing, dear. I'm just getting handsome for you. *(Returns to retching in the toilet bowl.)*

CINDY: You're already handsome. You don't have to make yourself more so. Can you just come to bed, please? It's late already.

TOM: Just a minute, darling. *(Stops retching and then straightens up and closes the toilet seat. Takes a pill bottle out of a pocket of his robe and pours out a handful of pills and takes them without bothering to drink any water.)*

CINDY: *(Gets up and walks to the bathroom door separating himself from TOM. Knocks on the door.)* Tom? What are you doing in there?

TOM: Nothing, dear. *(Replaces the bottle and smoothes out his hair and his robe. Opens the door.)* See! I'm here. Just for you.

CINDY: *(Looks at his disheveled appearance.)* Sorry, honey, but you look a little haggard. That was long time for such a casual look. What took you so long, anyway?

TOM: Nothing. *(Strides by CINDY and goes to stand by her side of the bed.)* Just come over here and get into bed. I've got a surprise for you.

CINDY: *(Returns and stands on her side of the bed.)* A surprise? What kind of surprise?

TOM: You'll see. Just get in bed! *(Gets in bed as he drops his robe to the floor and reveals skimpy, sexy, leopard underwear.)*

CINDY: Wow! That's pretty wild.

TOM: How do you like it?

CINDY: It's interesting. It's wonderful. It's sexy.

TOM: *(Turns on himself like a model.)* Do you think I look good in it?

CINDY: Yeah! Sure. You look great.

TOM: *(Climbs into bed next to CINDY.)* I just wish I didn't have these awful love handles. *(Grabs the tiny amount of fat at his waist.)*

CINDY: Ah, come on. You're beautiful, gorgeous, just perfect.

TOM: You're so sweet. Even if I know you're lying.

CINDY: I'm not. I'm not lying. You're really handsome.

TOM: That's okay. You can tell me the truth. I know I'm getting fat and flabby.

CINDY: No, you're not.

TOM: Too much cellulitis in the thighs. Too many wrinkles. Too much fat. God, what I wouldn't give to lose another twenty pounds.

CINDY: Twenty pounds! Tom, if you lost twenty pounds, you'd be nothing but skin and bones. You look great the way you are. Perfect.

TOM: Kiss me, you liar. *(They kiss.)* Now turn off that lamp. In the dark, you can imagine me any way you want.

(The lights dim to dark.)

SCENE II

(CINDY is now dressed in casual work clothes. She is standing in front of the desk on stage left. MR. BASTROP, dressed in a suit and tie, is seated behind the desk in the executive, high back chair. He rises and extends his hand to CINDY.)

BASTROP: Cindy. Come on in. Sit down. *(They shake hands and CINDY sits down in one of the chairs in front of the desk.)* How are you doing?

CINDY: I'm fine, Mr. Bastrop.

BASTROP: And your husband?

CINDY: He's doing fine. Thanks for asking.

BASTROP: Glad to hear it. *(Sits down and pauses a few seconds.)* You know, you're one of our best employees. You've been here over 17 years and have never let us down when we needed you for a special job. I value your opinion and appreciate your role as a leader among the other employees.

CINDY: Thank you, Mr. Bastrop. What exactly can I do for you?

BASTROP: I'm just sounding out a few key employees about some changes which may have to take place in our health insurance.

CINDY: What's wrong with the current one?

BASTROP: Nothing. It's great. But they just went up another 35% on the premiums. Castor Industries is already paying a bundle for health insurance and we can't go up that much. We will either have to pass the increase on to the employees or change plans. What do you think?

CINDY: I think you're going to get a lot of resistance from the rank and file. Folks don't want to have their health benefits touched. People consider health care a sacred cow. And most people think they pay plenty for medical care already.

BASTROP: We've already swallowed four consecutive price increases without passing them on to the employees. The board is screaming. A fifth of our production costs are tied up in health care. There's no way that can go on and have us remain competitive.

CINDY: What does this all have to do with me?

BASTROP: We are in a business to sell a product. That product must be competitively priced and what we have gained in productivity over the years, we're losing in health care costs. It can't go on.

CINDY: What am I supposed to do?

BASTROP: Talk to the employees and explain the problem. Prepare them for an increase in employee contributions, an increase in the deductible, and higher co-payments. That sort of thing.

CINDY: With all due respect, isn't that your job?

BASTROP: No, it's our job. And that's what we are going to lose, all of our jobs, if we don't find a solution. Can I count on you?

CINDY: I'd be glad to help out if I can. But that's going to be an incredibly hard sell to the workers. (*Pauses.*) Is that it?

BASTROP: Yes. Thanks for your help. We're counting on you to help our workers swallow the bitter pill. (*Laughs at his own joke.*) A little medical metaphor, get it?

CINDY: Yes, I got it. Now may I go?

BASTROP: Of course.

(*Lights dim to dark.*)

SCENE III

(*TOM is dressed and sitting on the bed, which is covered with bottles and pills. He is counting. There is a plastic box which is also filled with more bottles.*)

TOM: One. Two. Three. Four. Five. Six. That ought to do it. (*Pops the pills into his mouth, then looks at his watch. Continues to talk to the bottle.*) You little fellas should start working in about 20 minutes. (*Picks up another bottle and speaks to it.*) Then you guys should start to work. Some for shitting, some for peeing. Some for throwing up. (*Replaces the bottles in the plastic box and puts on the snap-on cover. Picks* up the box and starts to dance around the stage holding it. He sings "I Feel Pretty" from West Side Story in a sing-song voice) "I feel pretty. I feel witty. I feel pretty and witty and gay. I fell happy in an oh so very special way." (Stops singing.) You'll make me beautiful again, little friends. Like magicians, like tiny fairy godmothers. You little devils. I'll shit. I'll pee. I'll shit again. I'll puke. I'll shit. I'll puke again. Then I'll start all over again. (Stops spinning and looks up at the ceiling.) I wonder how long it will take to lose another twenty pounds? A week? Two weeks? A month? (Mimes looking into an imaginary mirror.) All that flab just has to go. It's so horrible. So hateful. Where did it all come from? How did I ever get to be so ugly? (Throws the box back onto the bed.) Cindy did it! Damn her! All that fast food. All those restaurants. All those all-you-can-eat buffets. And then that Caribbean cruise! Food in the morning. Food at noon. Food for snack. Food for dinner. Food at midnight. God! I know Cindy always means well. I know she wanted us to have a second honeymoon. But look at the results. I'm a blimp. A piglet. No, a gross, wallowing porker. (Clutches his stomach and tries pounding it in a frenzy and then stops suddenly.) Here it comes. A last. My God. Here it comes. (Rushes to the toilet which now becomes illuminated in a solitary pool of light. Drops down his pants and lifts the toilet seat cover and plops down on the toilet. Almost screams, moans and groans in sensual pleasure as he mimes filling the toilet with bowel movement. The light becomes a bilious, diarrhea green.) Oh God. Oh God. It's so good. So good. I love you. You're so good. More. More. More. Come on. Come on out. Get out of me. Oh. Oh. (Pants and hyperventilates, and then starts to sway back and forth. Finally clutches his stomach and pitches out onto the floor. Lights out.)

SCENE IV

(TOM is back in bed. But now it is a hospital bed. There is an IV pole, oxygen, and a heartbeat monitor. One of the chairs in front of the desk has been pulled over and CINDY is seated at the left side of the bed. TOM is sleeping. FOREST is standing on the other side of the bed. He makes a sign to CINDY to follow him stage forward to talk in private.)

CINDY: How's he doing, doctor?

FOREST: Better now, but he almost died.

CINDY: How could he get so sick?

FOREST: I'm sure he's suffering from anorexia-bulimia. He's been taking pills. Diet pills. Fluid pills. Laxatives. He must have been taking them by the handful.

CINDY: Bulimia? That's a problem for young girls.

FOREST: Usually, yes. But rarely men can suffer from it as well. And he has been taking lots of different kinds of pills.

CINDY: How can you tell?

FOREST: All of his lab tests were completely out of whack. His potassium, his sodium, his bicarbonate levels were all as abnormal as I've ever seen. There's no way to get so sick without taking gobs of medications. He's probably been vomiting and purging himself for weeks. Have you found any pills around the house?

CINDY: I've never seen any.

FOREST: I'd like you to go home and search your house. They'll be hidden somewhere out of the way: back of a closet, under the bed, in the attic, maybe. Just look everywhere.

CINDY: And if I find them?

FOREST: When you find them, bring them in to me. He needs to be confronted. He could have killed himself.

TOM: *(Wakes up and looks at CINDY and FOREST.)* Cindy?

CINDY: *(Rushes over and hugs him.)* Oh, Tom. I thought I'd lost you. You've been so sick.

TOM: Where am I?

CINDY: You're in the hospital.

TOM: The hospital?

CINDY: You were six days in the ICU. You were having heart problems and breathing problems. You were hooked up to all sorts of machines. You've been so, so sick.

TOM: Sick from what?

CINDY: The doctor thinks you may have taken something. Some diet pills or laxatives or something like that.

TOM: What? He thinks I did this to myself? Why would Dr. Forest say something like that?

CINDY: Why would he?

TOM: Maybe Dr. Forest just doesn't know anything. Maybe I wasn't sick at all. *(Turns toward FOREST.)* Why would you say something like that? I've know you for years. You took care of my parents before they died. They loved you. Our whole family does. Why would you want to say something like that?

FOREST: Tom, there are not that many diseases that make someone as sick as you were. I don't know why people do such things, but they can make themselves sick. Very sick.

TOM: Hospitals make people sick. Doctors make people sick. You read about it all the time. What about those horrible germs like staph? I don't know what happened, but I didn't make myself sick.

CINDY: Please, the doctor's trying to help you.

137

TOM: Help me? By blaming all this on me, the patient? Yeah, that's the way it is. I can see it. (*To CINDY.*) You've got to believe me. Please tell me you believe me.

CINDY: (*Hugs TOM and the doctor backs away discreetly.*) I believe you. I believe you. Please just rest and get better. This will all be like a bad dream, a nightmare. We'll get over it. We'll get through it just fine.

(*Lights out.*)

SCENE V

(*BASTROP's office. CINDY is seated in front of the desk. BASTROP is standing behind desk. He is looking out a window, then turns to face CINDY.*)

BASTROP: So what's the verdict? Will the employees accept the changes in health insurance or not?

CINDY: I don't know, Mr. Bastrop. There's been a lot of grumbling already. You can't take away an entitlement like that and expect people to accept it lying down.

BASTROP: Lying down! Did you see the sales figures for last quarter? Flat! They're dead flat! Now that's something that's lying down. (*Pauses.*) They can make the same products we do in Europe or China. Did you know that in those European countries they spend half of what we do per capita on health care? Did you know that those same countries spend only 8% or less of their gross national products on health care? Do you know how much we spend in this country?

CINDY: I don't know, Mr. Bastrop. Why don't you tell me?

BASTROP: Sixteen percent! Sixteen percent of the gross national product of the biggest economy in the world. Billions! And you know what percentage of that assumed by the private sector?

CINDY: How could I know that?

BASTROP: Fifty-five percent. Over fifty percent of that huge expenditure is assumed by the private sector. Not the federal government, not the state government, but us, the private sector.

CINDY: Is that bad?

BASTROP: No, but in Europe the government assumes over 80% of that same expenditure. Health care is considered a public cost, borne by the public. Not so here. *(Plops down in his executive chair.)* It's killing us. This health care thing is killing us in this country. And if we can't get a handle on it, we cannot compete. It's eating us alive. Your job. My job. All will go down the drain of health care. You know they project that health care expenditures will reach 20% of our gross national product by the year 2030?

CINDY: What can I say?

BASTROP: Nothing. But you can continue to talk to the other employees. *(Pauses.)* By the way, how is your husband?

CINDY: How did you know he was sick?

BASTROP: Through the grapevine. A lot of the people down here knew your husband was in the hospital. That's all. Nothing personal.

CINDY: What else did you know?

BASTROP: Nothing. Nothing at all. Don't get all riled up. I just heard he was sick and in the hospital.

CINDY: I hope that's all you know. His health is none of your business.

BASTROP: *(Sighs.)* That's the problem. It is my business and your business and all of our business. And that's what pays all of our health care premiums . . . this business.

CINDY: Is this a threat?

BASTROP: Calm down. Of course it's not a threat. I care about you. I care about your family. But I have a CEO and a board who care passionately about the bottom line. That is their business and if they don't take care of it, we're all out of jobs. Do you have any idea how much it would cost for you and your husband to buy health insurance now? And that's not even taking pre-existing conditions into account.

CINDY: No. I have no idea.

BASTROP: Thousands.

CINDY: A year?

BASTROP: No. A month.

CINDY: *(Pauses.)* Wouldn't we be covered even if we left the job? I thought that was the law?

BASTROP: Yeah, sure. That's COBRA and it's very expensive, plus it only lasts for about six months.

CINDY: Then what?

BASTROP: I don't know. But, you would no longer be covered by our insurance. You would just have to look around for something else, if you could find it. *(Pauses.)* For the time being, I know we're going to have to change our health care coverage here at Castor Industries. We will have to go for a thousand dollar deductible and some percentage copayments for office visits, hospital costs and medications. We don't have any choice.

CINDY: The employees here will never accept it.

BASTROP: So we close down? Just to prove a point?

CINDY: They'll never accept that kind of an increase.

BASTROP: They've already had to accept it in almost every industry around here. You're still among the privileged few. Work with me. Please work with me. Go back and try to convince the employees.

CINDY: *(Stands to leave.)* I'll see what I can do.

SCENE VI

(Tom and CINDY are in bed, center stage. They are illuminated by a single pool of light.)

TOM: After I got back from the gym, I helped down at the Manna House today.

CINDY: That's a nice thing to do.

TOM: I know. I'm a nice person. We served over 50 meals to the poor. You just can't believe the amount of poverty and hunger we have in this town. It's amazing.

CINDY: Does that bother you?

TOM: What? Poverty and hunger? Sure it bothers me. It's not their fault. Some of the people have mental illnesses. Some are between jobs or have health problems and can't get onto disability. You bet it bothers me.

CINDY: No, I mean does it bother you being around all that food all the time?

TOM: No, of course not. I never eat any of it? I just serve.

CINDY: Why do you do it?

TOM: I like to help people. I like to give them something they need and want like food. It makes me feel good.

CINDY: *(Sighs.)* Like throwing up or shitting?

TOM: What's that supposed to mean? I like to help people. I don't like to throw up or go shit.

CINDY: Really, Tom? *(Reaches under the bed and pulls out the plastic box filled with bottles of medications.)* Then what's all this about? Why do you keep all this? *(Picks up some bottles.)* Pills to poop. Pills to pee. Pills to vomit. Are you using it or just keeping it as a souvenir?

TOM: Where did you get that?

CINDY: Where you hid it, under the kitchen sink, way in the back behind the cleaning stuff.

TOM: You little sneak!

CINDY: Sneak? Why shouldn't I sneak? I saw you in the ICU last month on a breathing machine for three days because you were almost dead.

TOM: Dr. Forest told you to do this, didn't he?

CINDY: Yes, he suggested it.

TOM: He's a quack! He doesn't know anything about me or my body or my health or anything.

CINDY: He's trying to help you.

TOM: How? By making me miserable and fat? Yeah! He wants me to die of a heart attack with all my arteries clogged up with cholesterol. That's what he wants.

CINDY: Don't be ridiculous. Dr. Forest knows more than you want to give him credit for. And besides, he said that admitting that you had a problem was half the battle.

TOM: I do have a problem. I'm fat. I'm ugly. I'm hideous. But I don't take pills and I'm not anorexic or bulimic.

CINDY: *(Gets up and takes the box, then goes and opens the bathroom door and mimes flipping on the light. Now the toilet is also illuminated in a pool of light. Sets down the box, opens it and begins pouring the pills into the toilet.)* Then you won't need these, will you?

TOM: *(Screaming.)* What are you doing?

CINDY: I'm getting rid of this trash.

TOM: That's not trash. They're worth a lot of money. And you're just throwing it down the toilet. We don't have money to throw away like this.

CINDY: A lot of money? What are you talking about? Who cares about what they cost. This is poison for you. It's killing you and all you can do is worry about how much they cost. These pills are killing you and they need to get flushed down the toilet.

TOM: Don't! Don't do that! They're mine! I need those pills.

CINDY: *(Screams now.)* No you don't! They're killing you!

TOM: *(Gets up and watches CINDY from the door of the bathroom. Lurches forward and kneels by the toilet.)* Don't do this to me. I beg you. Don't condemn me to a miserable life of obesity. Please!

CINDY: *(Picks him up and hugs him.)* You don't need them. I love you. I need you. I don't want to lose you. You are beautiful. You are as handsome as the sun. You're perfect the way you are. Please believe me. Please work with me. Please try.

SCENE VII

(CINDY and TOM are standing in chairs in front of the desk, stage left. This time the desk is in the office of FOREST. He is dressed in a white lab coat and is standing behind the desk.)

FOREST: *(Reaches over to shake CINDY's hand, then TOM's hand.)* Tom, Cindy, nice to see you both. Please, sit down.

(CINDY and TOM sit down. Then FOREST sits in the executive chair and pulls out a folder. FOREST looks at some papers.)

FOREST: Congratulations, Tom. Your lab work looks excellent again this week. Potassium, sodium, creatinine, albumin . . . everything looks just perfect.

TOM: Of course it does.

FOREST: It's been almost three months now and your labs have been completely normal. That's a real accomplishment.

TOM: What did you expect?

FOREST: Patients with bulimia have a life-long disease. I know it sounds harsh, but by tracking your labs, I can make sure you're not abusing laxatives or diuretics. It's simple, but very accurate. If you start to abuse anything, it shows up in your labs.

TOM: *(To FOREST.)* I'm not a child. I'm not an invalid. I'm not a recovering addict. So why do I have to come here each week like a child and have my blood tested?

CINDY: It's working.

TOM: You shut up! I already have one prison warden. I don't need two. And I know you've been going through the house when I'm not there just to check if I'm stocking up with anything.

CINDY: How do you know?

TOM: Because I leave pieces of tape on the cupboards and drawers and every time I come back and you've been in the house, they're all pulled off. It makes me feel like I'm in prison. I'm miserable.

CINDY: But you look great. You've gained a few pounds and you look like a man again, not like a skeleton.

TOM: I'm a pig. A pig in prison. Look at this! *(Indicates his hips to both CINDY and FOREST.)* You both think you're so smart. You've got me cornered. You're probably videotaping me as well. But you can't do it. You can't force me to look fat and repulsive.

FOREST: The first step in your recovery is admitting what you have done is wrong and moving ahead. I thought you were well beyond that first step by now.

TOM: *(Screams.)* I admit it! I did it! I took pills. I puked and shit every day. *(Sulks.)* Now leave me alone. Let me be free just for awhile. Don't force me to live in this police state day and night.

CINDY: *(To FOREST.)* Can we try cutting down on the labs a little? Perhaps we can give him some more freedom. Maybe a month?

TOM: You want that for me?

CINDY: Yes, I do. I'm proud of you and I believe in you.

FOREST: Okay. Let's go a month before the next labs. But please believe me, we want you to live a happy, healthy, productive life. You have a disease, a chronic, debilitating disease. It's fatal in 50% of cases, sometimes more in men. More than one out of two bulimics will die from their disease. Your wife loves you and I care about you. We want you to choose life, not death. Please work with us.

TOM: *(Speaks to FOREST.)* I swear I will. *(Turns to CINDY.)* I swear I will. I won't let you both down. Thank you for believing in me. If only for a month. You won't regret it; I swear to God you won't regret it.

SCENE VIII

(CINDY and TOM are dressed and standing in the bedroom. She looks as if he is about to leave.)

CINDY: Are you sure I can leave you alone?

TOM: Of course you can. I even let you search the house, didn't I? Did you find anything?

CINDY: No.

TOM: Then go to your meeting. You said it was important.

CINDY: It's about health care premiums. You can't imagine what a mess all of this is.

TOM: You're smart. You can find a solution.

CINDY: Maybe, but it's a big problem. It's nationwide and it's overwhelming.

TOM: I have faith in you, even if you don't have faith in yourself. What's the worst that could happen?

CINDY: I could lose my job and we could lose our health insurance.

TOM: So? You find another job. We can get another insurance.

CINDY: It's bit more difficult than that. I've worked at Castor Industries for 17 years. Now I'm almost 43. Who's going to hire me?

TOM: You're smart. You can always find something.

CINDY: But I'm not young anymore. And if we had to buy insurance, they would see if either of us has ever been ill. They will put a pre-existing condition clause in the contract for anything related to bulimia.

TOM: They can't do that. Besides, I'm not sick anymore.

CINDY: Dr. Forest said anorexia-bulemia was a lifelong illness, like alcoholism. Once an alcoholic, always an alcoholic. Once an anorexic, always an anorexic.

TOM: You believe that crap?

CINDY: Yes, I do. And you scare me when you talk like that.

TOM: *(Approaches CINDY and gives her a loving hug.)* Have a little faith. People change. Can't you make that leap of faith?

CINDY: I want to, but I'm afraid.

TOM: Don't be. Just go to your meeting and solve the world's problems. I've got plenty of things to do here.

CINDY: *(Takes her jacket.)* Are you sure you'll be all right by yourself?

TOM: So sure it hurts.

CINDY: *(Kisses TOM.)* Take care of yourself. Bye. *(Leaves into the darkness stage left.)*

> *(As soon as she leaves, TOM sighs deeply and smiles. He goes into the bathroom. When he does, the light in the bedroom goes off. The toilet is illuminated in a single, brilliant pool of light. TOM goes over and lifts off the cover of the back of the toilet. He lifts out a plastic bag filled with bottles. TOM opens a bottle and fills his hand. Then TOM mimes looking in a mirror and scrutinizing the image. TOM speaks to his own image in the mirror.)*

TOM: I know I promised. I know I promised Cindy. But look at me. Look at my bloated face, my arms, and massive butt. *(Puts the plastic bag on the back of the toilet and begins to spin around the stage in a ballet which is both haunting and grotesque. Begins to sing "Oh What a Beautiful Morning" from Oklahoma.)* "Oh what a beautiful morning, oh what a beautiful day, I got a beautiful feeling, everything's goin' my way."

(The movements start slowly, but become faster and faster and more and more erratic. Finally TOM stops spinning. Looks wild, like a tracked animal. Returns to the toilet and begins opening bottle after bottle, swallows handfuls of pills, one after another. When TOM has taken several bottlefuls, he calmly closes the empty bottle, replaces them in the bag and puts the bag back in the reservoir of the toilet. Replaces the top. Then he lifts up the seat, pulls down his pants, and sits down. TOM looks up at the light so his face is illuminated.)

TOM: Oh great and merciful God. Let me shit and let me puke. Let me lose this horrible straight jacket of fat so that I may be beautiful again. All I ask is twenty pounds, God. Just dissolve away twenty pounds and let's flush them down the toilet. I promise to work at the Manna House every day. I will even go back to church. But please, God, just make me handsome again so I may be worthy servant of your will. In your Holy Name, amen. *(Starts to heave and moan. Clutches his stomach.)* Thank you. Thanks you for answering my prayer. Oh, thank you. *(Continues to heave and begins to retch without vomiting. The light turns green. TOM falls backwards with her arms outstretched.)* Thank you!

(Lights dim to dark.)

SCENE IX

(BASTROP's office, stage left. He seems to be staring out a window. His back is turned to the desk. CINDY comes in, but BASTROP does not turn immediately.)

CINDY: Mr. Bastrop?

BASTROP: *(Turns to face CINDY.)* Yes. Sorry. Sit down, please.

CINDY: *(Sits down while BASTROP remains standing.)* I guess it's about the health insurance.

BASTROP: Yes. As you know, the employees voted down the proposed changes.

CINDY: I know. I tried, but I couldn't convince them.

BASTROP: That's okay. I know you did what you could.

CINDY: So what happens now?

BASTROP: We impose the board's choice.

CINDY: And what if there's a strike?

BASTROP: We stay open awhile, and then we shut down, perhaps indefinitely.

CINDY: Mr. Bastrop. I can't lose my job. I can't lose my health insurance. My husband's ill. He's got an on-going medical problem.

BASTROP: I'm not making this call. But either way you're going to be in trouble. If there's a strike, you may have to cross the picket line. And even if we manage to survive, there will be down-sizing. You're already an expensive employee. Who do you think is going to be the first to be let go? The young man with no dependents and no seniority, or the forty-three year old woman at the top of her pay scale with a sick husband?

CINDY: Even if I promise to cross the picket line if there's a strike. Surely that would make a difference?

BASTROP: I wish I could tell you it would. But this is about profit margins, not loyalty. I wish I could say it would make a difference, but I doubt it. I like you, Cindy. You've always been a straight shooter and a good woman. I'm just letting you know what's happening. You might have to make other plans.

CINDY: What other plans?

BASTROP: For a new job. And some sort of health insurance after the six months of COBRA we are legally obliged to provide.

CINDY: You can't be asking me to choose between my husband and Castor Industries.

BASTROP: Of course not! No one is asking you to do that.

CINDY: *(Stands and raises her voice.)* You are! If I were forty and single or if my husband was in good health, would that make a difference?

BASTROP: No.

CINDY: This is crazy. It doesn't matter what I do, does it? This is just an advance warning.

BASTROP: That's what it is, an advance warning.

CINDY: That's crazy!

BASTROP: No, it's just economics. *(Turns and faces the window again.)* Health care costs per capita in the US are double those in Europe and ten times those in Asia. *(Turns to face CINDY again.)* We want it all, good salaries, the best in health care regardless of the costs, MRIs, CAT scans, genetically engineered medications, every imaginable transplant. We want it all and we want it now, and then we want the right to sue somebody if it doesn't go perfectly. It's a collision between unlimited demand and limited resources and we're both caught in the middle.

CINDY: Those are just words. My husband and I are people, like the rest of your employees. Real people with real problems.

BASTROP: I know, and I feel sorry for both of you. But when the cuts come, either way you are going to suffer.

CINDY: Suffer, eh? What do you know about suffering? You're just a lackey for the board. You're their hatchet man, that's all.

BASTROP: Are you done?

CINDY: Yes.

BASTROP: My son, Kyle, died of a liver disease seven years ago. My wife and I could not get a transplant for him because it was considered an experimental therapy at the time. We watched him die a slow, painful death. I have suffered. My wife and family have suffered.

CINDY: I thought he died of an accident.

BASTROP: That's what we told people here. What was the point of dragging our personal problem in front of everyone?

CINDY: I'm really sorry.

BASTROP: So am I. It's bigger and more complicated than either of us. And I would appreciate it if you keep the medical information about my son to yourself.

CINDY: Of course. Is that it?

BASTROP: Yes, and thank you for trying to save the company.

(*Lights dim to dark.*)

SCENE X

(TOM is now retching over the toilet. He is bathed in a pool of light. CINDY enters stage left and throws her jacket on the bed.)

CINDY: Honey, I'm home.

TOM: *(Gets up quickly. Staggers away from the toilet.)* Just a minute! *(Mimes looking in a mirror and smoothes his hair and clothes.)* I'll be right there.

CINDY: *(Approaches the door and listens.)* Are you all right in there?

TOM: *(Walks out as briskly and steadily as he can.)* Of course I'm all right. What do you think?

CINDY: *(Examines him from head to toe.)* How was your day?

TOM: Fine. What are you looking at? I'm fine. After the gym, I spent the whole day helping to get ready for the Cancer Survivors Support Group banquet.

CINDY: Doing what?

TOM: Making fancy hors d'oeuvres, chopping carrots and onions. Fixing little sandwiches with olive slices on top. That sort of thing.

CINDY: How'd you get involved in that?

TOM: Some lady I met at the Manna House asked me to come. She said I was good with food.

CINDY: *(Looks at him very closely.)* Did you lose any more weight?

TOM: Of course not? That's silly.

CINDY: Tom? Let's put you on the scales and weigh you.

TOM: They're broken.

CINDY: That's convenient. I'll get a new one this weekend. I know you're losing weight and you look terrible. You're taking something, aren't you?

TOM: I'm fine. And I'm not taking anything. If you don't believe me, just search the place again. Search me if you want to. *(Holds his arms out as if to be searched.)*

CINDY: I've already searched the house from top to bottom. I can't find anything. But I can see you're losing weight. You're melting away and I can't seem to do anything about it.

TOM: Then don't. I feel fine. I look better than ever.

CINDY: When do you have to go back to Dr. Forest for a blood test?

TOM: His nurse called and cancelled our next appointment. It's been rescheduled a month later.

CINDY: Why?

TOM: I don't know. I supposed he's on vacation or at a medical meeting or something. How should I know?

CINDY: But that's two months without a blood test.

TOM: I can get a blood test any time you want. But it still takes a doctor's order to get it. And even if I do, what makes you think you'd know what you're looking at? *(He pauses.)* And, by the way, how was your day, dear?

CINDY: *(Sits down on the edge of the bed.)* Not so good.

TOM: Oh? *(Sits down next to CINDY and massages her back.)* What's happening?

CINDY: I might lose my job in the next few months. There may be a strike and down-sizing or even a plant closure. It looks bad. Whatever I do, I'll still probably be fired.

TOM: So?

CINDY: So! I only get six months unemployment and six months medical coverage.

TOM: So?

CINDY: You're sick. If you get as sick as you did a few months back, you might have to go to the public hospital. And even there, they still charge proportional to your assets. We could be wiped out. Do you understand? We could lose everything.

TOM: You're smart. You're strong. You're not that old. Of course you'll be able to find a new job.

CINDY: Maybe. But even so, we're still going to have to change our current insurance plan. Bastrop told me so.

TOM: To what?

CINDY: Something with a five thousand dollar deductible, plus a percentage of hospital and office charges, and a restricted list of medications with hefty co-payments. That's for the time being.

TOM: You're tired. You're upset. *(Continues to massage CINDY and give her little kisses.)* Just let go. Relax. Your baby doll's here. He'll take care of you. He knows just what to do.

CINDY: *(Stands up abruptly.)* You can't even take care of yourself. What are we going to do if something happens to me? You haven't held a job in five years or more. You've never been able to do anything for more than six months. Plus you're sick.

TOM: *(Stands and goes to CINDY. Puts his finger to her lips.)* Ssshhhh. No more talking. *(Continues to caress CINDY and give her kisses. Begins to unbutton her blouse.*

(Lights dim to dark.)

SCENE XI

(TOM is in the bathroom. He undoes the back of the toilet reservoir and pulls out his stash of bottles.)

TOM: Come to momma. We've just got three more pounds to go. That will make the second twenty. We might even make it today. Think about it. Twenty pounds after the first twenty. It's more that we every hoped for, isn't it. We've done it in a record time and under very strict supervision. Such a pity Dr. Forest isn't on the new list of medical providers. That gave me a full extra month. How convenient for us. That has given us plenty of time, hasn't it. *(Smiles as he downs several handfuls of pills.)* I love the crunchy ones. So easy to take. Perhaps if we take an extra couple of handfuls, we'll get those three pounds off today. I'll be handsome again. Perfect. Cindy will love me. Everyone will love and admire me. *(Downs another couple of handfuls of pills.)* If she loses her job, who cares? We can run away somewhere and forget all these doctors and insurance plans and problems. Who needs it them? *(Talks to the bag of bottles.)* I don't need them. All I need are you. My friends. My helpers. Let's go for that last three pounds. *(Clutches his stomach with the first wave of cramping.)* Here we go, my little friends. *(Flips up the lid of the toilet, pulls his pants and sits down.)* Come on. Come on. *(Clutches his stomach and winces in pain.)* Oh lawdy, oh lawdy. *(The light now turns a very sick color of bilious green. TOM continues to writhe and groan. Starts to retch violently. The light now turns to blood red.)* Oh God. God help me!

(TOM stands up and staggers toward the bedroom. He only makes it to the edge where he falls to the ground as he pulls the bedspread off the bed and lies motionless.)

(Lights dim to dark.)

SCENE XII

(TOM is lying in bed. He is dead. The bedroom is now a funeral parlor, with a mortuary spray of flowers. It should be obvious that this is no longer the bedroom. The bed itself may be covered with a black sheet. He is dressed in a simple, gray suit. FOREST, BASTROP and CINDY stand around the bed. FOREST and CINDY are on one side, BASTROP on the other.)

BASTROP: I'm sorry. *(Moves to the head of the bed. CINDY moves forward and they shake hands.)*

CINDY: Thank you.

BASTROP: I know it might not be the time or the place, but I wanted you to know that his last hospitalization will be covered in full. Our carrier chose to over-look the clause which excluded coverage for self-inflicted injuries.

CINDY: I appreciate it. I really do. But I don't want to talk about that now, if you don't mind.

BASTROP: Of course. *(Moves away, back to the side of the bed.)*

FOREST: *(Moves over toward the head of the bed and puts his hand on CINDY's shoulder.)* You did everything you could.

CINDY: Did I? Did I really? I didn't look in the back of the toilet. That's where he hid the pills. I left him that afternoon. I could have stayed. Did I really do everything I could have?

FOREST: Some people are so determined to die that all the caring and all the love in the world will not prevent it. You did everything you possibly could.

CINDY: I failed him. I couldn't give him what he really wanted.

FOREST: What did he really want, a perfect body?

CINDY: Yes, he did. He wanted a perfect body and I could never convince him that he already had it.

FOREST: That's the whole point. You could never convince him, even in a whole lifetime of trying.

CINDY: (*Looks over at TOM.*) Maybe he's got it now.

BASTROP: Got what?

CINDY: The perfect body. Tom's perfect body. Maybe he's finally got the perfect body in heaven. That's where he is, isn't he?

BASTROP: Of course.

FOREST: I'm sure he is. And that's where you have to think of him . . . . in heaven with a radiant smile and a perfect body.

BASTROP: (*To CINDY.*) I know you don't want to talk about office matters, but I wanted to tell you that the employees finally voted to accept the latest health care package. Your job is safe.

CINDY: (*Looks at TOM.*) Safe for me. But it doesn't help him.

BASTROP: No it doesn't and I'm sorry for you and for him. (*Turns to speak to FOREST.*) Bye the way, Dr. Forest, I'm Mr. Bastrop, Chief of Human Resources at Castor Industries.

FOREST: Nice to meet you. (*They shake hands.*)

BASTROP: I just wanted to let you know that you have been included in the new list of preferred providers in our insurance plan. You'll be able to continue to see Cindy as a patient, if you both think that's appropriate, of course. You have an outstanding reputation in the community, Dr. Forest, and we want to make sure you could continue to see our employees. Congratulations and thanks for your help. *(Turns to CINDY.)* We'll look forward to seeing you back at work when you feel up to it. I know you are going to have other things on your mind for the next couple of weeks. Again, accept my sincere condolences. *(Shakes CINDY'S hand, then DR. FOREST'S hand.)* Goodbye. *(Leaves stage right.)*

FOREST: *(Shakes CINDY's hand.)* I have to get back to the clinic. I know you understand. Life goes on and the sick just keep on coming. My place is there, with the living. If you need anything for sleep or depression, just let me know. Goodbye. *(Leaves stage left.)*

> *(CINDY is left alone in the room with TOM'S body. She takes one of the chairs near the desk and puts it at the bedside. CINDY sits down and takes TOM'S hand.)*

CINDY: A perfect body. *(CINDY touches it to her forehead and shakes her head.)*

> *(Lights dim to dark.)*

THE END

FRANZ JOSEF'S WATCH

CAST OF CHARACTERS

MRS. CERENISKY: A 90 plus year old lady with a very thick Eastern European accent.

MRS. DUDACHKA: Cerenisky's daughter, already in her late 60's. No accent.

DR. SMITH: Middle aged doctor. Very good dancer, a Slavophile.

NURSE: Dressed in scrubs. Casual language

SETTING

The initial stage setting is a stage illuminated by a single pool of light.

(SMITH is dressed in black boots with black pants, tucked inside the boots. He wears a white shirt with puffy sleeves, a short black vest, and a black hat decorated with feathers. He dances on stage with CERENISKY. She is dressed in a red, folk skirt, a white, short sleeved blouse, and a red or black vest. She may also be wearing black boots. These are both typical Czech costumes. The scene begins with the cheerful music of "Pardubacka," a Bohemian folk dance. The couple dances the short dance. When they finish, SMITH takes off the hat and vest, pulls his pants out of the boots and puts on his lab coat which he smoothes out. CERENISKY goes to the hospital bed and gets in, covering her costume with the sheet. DUDACHKA, her daughter, is seated next to the bed. CERENISKY has an IV in her arm and oxygen tube in her nose.)

SCENE I

CERENISKY: *(Sits in a hospital bed and speaks in an animated way.)* And it was given to my grandfather by the Archduke Ferdinand himself, you know, the one they shot at Sarajevo. That started the war, you know, not the watch, of course, but the shooting of the Archduke at Sarajevo in 1914. Yes, that started the Great War, the first one. Well, anyway, the Archduke had gotten the watch as a gift from the Emperor Franz Joseph himself in Vienna. (*Pauses as if to catch her breath.*) And Archduke Ferdinand gave it to my grandfather who was a metal worker. My grandfather was a skilled man who made fancy metalwork for balconies and stairways. He worked at the palaces in Vienna and at the royal hunting lodge in Transylvania, near Cluj. That's where he met my grandfather. (*Pauses.*) I know it's complicated. Anyway, my father told me that my grandfather was an artist, not just a metal worker. Yes, a real artist. We have artistic blood in our veins. And my grandfather received the watch for being an artist, too, right from the Archduke Ferdinand, who got it from the Emperor Franz Josef. Did I mention that?

> (*CERENISKY holds her hands as if she actually held the watch.*
> *CERENISKY sinks back into the chair. She breathes heavily,*
> *trying to catch her breath. DUDACHKA, sits at attention on a*
> *chair by the hospital bed.*)

DUKACHKA: Yes, Mother, you did.

CERENISKY: (*Continues after a moment's pause.*) I was really born in Rumania, even though my parents were Czech. My father made sausages, not metalwork. After my grandfather died, we moved from Bohemia to Bucharest in Rumania, where he started a sausage factory. King Karl I ruled Rumania at that time. Lots of Czechs moved around Eastern Europe in those days to find work because they were smarter, better educated, and sometimes very artistic. (*Nods her head and winks at SMITH.*) Did I tell you that already?

SMITH: (*Smiles and looks over at DUDACHKA.*) Yes, I believe you did mention that.

CERENISKY: Well, my parents stayed in Bucharest where my father's sausage factory produced the best sausage for all the fancy restaurants. They called Bucharest the "Paris of Eastern Europe" at that time, you know. There were wide boulevards with trees and fancy shops. I can still see the trees. We would walk under them and look at the windows of the shops, filled with fancy things, just like in Paris, I suppose. We would eat ice cream in a shop with chandeliers and mirrors. *(Pausing again, moistens her lips and wipes the corners of her mouth.)* But in the years before the Great War, everything was changing. So many poor people, so little money. The sausage factory closed. No one could afford such fancy sausage anymore. And since we were Czechs and not Rumanians, we weren't really welcomed there anymore. I could speak Rumanian without accent, but not Czech. Did I mention that?

SMITH: *(Makes a few notes, while CERENISKY continues.)* Yes, I think you did.

CERENISKY: Rumania was nice, but they knew from my name that I was Czech, not Rumanian. Everyone was so poor and angry before the Great War, the first one. It's then that my parents began talking of coming to America. America seemed young and untouched by trouble. America had opportunity. America had freedom. Everyone was equal. Everyone had the same rights. My parents dreamed of what they could do in America. So they wrote to an uncle in Chicago and asked if he would help them get started. Everyone seemed to have an uncle in America. And all the uncles seemed to be rich, at least for us. For a long time, my parents waited. Then the letter came. It was not so friendly as my parents had imagined, the letter I mean. My uncle had lots of people asking him for help and he could only help us out a little with a sponsorship and some money for tickets. So we came to New York on a boat with a thousand of other people from Europe: Czechs, Hungarians, Russians, Ukrainians, and many Jews with their beards and shawls from all over Eastern Europe.

> *(SMITH cradles the medical chart in his hand and leans against the edge of the sink.)*

CERENISKY: Am I boring you doctor?

SMITH: *(Shakes his head.)* Of course not. How could I pass up an opportunity to soak up such an amazing tale from such an amazing woman? I really enjoy listening to you. Central Europe seems so far away from Central Louisiana. Your stories and your accent make me think of emperors in their courts with lots of gold braid and peasant women dancing in their folk costumes. I love that stuff. (*Pauses.*) I'm sorry. Now I'm the one probably boring you.

CERENISKY: (*Dismisses the idea with a wave of her hand.*) Of course not, Doctor. I love to think about those old times and those old dances. They were so beautiful. And I was beautiful, too, at least I thought so, and so did my parents. I learned lovely dances for girls. The young women would dance them in the villages, so the boys could look at them after church. We learned to dance in school in Bucharest. My teacher, a good man, a Hungarian from Bratislava, taught us dances and he even taught us a Czech one, just for me, because he knew my parents were Czech. I think he thought I was beautiful too, at least a little and I thought he was so handsome and graceful.

(*CERENISKY closes her eyes and remembers. There is a women's dance "Louky." Several women can dance with or without SMITH. It can also be performed as a couple dance. When it finishes, CERENISKY opens her eyes.*)

CERENISKY: You know, Doctor, I did not speak English back then when we came here. I even had to learn Czech because my parents only started speaking Czech at home instead of Rumanian when we came to America. Imagine, not really knowing how to speak Czech or English. I felt so stupid. The only language I spoke without accent was Rumanian and I couldn't even talk to anyone in that. (*Laughs and sighs.*) When I was in school in New York, I made one of those Rumanian blouses all embroidered up the front and the sleeves. It was for a school fair and it was to show pride in the countries we came from. So I embroidered a blouse. It was beautiful, with geometric designs. But I only finished the front and one of the sleeves when it came time for the school fair. And you know, somebody stole it right from the school. It wasn't even finished and they stole it. Why would anyone want to steal from a school girl? Can you believe such a thing?

SMITH: (*Nods his head.*) Yes, I'm afraid I can believe it. Some people will steal just about anything.

(There can be a projection of an embroidered Rumanian blouse projected over the back of the center stage. It should have thick cross stitching winding up the sleeves and front in diagonal patterns, typical of Rumania.)

SMITH: *(Clears his throat, looks at the medical chart and frowns.)* I'm afraid we have to discuss a little medicine here. Your creatinine is starting to rise. Creatinine is a measure of your kidney function. When it goes up like this, it sometimes means renal failure. You've been started on fluid pills to help the kidneys get rid of water, but if we use too many, you may get dried out. Before now, you've had too much fluid, but now you're getting a little dried out.

(CERENISKY looks at DUDACHK, who smiles and nods. The two women are holding hands. SMITH steps back and motions to DUKACHKA to follow.)

SMITH: Can I speak to you privately? *(Moves further away from the bed.)* I didn't want to talk to you about this in front of your mother, Mrs. Dudachka, but your mother's going down.

DUDACHKA: Down where?

SMITH: She's going down hill. You're mother's deteriorating and I think she's going to die soon.

DUDACHKA: When?

SMITH: If she continues like this, she'll probably die in the next few days. Her heart and kidneys are both failing rapidly.

DUDACHKA: *(Touches her lips and then pulls away her fingers.)* Doctor, she hasn't had a bowel movement in almost three days. Do you think it would help if she had one?

SMITH: *(Pauses and then clears his throat.)* We can certainly work on that, but if her heart stops, we would be obliged to give your mother CPR . . . life support. That means we might have to break her ribs and

164

shove a tube down her throat and give her painful electrical shocks. Personally, given her age, I would not recommend CPR, although it has to be a family decision. What are your feelings?

DUDACHKA: She's tough, Doctor. It would be a pity not to give her every chance.

SMITH: If we do try and resuscitate her, we will inflict pain and probably not prolong her life. Only five percent of resuscitated patients survive to leave the hospital. I'm sure it's even less in her age category. She's ninety one, after all.

DUDACHKA: No, ninety-two. (*Ponders the question a few seconds.*) Why don't we leave the decision to you?

SMITH: I can't make that decision for you. Remember, there is no right or wrong decision, but the patient and their family have to make it, not the doctor.

DUDACKHA: What if she were your mother?

SMITH: Doctors are never supposed to take care of their own families. We're not supposed to do it because we lack objectivity when we treat our own family. So you will have to make the decision for her, unless you think she can make the decision herself. All I can do is explain the options to you.

DUDACHKA: (*Pauses.*) Let's give her at least one chance. But no long-term life support. After all, doctor, she is ninety-two years old.

SMITH: (*Flinches.*) Are you sure you want that for your mother? You do have the final decision, whatever it may be.

DUDACHKA: Is it always brutal? Do you always break the ribs and teeth?

SMITH: Not always, but often.

DUDACHKA: Does it always fail?

SMITH: No, sometimes we get people back. Sometimes they do start breathing again. But often they are so sick that they get stuck on the ventilator. And the decision not to intubate is always easier than the decision to take someone off the ventilator once they're on. Remember, only five percent of those who get CPR in the hospital ever leave the hospital alive.

DUDACHKA: (*Pauses.*) Let's still give her one chance, just one chance. She's my mother and I'm not ready to lose her yet. I know she's old and frail and I know she's already led a good, long life, but I have to give her that once chance.

SMITH: Okay, just one chance.

(*DUDACHKA returns to her mother's bedside, while SMITH goes off stage. (*

(*Lights dim to dark.*)

SCENE II

(*CERESNICKY is in the bed. DUDACHKA is at the bedside as at the end of the previous scene. SMITH, carrying a clip board, enters from off stage.*)

SMITH: Mrs. Cerenisky, it looks like you've only taken a few sips of water since yesterday. You've hardly put out any urine at all. Your lab values show a doubling of your creatinine. It went from 2.0 to 4.0.

DUDACHKA: What does all that mean?

SMITH: It means that your mother is going into complete kidney failure if things don't turn around. The kidneys are only working less than a fourth of normal.

DUDACHKA: Can't she just drink a little more?

SMITH: I'm afraid she would have to drink quite a bit more. And then she'll probably go back into congestive heart failure. (*Sighs and sits down. Fumbles and flips through the chart. Speaks to CERENISKY.*) How exactly did you get to Louisiana anyway? It seems so unlikely and isolated.

CERENISKY: My father brought us here from New York to help start the new Czech village of Vitr. That means "the wind," you know. The brochure from the Czech agricultural society promised good land and a good climate, two or three crops a year. The land was very cheap, too. So we moved again and came down to join a few hundred other Czech families. They came from all over, some from Bohemia and Moravia, but mostly from other parts in the United States, Nebraska, Iowa, Indiana. We had a school taught in Czech back then, the Komensky School. My parents wanted us to learn Czech and to keep the old traditions. But, you know, after a few years, the children didn't want to learn Czech anymore. Even their parents wanted them to learn good English, without an accent, so they could move up in the world. So they started sending their children into Fulton to go to school. Then the old Komensky School blew down in a hurricane, and that was the end of the Czech school. (*Makes a sweeping gesture and then settles back.*) I was already too old for the school anyway. And I just went to work right away with my first husband in the feed store. Yes, the school's gone, the store's gone, and I'm already past my third husband.

SMITH: Weren't you bored here? So isolated? It's not exactly the Paris of Central Louisiana.

CERNISKY: Bored? Sometimes, a little. It was quite a shock from Bucharest and New York to Louisiana. But then again, we had so much work on the farm and in the store that I hardly noticed the years go by. And we knew all the people. So it was like a village in many ways. And we did have to stick together, you know. The Americans sometimes didn't like us and called us "Bohunks" or worse. They didn't like our dances or our beer drinking and sometimes there were even fights. But we worked hard, but we had fun, too. We had dances in the hall and would polka and waltz all night. We had good musicians, too, violinists and accordionists and drummers and even a saxophone and trumpet player. Old Mr. Voda made cabinets at his shop during the day and instruments at night. And all his children learned to play an instrument. Music was very important. No one wore the old time costumes, but everyone still danced, even the little ones. You should have seen those dances. I think you would have really enjoyed them.

(*The music of "Studenka," a simple dance from Pilzen begins. It's a circle dance and everyone can dance, SMITH, CERENISKY, NURSE and DUDACKA. No one needs to be in costume. The dancers yell "Pivo!" (Beer!) from time to time while dancing. When it's finished, everyone goes back to there places.*)

CERENISKY: (*There can be a projection of the Rumanian mountains with a forest and possibly a castle.*) When I look out the window at our house here in Vitr, I think about the forest back there in Rumania, so long ago. You could see the mountains and trees out of our country house in the hills near Cluj. Cluj is in Transylvania, you know. Our summer house was really very close to the old royal hunting lodge. That's where my grandfather got the watch, you know, the one Franz Joseph had given to the Archduke Ferdinand before he gave it to my grandfather. (*Pauses.*) We followed the Great War, the first one, from the safety of Louisiana. Czechoslovakia became a new state. I sometimes dreamed of going there to Czechoslovakia, but my father and mother never wanted to. It was the Old World to them, with all of its problems. We had a new life in a hard new land. (*Pauses.*) I would sometimes walk in the woods around our house here in Louisiana and try to imagine myself in the forest near our country house in Transylvania. But here it was so hot and humid, and the red bugs and mosquitoes bite you. And I would be sweating and looking out for poison ivy and snakes and sometimes I would cry, all by myself, in the woods of Louisiana and dream about the forest in Transylvania and the great boulevards in Bucharest.

DUKACHKA: She's not eating well, Doctor. I even tried bringing in some kolaches, but she wouldn't even try a bite.

CERENISKY: Bucharest, indeed, but I was here, now, in Louisiana. And I never cried in front of my parents, or my husbands. I wanted to be cheerful and helpful to everyone. And everyone felt I was their friend. I listened and smiled and never repeated the stories they told about their wives and husbands and children and money and drinking problems. Some nights I felt like the weight of all these problems would pull me down. But I had my lovely daughter to raise to be a good American. *(Takes DUDACHKA's hand and squeezes.)* She needed to speak Czech and English without accent, not like me. It took a lot for me to smile sometimes, but I always smiled. No one knew how tired I was sometimes. I even felt as of my own heart was tired and I feel that now, too, but in a different way.

SMITH: It's true. Your heart is weak and tired. The muscle itself is weak. It can't pump the fluid and when there's too much fluid in your body, it fills up the lungs. And if there's too little fluid, it's like a motor running dry. In either case, the kidneys don't get enough blood flow, and they fail as well. That's a no-win situation. You are too old and weak for dialysis.

DUDACHKA: Just a tired, old heart, Mother, a wonderful, tired, old heart.

SMITH: Yes, just a tired, old heart, wonderful and tired.

(Lights dim to dark.)

SCENE III

(SMITH enters on stage to find CERENISKY poking around in the air as if she were drawing imaginary figures on the ceiling.)

CERENISKY: Doctor, do you know I have a watch from the Emperor Franz Joseph?

SMITH: Yes, I remember you telling me. It's a fantastic story. (*Looks over the medical chart and shakes his head.*)

DUDACHKA: My grandfather got it from the Archduke Ferdinand, who had received it from the old emperor himself before the Great War, the first one.

SMITH: (*Flipping through the chart*). Does it still work?

CERENISKY: Of course, it still works! My daughter has it now. You know, I remember our house in Transylvania. We lived well then, when my father owned the sausage factory in Bucharest. My grandfather was an iron smith for the Archduke and worked at the hunting lodge near our country home. Then we came to America. It was so hard, especially in the beginning. New York was so busy and full of people and my father struggled to find work. I didn't understand a word in English and everyone seemed to make fun of me. And then Louisiana just seemed like the end of the earth. I was a young woman when I came here. Everyone said I was a real beauty. And at least three men thought so. (*Pauses.*) Now they are all dead and gone. (*To DUDACHKA.*) Who will take care of you when I'm gone? What will happen to you when I die? You'll have nothing left to do, you poor girl.

DUDACHKA: Don't say things like that. You know you'll get better and be going home in just a couple of days.

CERENISKY: (*To DUDACHKA.*) No one lives forever! We all die sometime. I've seen so many people go already. I've outlived them all. It's my time, you know. (*Pauses for a second, catches her breath.*)

SMITH: (*To CERENISKY.*) If your heart should stop, we would have to perform CPR on you. That means pushing on your heart and maybe putting you on a breathing machine. Would you want us to do that?

CERENISKY: (*Looks bewildered.*) Pushing on my heart and a breathing machine? (*To DUDACHKA.*) Do I need a breathing machine?

DUDACHKA: No, mother, not yet. But you are getting very sick and the doctor will have to do some things to you if your heart stops ticking. He needs to know what you want done.

CERENISKY: Is that old watch still ticking? You know the one, from the Emperor.

DUDACHKA: Yes, of course it is. *(Looks from CERENISKY to SMITH.)*

CERENISKY: It's still beautiful, you know. It's pure gold, covered with fine filigree and engraved with the letters 'F.F.,' for the Archduke Franz Ferdinand. *(Abruptly turns to DUDACHKA.)* I'd like to see it. Could you bring it here? I'd like to see it and show it to the doctor now.

DUDACHKA: *(Appears startled with the request.)* Of course, mother. It's in the safe deposit box at the bank, but I can get it. It just needs a little polishing and winding, that's all.

CERENISKY: *(To SMITH.)* You'd like to see it, wouldn't you?

SMITH: Yes, of course. Yes, I think it would be interesting. A real bit of authentic history. But what about your code status? Do you want CPR?

CERENISKY: *(Ignores SMITH. To DUDACHKA.)* Bring it, please. I think the doctor would enjoy seeing it.

DUDACHKA: *(Takes her mother hand.)* Certainly, Mother. I'll bring it over tomorrow.

SMITH: *(Turns to DUDACHKA.)* Your mother's lab work is getting much worse. We're looking at complete renal failure. We cannot do dialysis on ninety-two year old women. It's too hard on an old body and your mother's body is just too frail. *(Fixes DUDACHKA with his eyes.)* I don't think you have to be a doctor to appreciate the seriousness of the situation. If your mother cannot decide, then you have to. Have you made up your mind concerning her?

DUDACHKA: *(Looks at SMITH.)* Made up my mind? Of course I have! I'm going over to the bank today and get the watch. There's really no time to lose.

> *(DUDACHKA exits hurriedly. SMITH walks off stage as he shakes his head. Lights dim to dark.)*

SCENE IV

> *(SMITH returns to the hospital room. CERENISKY is seated bolt upright in the bed and is making an ominous gurgling. While SMITH listens to her bubbling chest, DUDACHKA comes into the room and waves to both CERENISKY and SMITH before sitting on the couch by the hospital bed. A projection of the famous golden watch gleams in the background.)*

DUDACHKA: *(To SMITH.)* How does she sound today?

SMITH: Very congested.

> *(SMITH forces a smile. CERENISKY tries to imitate, but only manages a grimace.)*

CERENISKY: *(To DUDACHKA.)* Did you bring it?

DUDACHKA: Yes, mother, I did. *(Reaches into her purse and pulls out a small velvet sack. Unties the drawstring and withdraws the golden watch from the sack. Puts it in CERENISKY's outstretched hand.)* I polished it so it would really shine.

CERENISKY: *(Takes the watch and turns it over and over in her hands. After several turns, opens up the cover and looks at the face. Looks around the room for a clock. Turns back to DUDACHKA.)* What time is it?

DUDACHKA: About ten o'clock.

CERENISKY: (*Fumbles with the watch, and then hands it back to DUDACHKA.*) Here, set it on time and wind it up, then give it back to me, please.

DUDACHKA: (*Takes the watch, and then adjusts the hands. Afterwards, DUDACHKA winds the knob back and forth, places the watch to her ear, and listens attentively for a few moments, and then hands the watch back to CERENISKY.*) Here, Mother, it's working fine, just as good as new.

CERENISKY: (*Seizes the watch and places it next to her ear. Wrinkles her brow in concentration. After a few seconds, switches ears and continues to listen.*) It's broken! It's finally broken! It's stopped after all these years! (*Hands the watch to SMITH.*) You listen, Doctor. I don't think it's working anymore. Tell me if it's still working, please!

SMITH: (*Takes the watch. Closes the cover and places the watch to his ear. Pauses and listens. To CERENISKY.*) It's working. I can definitely hear it ticking.

(*CERENISKY does not seem to hear. CERENISKY stares forward blankly.*)

SMITH: (*To CERENISKY.*) You probably just can't hear it ticking! It's working!

(*SMITH hands CERENISKY back the watch and clasps it in her open hand. CERENISKY stares at him and then her mouth drops open and her eyelids sink down. CERENISKY slumps down in the bed. SMITH jumps forward and shakes CERENISKY.*)

SMITH: Can you hear me? (*Grabs the call button and jams it down.*)

INTERCOM VOICE: Can I help you?

SMITH: Call a CODE BLUE! Send the nurse down here STAT! Tell her to bring the crash cart! (*Glances over to DUDACHKA who is backing toward the door.*) Mrs. Dudachka, please step out for a few minutes.

Call your family to come to the hospital now if they possibly can. I don't think she's breathing anymore.

DUDACHKA: Is she . . . ? (*Manages to say before backing out into the hallway.*)

NURSE: (*Pushes a large red cart filled with drawers and covered with various resuscitation equipment from offstage. Checks for a pulse. Grabs the intubation equipment in the top drawer of the cart and shoves it toward SMITH.*) Straight blade O.K?

> (*SMITH looks first at the shiny intubation blade, then back to CERENISKY who is already making jerky motions with her head in respiratory spasms. SMITH takes the handle.*)

NURSE: Is she a DNR?

SMITH: No.

NURSE: You talked to the family about it?

SMITH: Yes, I talked to the old lady and her daughter about it several times. The daughter wants us to give her one chance. Once chance at resuscitation. (*Looks at NURSE and then back to CERENISKY.*)

NURSE: Are you all right, Doctor?

> (*SMITH nods, then motions with his hand in a half-hearted gesture of reassurance and sits on the edge of the bed. SMITH reaches over and pushes CERENISKY's head back against the pillow. SMITH brushes a few tangled strands of her hair back on her forehead. CERENISKY's breathing is nothing more than useless gasps. SMITH looks at CERENISKY's face.*)

NURSE: Aren't we legally obliged to do something? She's technically a full code if there's no written DNR? That might be malpractice and cause a lawsuit.

SMITH: (*Looking at CERENISKY.*) Full code, chemical code, DNR status, malpractive, lawsuits? What have they to do with this amazing life that's sputtering out before our eyes? (*Looks up at NURSE and sighs.*) Break her ribs? Shove a plastic tube down her throat? Shock her body? I can't do that to her. I won't do that to her. She doesn't deserve that indignity.

(*SMITH hands the intubation tube and laryngoscope back to NURSE, who turns away and begins replacing the various equipment in the crash cart. CERENISKY heaves a final, rasping breath and dies. SMITH reaches up and feels the side of the neck.*)

SMITH: (*To NURSE.*) She's dead. That's it. Thank you for your help. Just write what happened in the code note. I made the call, not you.

(*NURSE continues arranging their various instruments. SMITH sits on the edge of the bed, sharing it with CERENISKY. SMITH glances down among the rumpled sheets. The watch lies near CERENISKY's outstretched hand. SMITH picks it up and puts it to his ear.*)

SMITH: The damn thing's still ticking. Can you believe that? It's still ticking.

(*NURSE looks over at him. Shows NURSE the watch.*)

SMITH: It's a watch her grandfather got from the Archduke Ferdinand who received it from the Emperor Franz Joseph. Can you believe it? After all this time, it's still works.

(*NURSE turns back to her task and completes arranging the Code Cart. NURSE pushes the cart out off stage. SMITH stands up and walks out to where DUDACHKA stands.*)

SMITH: She's gone. I'm so sorry. (*Gives DUDACHKA a hug, and then extends his hand and gives DUDACHKA the watch, which she take, cradling it in both hands.*)

DUDACHKA: It was the Archduke's, you know, a gift from the Emperor Franz Joseph himself. He gave it to my great grandfather for work he had done at the hunting lodge in Translyvania. (*Her voice trails off. DUDACHKA holds the watch up to her ear*). It's still ticking, isn't it?

SMITH: Yes, it is. I listened myself. It's still ticking.

DUDACHKA: (*Looks at SMITH.*) Did you try and bring her back?

SMITH: (*Pauses a long time.*) I did everything I could. I did everything I could and no more.

DUDACHKA: (*Looks from SMITH to the watch and back again.*) I know you did, Doctor, and we appreciate everything you've done for mother over the years. She loved and trusted you. We all do.

(*SMITH turns to go down the hall. DUDACHKA watches SMITH disappear off stage, and then walks over to the center. The light centers on DUKACHKA.*)

DUDACHKA: I know the good doctor is sad. He's sad to lose a patient. He's sad for me and my family. But I'm sure he will console himself with mental images of the glittering golden court of the long-dead Emperor Franz Joseph and the doomed Archduke. (*Pauses.*) Mother's grandfather and her parents are long dead and now she is dead, too. (*Looks at the watch.*) Perhaps I should dwell on the imperial court and the glamour of old Austro-Hungary and Rumania. Or maybe I should console myself with some cheerful Czech folk tune, some fast-paced little polka, like we still do here in Vitr. (*Pauses.*) But all I can think of is my wonderful, loving mother standing at our bedside when we were sick or making kolaches in the kitchen as she sang Rumanian folk songs from so long ago. (*Looks at the watch.*) I feel cold. I feel cold and the only warmth I still feel is my mother's lingering warmth in this magnificent watch. (*Pauses.*) And that, too, is growing cold. (*Looks offstage.*) I best be going back to my family. They need me now. (*Walks offstage.*)

(SMITH returns and walks back to the bed. SMITH is dressed in the vest and feathered hat. SMITH pulls CERENISKY, who seems to rise from the dead, off the bed. CERENISKY nods and they dance "Vitr," the Wind, a slow Czech waltz. Toward the end, CERENISKY separates from SMITH and drifts away into the shadows. SMITH removes his hat and bows in the direction of CERENISKY. Lights fade to darkness).

THE END

Choreographic note: There are four Czech dances:

1. Pardubachka (a couple dance taught by Vonnie Brown, Baton Rouge, Louisiana)

2. Louky (a women's circle dance taught by Vonnie Brown)

3. Studenka (a couple dance, modified as an easy circle dance, originally taught by Vonnie Brown)

4. Vitr (taught by Frantisek Bonus of Prague, Czech Republic)

TAKING CARE OF CHARLENE

CAST OF CHARACTERS

MARGARET (MAGGIE) HANLEY: Sister of Charlene Mason. A dumpy middle-aged woman with no distinguishing qualities.

CHARLENE (CHARLIE) MASON: Sister of Margaret Hanley. An older middle-aged woman with some breathing difficulty. No distinguishing qualities. Speaks with some English errors and sloppy pronunciation.

DR. PAUL COOK: Primary care physician. He wears a tie and white coat and not scrubs. Doctor to both Margaret and Charlene.

JASON MORTIER: Attorney. He wears flashy, expensive clothing and speaks quickly. Looks a bit vulgar despite his best attempts at respectability.

SETTING

Margaret and Charlene are seated at a breakfast table. There are a couple of coffee cups and some medicine bottles. Minimal set elements are needed.

MARGARET: It cost's how much?

CHARLENE: Over seven dollars a tablet. And you're supposed to take it twice a day.

MARGARET: But that's over $420 a month!

CHARLENE: That's right, Maggie. Actually, it costs closer to $500 when you add on the taxes.

MARGARET: What's the name of this wonder drug?

CHARLENE: Curital.

MARGARET: Curital. Catchy name. Where'd you get this bottle? (*Examines the medicine bottle.*) This one doesn't even have your name it. It say "Sally Perkins."

CHARLENE: Dr. Cook gave me a prescription, but I never got it filled. When they told me how much it would cost at the pharmacy, I just told them to forget it. Sally Perkins, a lady down the street, gave me what was left in her bottle. She said it hurt her stomach, so she stopped taking it. She said it really helped her arthritis, but she didn't want to risk getting an ulcer.

MARGARET: So, did you try it? Did it help?

CHARLENE: Of course I tried it. And it's great. I can finally move around a little. And it's supposed to be a lot safer on the stomach than all those other kinds of arthritis medications.

MARGARET: You mean the cheap, over the counter ones like ibuprofen?

CHARLENE: Exactly. Curital is supposed to be much better.

MARGARET: How is it better? Just because it's new and cost so much?

CHARLENE: No! Really! Curital is not supposed to hurt your stomach, despite what Sally Perkins says. It's some sort of new class of arthritis medication. And it really works for me. I don't even have any heart burn and I'm not taking anything for my stomach, not even Mylanta.

MARGARET: If your stomach is the problem, why not just take something over the counter for your arthritis and something else for your stomach. It would still be cheaper.

CHARLENE: I tried that already. Don't you remember my bleeding ulcer? I almost died.

MARGARET: Right, how could I forget all that? You were pooping clotted blood. I'm sorry I didn't think about that. It was really pretty horrible.

CHARLENE: Don't worry about it. You had a lot of things going on at the same time. Edgar was dying and your son was getting divorced. That's a lot of things to keep track of.

MARGARET: Yes, I did have a lot of things going on. Edgar was in the VA hospital in their intensive care unit and you were both hooked up to breathing machines at the same time. My God, what a nightmare! But he died and you lived and heaven forbid you should ever get in that situation again. I don't care what it costs.

CHARLENE: Speaking of the VA, do you still go out there to get your medicines.

MARGARET: No, I go to Fort Truman. You need to be a veteran to use the VA pharmacy. But as a retired service man's wife, I can get my medications free at the pharmacy at the military base. Dr. Cook writes the prescriptions and they fill them out there.

CHARLENE: Are they really free?

MARGARET: I pay a couple of bucks if it's a brand name medication and nothing if it's a generic. Thank God I don't have to take much of anything, just something for dizziness and my allergies.

CHARLENE: And you never get stiff in your joints?

MARGARET: Sure, but not like you. I lead a healthy life, remember. Since Edgar died, I only go out dancing once a week. *(Gets up and twirls around, doing a few dance steps.)* Before Edgar died, we used to dance twice a week at the VFW hall. And did we dance!

CHARLENE: I could dance, too, you know. *(Stands and approaches MARGARET.)* The only problem was that Herbert had two left feed and a bad attitude. But I used to love it back before we were married. You remember the jitterbug?

MARGARET: Sure I do.

(MARGARET and CHARLENE dance together and do a few turns. MARGARET turns CHARLENE around under her arm. CHARLENE breaks off and goes to sit down.)

CHARLENE: Wow! My knees are killing me.

MARGARET: Even with your miraculous Curital?

CHARLENE: It doesn't help me if I can't get it.

MARGARET: But why? Just ask Dr. Cook to give you a prescription. It's only $420 a month. You have that don't you?

CHARLENE: Sure, I have that. But I also have to buy this expensive medication for my blood pressure. And there are two pills for my diabetes, both over a hundred dollars a month. And don't forget the one for my cholesterol. Dr. Cook says I have to take that one if I want to live a long life with my diabetes and high blood pressure. They already cost over $700 a month. Just for those.

MARGARET: You're kidding?

CHARLENE: I wish I were. And then there are my cigarettes. Of course that's my own problem, but they are pretty expensive now.

MARGARET: How can I help?

CHARLENE: I don't know. You don't get any more for your pension and social security than I do. There's no way you could afford to shell out several hundred dollars a month for the rest of our lives. Besides, you have your own problems.

MARGARET: Yeah, but they don't include hypertension, diabetes, high cholesterol or crippling arthritis.

CHARLENE: How was I so lucky to inherit all the bad health genes? I think Dad gave me all the bad ones and Mom reserved all the good ones for you.

MARGARET: You were always Daddy's little girl, remember? I always envied your close relationship. He really had some special feeling for you. I really made me jealous.

CHARLENE: Yeah, but I didn't know his affections came with so many genetic strings attached.

MARGARET: *(Picks up the various medicine bottles on the table and examines them.)* Two for diabetes, two for blood pressure, one for cholesterol and one for arthritis. *(Pauses.)* You know, maybe Dr. Cook can write me a prescription for some of this stuff. I can get it free at Fort Truman and then give it to you. How about that?

CHARLENE: Can you do that?

MARGARET: Well, I can't do it for the diabetes, hypertension or cholesterol medications. I don't have any of those problems. But how would Dr. Cook know if I have any arthritic aches and pains? I could just tell him I was hurting in this joint or that and ask him to prescribe some Curital.

CHARLENE: Would you do that for me?

MARGARET: Of course. I would do more than that if I could. But I can't make my cholesterol or blood pressure go up just to get a prescription.

CHARLENE: But what if he does an x-ray or something? Can't he tell if you don't have arthritis?

MARGARET: So what? He can't tell if I'm hurting somewhere.

CHARLENE: And what if they don't have Curital out there at the base pharmacy?

MARGARET: Of course they will. Nothing is too good for veterans and their wives.

CHARLENE: Damn Herbert! Why didn't he just go into the service and stay there like Edgar?

MARGARET: Sure. He could have stayed in the service like Edgar and develop post-traumatic stress syndrome and drown his woes in cases of cheap booze from the commissary. Yeah, he could have done that. But I doubt it would have been worth a lifetime of free medicine.

CHARLENE: Sorry, I just feel trapped in this sick body of mine.

MARGARET: Don't worry. Let me get this Curital stuff for you. Then we can decrease that medicine bill for yours to only $700 a month.

CHARLENE: Right. (*Pauses.*) Only $700 a month. It will still be a help. I just hope you're able to do it.

MARGARET: Leave it to me. I've got young Dr. Cook wrapped around my little finger.

CHARLENE: He's cute, isn't he?

MARGARET: You little devil, you. He's way too young for you. Besides, he's happily married and has a couple of kids.

CHARLENE: So when has that stopped anyone from trying? If you can figure out how to get rid of the wife and children, maybe I'd stand a chance. (*Tries to look sexy and alluring.*)

MARGARET: (*Laugh.*) Sure, that'll get him. Now, let's get back to the problems at hand. I'll get the Curital taken care of. Then we can go on to seducing Dr. Cook.

CHARLENE: (*Hugs MARGARET.*) Thanks, Maggie. You're a life saver. (*Knocks the pill bottles over in the process and both CHARLENE AND MARGARET scramble to retrieve them.*)

MARGARET: Can't let any of these get lost. They're worth their weight in gold.

CHARLENE: (*Looks at the bottles.*) Nothing lost. Thank goodness for child-proof bottles. The only problem is that I can't even get them opened myself. (*Laughs.*)

(*Lights dim to dark.*)

SCENE II

(*COOKS's office. Just a desk and three chairs. Perhaps some papers.*)

COOK: Good morning, Mrs. Hanley

MARGARET: Good morning, Dr. Cook. And for heaven's sake, would you please call me Maggie.

COOK: Okay, Maggie, but I was always trained to address my elders by their family name, not their first names. And, besides, how come you call me Dr. Cook instead of Paul? Familiarity goes both ways, doesn't it? And I do believe you are older than me by a few years, even though you look much younger.

MARGARET: You're such a shameless flatterer.

COOK: Flattery will get me everywhere, don't you think?

MARGARET: Maybe. But not when you tell a woman she's old, even if she looks younger. When you call me Maggie, I just feel younger. And when I call you Dr. Cook, it makes you sound smarter and more important.

COOK: (*Laughs.*) More important, eh? And smarter? So I don't strike you as that smart?

MARGARET: Oh no! I think you're very smart as doctors go. And I've certainly seen enough of them in my time.

COOK: Now look who's flattering whom. You know that all flatterers live at the expense of he who listens to them?

MARGARET: You made that up.

COOK: I certainly did not. La Fontaine, a French writer, wrote that. And he borrowed it from the Aesop, the Greek writer. So it goes back a long way.

MARGARET: See! I said you were smart and you really are. Quoting French people and Greeks. You are really very cultivated.

COOK: What can do for you today? You look as fit as a fiddle. (*Looks at her chart.*) Cholesterol, good. Blood pressure, good. Weight, good. What more could you want?

MARGARET: Doctor Paul, I need something for my arthritis.

COOK: What arthritis?

MARGARET: My hips. My shoulders. My knees. My back. Just about everywhere. It keeps me from sleeping at night and it really bothers me when I get up. Throughout the day, I just drag around in pain. I really need something for it.

COOK: You never complained about arthritis before. Did you do something out of the ordinary?

MARGARET: No, nothing special. It's been developing over months, maybe years. But I just thought it was old age. I really didn't want to bother you with it before.

COOK: Have you tried any over the counter medications? Ibuprofen or naproxen?

MARGARET: Sure, I tried them all. Those things just don't work. Besides, they hurt my stomach after I use them for awhile.

COOK: Do you want to try some physical therapy?

MARGARET: No!

COOK: Well, I guess we could try some Piroxacam or Indomethacin, they sometimes work.

MARGARET: No.

COOK: No? Why not?

MARGARET: Because they'll hurt my stomach. I don't want to get a bleeding ulcer and die.

COOK: How do you know you'll get an ulcer and bleed to death?

MARGARET: Because all those medication do that. They all cause ulcers. Or at least they can. I know, because I look them up on the internet.

COOK: Then what exactly do you want? It seems you have something specific in mind.

MARGARET: I want Curital. That new one you see in the television ads all the time.

COOK: Curital?

MARGARET: Yes, I want Curital and I want the highest dose. I've heard that it works really good and doesn't cause stomach problem.

COOK: And where exactly are you getting your medical information these days? Over the internet? Or from all those slick adds on television and in every magazine?

MARGARET: All of them, of course. You see it advertised all the time on the television, in magazines, on the internet. Curital's supposed to be better and safer than all the others.

COOK: Yes, and it's much more expensive than the others, too. Do they tell you that on the internet and in the television ads?

MARGARET: So what? I only pay a ten dollar co-pay for a three month supply at the base hospital.

COOK: That stuff costs around seven dollars a tablet, Maggie. Why don't we try something else first? The worst that can happen is that you'll have to stop and change medication. All that publicity and this army of drug reps that come through my office are just trying to convince me to use the latest and most expensive medication. These companies spend billions on research and you better believe they want to make some money for their shareholders. Let's try with something older and less expensive first, okay?

MARGARET: No! I want Curital. And if it makes me sick, I'll come back and try something else later. What do you care if it's expensive? Are you trying to save money for someone? The insurance company? The government?

COOK: What's wrong with worrying about the health care budget or the national debt? If everyone uses the most expensive drugs, who's going to pay?

MARGARET: Dr. Cook, Paul. My Edgar, God keep us soul, wore himself out in the service of this country. He served for you, for me, for all Americans. He died in peace, knowing that his widow would have free health care, including medications, for the rest of her life. Now you are worrying about some hypothetical national debt. Whose advocate are you anyway, your patient's or the national debt? You should be ashamed of yourself!

COOK: (*Pulls out his prescription pad and begins to write.*) Okay, you win. I suppose it is unreasonable of me to consider the economic consequences of medical costs. You are right; I am your advocate first. I guess the politicians are going to have to sort out the economics. (*Hands MARGARET the prescription.*) Here's your prescription. If it doesn't work well, then let me know. If it causes any stomach problems, stop taking it immediately, okay? And don't take any more than you're supposed to. You just never know about new drugs.

MARGARET: (*Takes the prescription and puts it into her purse.*) Thank you so much. You don't know how much this means to me.

COOK: Perhaps you're right. But I do know how much that medication's worth.

MARGARET: It's not your problem. Repeat after me, Paul, "It's-not-my-problem."

COOK: It will be my problem if there isn't any more Medicare money when I reach your age. I'll know who to thank.

MARGARET: I doubt whether I'll be around when you do get my age. Anyway, always glad to be of service. See you in four months.

(*MARGARET gets up and leaves. COOK rises to see her out.*)

(*Lights dim to dark.*)

SCENE III

(*MARGARET and CHARLENE are back together. They are seated around the same kitchen table as in Scene I. MARGARET tosses a medicine bottle over to CHARLENE who catches it in mid-air.*)

190

MARGARET: Your wishes are my commands. I told you I could do it.

CHARLENE: It's three months worth! (*Hugs MARGARET and gives her a big kiss.*) You're a life saver, a real angel.

MARGARET: Yeah! With a little devil inside.

(*MARGARET and CHARLENE sit down at the table.*)

CHARLENE: Was it hard to get Dr. Cook to write the prescription?

MARGARET: Naw, Dr. Cook's an old softy.

CHARLENE: Not that old, is he?

MARGARET: No, not really. He's somewhere in his mid fifties I imagine.

CHARLENE: Too young for you, anyway.

MARGARET: (*Pats her hair and tilts her head.*) You think so? I've still got a little sex appeal left, don't I?

CHARLENE: (*Laughs.*) Sure. With sagging boobs, wrinkles, varicose veins and a touch of Alzheimer's Disease.

MARGARET: Whoa! It's all true except the last part. How do you think I could have gotten you your Curital if I was losing my mind?

CHARLENE: (*Fingers the medicine bottle.*) This stuff is worth its weight in gold. Did Dr. Cook just give you the prescription right away?

MARGARET: Heck no! I had to beg and twist his arm. He gave me a bunch of crap about it being too expensive and how the drug companies just want everyone to use the newest and most expensive medication so they could make a lot of money.

CHARLENE: But this medication really works.

MARGARET: Sure it works. But he still gave me even more crap about the national debt and the soaring Medicare budget and there not being any money left for people down the road. It was a real tear jerker. I've got to hand it to him.

CHARLENE: Was any of what he said true?

MARGARET: Who knows? Who cares? I want you to get the best for whatever the cost and to hell with the national debt.

(*MARGARET AND CHARLENE take their coffee cups.*)

CHARLENE: To us! And to hell with the national debt!

MARGARET: When do you go back and see him, anyway?

CHARLENE: Some time next month.

MARGARET: Does he even know we're sisters?

CHARLENE: How could he not? We look like sisters, don't we? We act like sisters, don't we? We even dance like sisters?

(*CHARLENE pulls MARGARET up and they do a little two-step to the tune "Me and My Shadow." They sing the words. The music starts as the two begin dancing together.*)

(*Lights dim to dark.*)

SCENE IV

(*CHARLENE is in COOK's office. There is a desk and three chairs.*)

COOK: Well, Mrs. Mason. Anything new with you?

CHARLENE: Mrs. Mason, Mrs. Mason. For heaven's sake, Dr. Cook, can you just call me Charlie like everyone else?

COOK: Okay, Charlie, but you have to call me Paul. Fair's fair.

CHARLENE: All right, Paul. And there's absolutely nothing new.

COOK: What about your arthritis? That's been a really ongoing problem for you.

CHARLENE: It's much better, doctor. I can even do a little dancing now.

COOK: I guess it's that Curital I prescribed for you.

CHARLENE: No way! That stuff was just too expensive. They told me how much it would cost at the pharmacy and I never even bought it. I hope you're not mad?

COOK: Of course I'm not mad. But you're the one who asked for Curital a few months ago.

CHARLENE: Yes, I did ask for it. But that's before I found out it cost over seven dollars a tablet. Can you imagine that, doctor? Seven dollars a tablet for an old widow woman with no medicine coverage? It looked great on television, but they never talked about the price.

COOK: They never do. The drug company's job is to sell medications, the more expensive the better. You should hear some of those guys that come in here to sell that stuff. They are as slick as slick can be. (*Pauses for moment.*) And what about your sister?

CHARLENE: (*Fidgets a little. Looks nervous.*) Who?

COOK: Your sister, Margaret, of course.

CHARLENE: Oh, THAT sister.

COOK: You have more than one?

CHARLENE: No, only the one.

COOK: So she's doing okay with her arthritis?

CHARLENE: I think she's okay. We hardly ever talk about our health. Why to you ask?

COOK: Well, it was strange. She started to complain bitterly about her own arthritis. In fact, she pretty much demanded I prescribe her Curital. You know, the medication you never bought.

CHARLENE: Oh really? That's interesting.

COOK: You ladies must not talk too much together.

CHARLENE: No, we don't. It's a pity, but we've really grown apart since our husbands died. *(Pauses and looks thoughtful.)* Yes, since my hubby died, we've just drifted apart.

COOK: That's too bad. You both seem like such nice ladies. *(Jots something in the chart.)* So what are you doing about your arthritis these days?

CHARLENE: I bought some of that shark cartilage stuff. And there's my magnetic bracelet and water aerobics. They seem to work pretty well. What do you think?

COOK: Who knows? The water aerobics will probably help, but I can't say much about the bracelet and the shark cartilage. That's more in the realm of voodoo than science. Some people swear they both work. And I'm sure the manufacturers are just laughing all the way to the bank.

CHARLENE: But if they don't work, why do people buy them?

COOK: Because people think they'll help, even when they don't.

CHARLENE: But if they don't work, doesn't the FDA or someone have to control that sort of thing?

COOK: Magnetic bracelets are just toys, not medications. The FDA only approves medications that are both safe and effective.

CHARLENE: So doesn't that mean that the miracle shark cartilage has to be safe and effective?

COOK: Great question. And they don't have anything to say about shark cartilage because it's considered a food supplement and not a medication. So the company doesn't have to prove anything to anyone.

CHARLENE: That doesn't make sense.

COOK: No it doesn't. But the laws were changed a few years ago to get food supplements out of the jurisdiction of the FDA. A few well placed congressmen from certain states that made a lot of this sort of thing made sure the law passed. Now there's no safety controls at all on thousands of so-called food supplements, which can contain all sorts of dangerous substances.

CHARLENE: That all sounds pretty sleazy.

COOK: Ah yes, sleazy it is. The sleazy business of health care.

CHARLENE: At least the FDA controls real medications. That's a relief, anyway.

COOK: They do the best they can. But the problem is that new medications are only tested in several thousand patients. When they start being prescribed to hundreds of thousands, there's a lot greater chance of discovering some adverse drug reaction. Some unpleasant idiosyncratic reaction.

CHARLENE: Like what?

COOK: Remember Thalidomide? All those babies born with no arms and legs? It was a great medication with some really nasty side effects.

CHARLENE: So how do you know? Maybe Curital isn't safe for my sister?

COOK: (*Shrugs.*) Sometimes we just don't know for years. All doctors come under huge pressure to prescribe these new medications by the pharmaceutical industry and by patients themselves. You've seen the ads. Use Wonderdrug X. Great results. No side effects. Much better than those old, cheaper, generic medications whose patents have run out. You don't see that, but as soon as a medication goes off patent, it disappears from the lips of the drug reps. They bring in the famous doctor so-and-so who explains the merits of the latest medication which has all the virtues and none of the inconveniences of its predecessors and competitors. And you get all this objective information in a lovely dinner at the fanciest restaurant in town. It's gross and expensive!

CHARLENE: Good heavens, doctor. You seem so passionate about this. Are the drug companies really so sinister?

COOK: They're just an industry, like every other industry. And the drug reps are just salesmen, like for any other product. They just happen to be selling medications. I understand the companies have a few years to recover their huge investments in research and development. But they are also tempted to push drugs on the market to recoup some of those costs. God forbid there's some sort of problem. Then you have this army of personal injury lawyers ready to sue the company for everything they can get. It's gross. And it's expensive. Trust me, Charlie. (*Pauses.*) Bye the way, what else can I do for you today?

CHARLENE: Not a thing, doctor. I think I'm good for my other medications.

COOK: Your diabetes could be better controlled. Your weight is not down. And I bet you're still smoking. Those are all tremendous risk factors. Are you still smoking?

CHARLENE: Come on, doc, give me a break. We were having such a pleasant conversation.

COOK: Mrs. Mason?

CHARLENE: Charlie.

COOK: Charlie? Are you still smoking? Because if you are, it's going to kill you.

CHARLENE: But I only smoke a half a pack a day and never inside the house. Maggie won't even let me smoke around her anymore.

COOK: I thought you said you hardly ever saw your sister anymore?

CHARLENE: In my rare visits. That's all.

COOK: You're doubling your risk of heart attack, stroke and peripheral artery disease. And all those risks are already doubled because you're diabetic. You're just asking for trouble. And we haven't even talked about the risks for emphysema and lung cancer.

CHARLENE: I know, I know. I've heard it all before.

COOK: Well, you have to hear it again. You know, women didn't even used to get lung cancer before they started smoking in the forties. And now lung cancer cases in women outnumber cases of breast cancer, colon cancer and pancreatic cancer combined.

CHARLENE: If smoking's so bad for us, why don't they just outlaw cigarettes?

COOK: They should!

CHARLENE: I doubt whether I'd go to Mexico or Canada to get cigarettes. Even though I might go down there for my medications.

COOK: I don't know why we don't outlaw cigarettes. Ask the state legislature. I think they should. But maybe the politicians just want people to die earlier so they don't get as many social security payments? Who knows?

CHARLENE: That's an awfully cynical thought, doctor. And maybe I just should go down to Mexico where medications cost a third of the cost as here?

COOK: (*Glances at his watch.*) Mrs. Mason. Charlie. I think we've delved into as many social issues as we can for one day. I'll see you in six months . . . ten pounds lighter and smoke-free, okay?

CHARLENE: I'll try my best. (*Stands up to leave.*)

(*Lights dim to dark.*)

SCENE V

(*Emergency room waiting area. Several chairs are lined up and MARGARET is waiting. She stands up as COOK walks in.*)

MARGARET: Is she going to be all right?

COOK: (*Motions to MARGARET to sit down and he sits down next to her.*) She'll live. But she lost a good part of her heart function. That was a very massive heart attack. She's really lucky to have survived.

MARGARET: So she'll be all right?

COOK: The cardiologists managed to open up a couple of arteries and put in some stents. But she will still have to undergo bypass surgery in the future. There were just too many diseased arteries in the heart.

MARGARET: If she had so many blockages, how come she never had any chest pains? Or any symptoms?

COOK: Diabetics often don't have any symptoms. Even when they're having a heart attack, they may not feel anything at all, or just get short of breath like your sister did. It's actually pretty common.

MARGARET: Thank God she got here on time. She just got short of breath all of a sudden. I thought she was going to suffocate in front of me. It was horrible.

COOK: Was she still smoking?

MARGARET: Of course.

COOK: How much?

MARGARET: You don't want me to snitch on my own sister, do you?

COOK: Of course.

MARGARET: A pack a day.

COOK: And was she at least still taking all of her medications?

MARGARET: Oh yeah, even the Curital.

COOK: The Curital?

MARGARET: Sometimes. Off and on.

COOK: She told me she never took that medication because it was too expensive to buy.

MARGARET: She was using mine.

COOK: Why did you do that?

MARGARET: Because she needed it and it was too expensive for her to buy, so I just gave her mine. Is that some sort of crime?

COOK: You know you shouldn't do that.

MARGARET: I know, but it helps her so much. She can't even move when she isn't taking it. And the darn stuff's just too expensive for her to buy. Doctor, it's really changed her life and I knew you would be willing to help us. No one will know. It's the government that's paying anyway. It's not like stealing or anything.

COOK: *(Stands to leave.)* Let's talk about this later. Right now your sister is surviving an acute heart attack and she will undoubtedly need bypass surgery in a few weeks if she hasn't had too much damage. She's still on a balloon pump in the ICU and her arthritis medications are the least of our worries. Let's just hope and pray she makes it through this part of her illness.

MARGARET: Doctor, thank you. Thank you for everything you've done for my sister and me. Thanks for the Curital, too. You've been a real life saver in the past and I know you will just go on being one in the future. *(Takes his hand.)* And don't be mad at me about the Curital. I'm only trying to help out my sister in any way I can. That can't be wrong, can it?

COOK: I suppose not. You ladies are a couple of real works of art. *(Pauses.)* Let's worry about Charlie now. I won't consider her cured until I see her walk out of this place on her own two feet.

MARGARET: Doctor, I know I shouldn't worry about any of this now, but all Charlie's got is Medicare. She doesn't even have a supplemental health insurance. What is all this going to cost?

COOK: Cost? We can worry about that later. Let's make sure your sister survives and that she goes on to her surgery and rehabilitation. It may take weeks and certainly hundreds of thousands of dollars. And that's if there aren't any major complications along the way.

MARGARET: But Charlie will be responsible for 10% of the hospital bill. It could run in the thousands, doctor. She doesn't have a Medicare supplement policy like I do.

COOK: Please, Maggie. I don't think this is the time or the place to discuss that sort of thing. Right now her survival is in the hands of the cardiologist and it will be in the hands of the surgeons later.

MARGARET: And your hands.

COOK: A little bit.

MARGARET: And God's.

COOK: And God's, of course.

(*Lights dim to dark.*)

SCENE VI

(*COOK's office. The desk is there, with three chairs, one for COOK and two others for MARGARET and CHARLENE.*)

COOK: So good to see you ladies. And thank you, Maggie, for bringing Charlie in.

MARGARET: It's the least I can do for my sister.

COOK: (*To CHARLENE.*) And how are you today?

CHARLENE: (*Talks with markedly slurred speech. Right side, both arm and leg, hangs limply.*) I'm doing okay. I can walk a little now with a cane. And my speech is a little better, too.

COOK: Are you able to help with anything around the house?

CHARLENE: I can do a little light housework, ironing, dusting, cooking. That is if Maggie lets me. She really waits on me hand and foot.

MARGARET: She really does want to help. But I'm not sure I can afford to buy anymore dishes to replace the ones she's broken. And as for ironing, she can burn the meanest hole in a dress that I've ever seen.

CHARLENE: *(Laughs.)* So that's why you took the iron away? And keep me away from the dishes. I thought you were just spoiling me.

MARGARET: It was that or switch to plastic plates.

CHARLENE: I can't really fold clothes anymore with only one good hand. And Maggie always hated my cooking, anyway. So I guess I just have to be the princess with my little lady in waiting.

COOK: I was so sorry when you had the stroke after the open-heart surgery. Everything went so well in the beginning, and then WHAM, a big stroke, on the left side, too.

CHARLENE: No. It affected my right side.

COOK: Well, the stroke was on the left, but the wires are crossed in your brain, so it affected your right side, and your speech, unfortunately. It was just unlucky.

CHARLENE: Yeah. I've always been the unlucky one.

COOK: You had one chance in five of having a permanent neurological event. It's a sad reality of open-heart surgery. It's as sad as it is unavoidable.

CHARLENE: Buy why me? First a big heart attack, then a big stroke. What a rotten combination. And that doesn't even include the twenty-two thousand dollars in hospital bills beyond what Medicare paid for me. Does that figure surprise you, doctor?

COOK: No. that doesn't surprise me.

CHARLENE: And that's only my 10% of the total hospital bill. $220,000. It's unbelievable.

COOK: Ten days in the ICU. A major surgery. Another week in the ICU. A month in rehab. To be honest, I'm surprised it's not more. I know it's none of my business, but do you have that kind of money to pay?

CHARLENE: No, I don't have that kind of money. But I got it anyhow. I sold my home and moved in with my sister. At least she can pay her bills with her husband's pension. And her house is already paid for.

COOK: It's not fair, is it?

MARGARET: No, it's not fair. I've got a full Medicare supplement and Charlie's just got Medicare. I wouldn't have to pay a dime and she had to cough up $22,000. And she's still got $500 a month in medication bills that she can hardly pay for. And that's not even including Curital. *(Pauses.)* By the way, doctor, I'm out of Curital. Would you mind writing me a little prescription?

COOK: Are you taking it? Or are you still giving it to your sister?

MARGARET: Of course I'm giving it to my sister. You can't give me diabetic medication or cholesterol medication of blood pressure medication because I'm perfect, at least on paper. But you can sure as heck give me Curital for my arthritis. Everyone's got arthritis, doc.

COOK: It's illegal, Maggie. It's one thing when I didn't know about it. It's something altogether different when I know what you're doing. I can get into a heap of trouble. It's fraud.

MARGARET: Fraud! It's just a prescription from your pad. Look at my sister, for God's sake! She's lost her home. She can't pay for her medications. She's had bypass surgery and ended up getting a horrible stroke. What big moral dilemma is it for you to bend the rules a little bit? Just give me a prescription. I'm not going to tell anyone. Charlene's not going to tell anyone. Look at this poor woman and tell me you're going to refuse our request based on some abstract moral principle.

COOK: *(Writes a prescription and hands it to MARGARET.)* It's still wrong, Maggie. But it's also wrong for Charlie to lose her home, her life savings, and her health. I just hope I don't burn in hell for this.

MARGARET: Don't worry, doc. You're not going to hell for a prescription. You're a good man. Thank you. We won't forget this. Every little bit helps us out a lot. And that's what's important, isn't? Helping each other out?

(Lights dim to dark.)

SCENE VII

(CHARLENE and MARGARET are at the kitchen table again. They have cups of coffee and are looking at a newspaper.)

MARGARET: Look at this, Charlie. It says that Curital can cause heart attacks and strokes and that there's going to be a class action suit against the manufacturer.

CHARLENE: *(Takes the paper to read. Her voice is still markedly slurred.)* Let me see. *(Reads the article.)* "If you or a loved one has taken Curital in the past six months and suffered from a stroke or heart attack, you deserve compensation. Call the law offices of Mortimer, Caussey and Chapman at 1-800 696-5555. Call today. There are statutes of limitation."

MARGARET: Maybe you can get your $22,000 back and then some. Think of all your pain and suffering. My God, Charlie, this might be worth millions. This is that gift from God you're always praying about.

CHARLENE: But I was taking your medication, Maggie. It was under your name. How would anyone know I was taking it all along?

MARGARET: Dr. Cook knew you were taking the medication.

CHARLENE: But it was not in my record. It was in yours.

MARGARET: So what? What does it matter if Dr. Cook testifies that you were taking the Curital.

CHARLENE: I guess you're right. Do you think I should call this number?

MARGARET: Sure! Let me call. *(Takes a cell phone and makes the number.)* Hello, is this the law firm of Mortimer, Caussey and Chapman? Yes. It is about the Curital case. *(Pauses.)* Yes, but it was my sister. She was taking Curital for over a year and she went on to have a terrible heart attack, then bypass surgery, then a terrible stroke. *(Pauses.)* So you think we have an excellent case. *(Pauses again.)* Of course we can come in. Next Friday would be fine. At ten o'clock. *(Pauses.)* I'll see if we can bring in her medical records from St. Caritas Hospital. Thanks you. See you then.

CHARLENE: So?

MARGARET: So. He thinks we have a great case and should get a handsome settlement although it might take some time to work it through. It's going to be all right. We can get your medical records from the hospital. Then we can get Dr. Cook to say you were taking the medication. Then we can cash the check and buy a home, or maybe a condominium in Florida? Or maybe something chic downtown, handicapped accessible and ready to go.

(MARGARET grabs CHARLENE and begins to dance with her. CHARLENE keeps up as well as she can. MARGARET sings "Yes sir, that's my baby. No sir, I don't mean maybe. Yes, sir, that's my baby girl.")

(Lights dim to dark.)

SCENE VIII

(MORTIMER's law office. There is a conference table and six chairs. Perhaps an eagle on the wall or some other art of dubious quality.)

MORTIMER: I'm Jason Mortimer. And you must by Charlene Mason.

CHARLENE: Yes, pleased to meet you.

MORTIMER: And you must be her sister, Margaret Hanley?

MARGARET: Yes, pleased to meet you.

MORTIMER: Well, let's all sit down. *(Helps CHARLENE get seated and then takes his place next to a pile of assorted papers.)* My paralegal has already reviewed your hospital file, Mrs. Mason. There is irrefutable evidence of heart attack and stroke. This should make you an excellent plaintiff in this upcoming class action suit. *(Pauses and flips though some papers.)* There is one thing that troubled us about this case. We reviewed your chart from Dr. Cook's office and there is no reference to your Curital use. In fact, it states that you received a prescription and did NOT take the medication because of its expense. Yet, in the hospital chart, it states that you had been taking Curital regularly up to six months prior to the heart attack. Could you clarify that?

MARGARET: Oh, that's easy. She was taking my medication.

MORTIMER: *(Turns back to look at CHARLENE.)* Mrs. Mason, if you were taking your sister's prescription medication without your doctor's knowledge, then I'm afraid there would be no grounds for your participation in this class action suit.

MARGARET: But he did know! Well, maybe not in the beginning, but at least after Charlie's hospitalization. It's kind of complicated, but Charlie has no supplemental insurance, just Medicare. And that doesn't include a medication plan. But I have government supplemental insurance for life because my husband was retired from the military. So, Dr. Cook wrote prescriptions for me and I gave the medications to my sister because she couldn't afford to buy them herself.

MORTIMER: And did Dr. Cook know you were not taking the Curital.

MARGARET: Not at first. But he felt sorry for my sister. She ended up losing her home, her savings and her health. She lost everything, except me. He was just trying to help us out a little.

MORTIMER: This is very complicated, Mr. Mason. In the absence of any documented use of Curital prior to your heart attack, you may not even have case. Dr. Cook would have to testify that you were, in fact taking the medication and that he was aware of that fact.

MARGARET: Of course he will.

MORTIMER: If he testifies that Mrs. Mason was taking the Curital prior to her heart attack, it means he must have known that she was receiving them from you.

MARGARET: So?

MORTIMER: So, that's fraudulent, Mrs. Hanley. If he knew he was giving you a prescription, paid for by the government, and then passing that medication on to your sister, Mrs. Mason, that's insurance fraud. He could be fined or jailed or lose his medical license.

CHARLENE: We can't risk that.

MARGARET: But he didn't know before your heart attack, Maggie, only afterwards.

MORTIMER: Yet he continued to prescribe the Curital to you, Mrs. Hanley, knowing that you were giving the medication to your sister.

MARGARET: Can we force him to testify to that?

CHARLENE: Maggie, we can't do this to Dr. Cook.

MARGARET: Charlie, you've lost everything. This can be your ticket to independence. A new home. Enough money for medications until you die, God forbid.

CHARLENE: And if Dr. Cook loses his license?

MARGARET: We're doing this for you, not for him.

MORTIMER: I think you ladies need to discuss this. I'm willing to go forward with the case. There has been irrefutable evidence of damage and I think a handsome settlement can still be obtained which would give you, Mrs. Mason, financial security for years to come.

CHARLENE: And Dr. Cook?

MARGARET: Let's go talk this over. We can meet with Dr. Cook at the next appointment and let him know what's happening. Will that help you feel any better about this whole thing?

CHARLENE: Yes, it would.

MORTIMER: *(Rises and shakes hands with MARGARET and CHARLENE.)* Thank you ladies for coming in. We expect to hear from you shortly.

(Lights dim to dark.)

SCENE IX

(COOK's office. COOK enters. MARGARET and CHARLENE are seated, but both rise when COOK enters. COOK pulls up a chair.)

COOK: Sit down. Sit down. I'm not the king, you know.

MARGARET: Oh yes you are.

COOK: Sure. And all flatterers live at the expense of he who listens to them, remember that one, Maggie?

MARGARET : Voltaire?

COOK : No, La Fontaine, now what can I do for you ladies? Who's the sick one today? *(A silence follows.)* No one sick? Well, I guess I can move on to me next patients.

CHARLENE: (*Her speech is still slurred.*) We need to ask if you could help me.

COOK: Of course. What can I do for you?

MARGARET: You can testify that Charlie was taking Curital before her heart attack and stroke.

COOK: Testify? To whom? Why?

MARGARET: To our attorney, Mr. Mortimer, in a deposition at his office.

COOK: Who's being sued?

MARGARET: The makers of Curital, of course. You must know about all this. You sent out that letter telling everyone to stop it. And it's been on the news for weeks. Surely you're aware of all that?

COOK: Sure, I know about it. That's why I sent the letter to everyone who was taking it. You got a letter, too, Margaret, even though your sister was taking your medication. Charlene's been off that stuff for months. At least I hope she has.

MARGARET: Of course she has. But look what that poison did to her, doc. She can't even talk right. She can't walk right. She's lost her home from all the bills and has to live with me. And all because of that poison she took. That Curital, it nearly killed my sister.

COOK: Mrs. Hanley!

MARGARET: Why so formal all of sudden, Dr. Cook?

COOK: Margaret. No one knows for sure if that medication was really that dangerous. In any case, the company pulled if off the market as soon as they thought it might be causing harm. Now you have this army of sleazy lawyers coming out of the woodwork and all ready to cash in on the miseries of unfortunate patients like your sister.

MARGARET: And why shouldn't they pay? The manufacturers wanted to make millions. They wanted the profits. So they rush this dangerous stuff out on the market and created a lot of demand by advertising. They get millions of people to take their poison. Why shouldn't they pay for the consequences?

COOK: The FDA approved Curital and said it was both safe and effective.

MARGARET: And we ought to sue the FDA as well if we could. Look at her. (*Points to CHARLENE.*) She's crippled. Her life's ruined. And we're supposed to shrug our shoulders and say so what? That's too bad. Just an honest mistake by the drug companies!

CHARLENE: (*To MARGARET.*) You're yelling at the doctor.

MARGARET: Yes, I'm yelling. And you should be too, if you could. (*Turns back to COOK.*) You need to testify that you prescribed me the medication and that I gave it to my sister. And that you think that medication caused her heart attack and stroke.

COOK: I did not know you were giving your Curital to you sister. At least not in the beginning.

MARGARET: But you did afterward. Not only did you know, but you continued to give me prescriptions that you knew I was giving to her up until that poison was pulled off the market. You sat right there at that desk and wrote prescriptions knowing full well it was going to Charlie. Didn't you, doctor?

COOK: Yes, I did.

MARGARET: And why did you do that?

COOK: Because I was trying to help you both out.

MARGARET: Help her out. Yeah, some help. You gave her poison and now she's crippled.

CHARLENE: Maggie! (*To MARGARET.*) He wanted to save me some money. He wanted to help me out.

MARGARET: Well, it turns out it was the wrong thing to do.

COOK: Why was trying to help your sister the wrong thing to do?

MARGARET: Because Curital nearly killed her. And besides, it was insurance fraud.

COOK: And you want me to testify that I knowingly committed insurance fraud against the federal government? You want me to put my license and my livelihood in jeopardy so your sister can get on a class action suit and make some money off this tragedy?

MARGARET: And why not? Wouldn't you do the same if you were in our situation?

COOK: Mrs. Hanley, I have known you and your sister for many years and have done my best to treat you both. And you would make me jeopardize my career to enrich some sleazy lawyer?

MARGARET: No, not to enrich a sleazy lawyer, but to help my sister. The lawyer just happens to make money off the deal because that's the way it works here.

CHARLENE: (*Looking nervously as she follows the conversation to MARGARET.*) Let's go. I want to go. We can talk about this later. (*Gets up to leave and stumbles, falling to her knees.*)

COOK: (*Rushes forward and helps her up.*) Are you all right?

MARGARET: (*Grabs CHARLENE's arm.*) Of course she's not all right. She can't walk right. She can't talk right. She's depressed and from what I can see, you're not really interested in helping her anyone. I think you can expect to hear from Mr. Mortimer whether you want to or not. Goodbye, doctor.

(*MARGARET leads CHARLENE offstage.*)

(*Lights dim to dark.*)

SCENE X

(*MORTIMER's law office. There is a conference table with chairs around it. MORTIMER, MARGARET and CHARLENE are already seated when COOK, dressed in a suit, comes in. MORITMER rises and extends his hand to COOK.*)

MORTIMER: Dr. Cook. How nice to meet you. I'm Carl Mortimer. Have a seat, please.

COOK: (*Turns and greets the ladies.*) Mrs. Mason. Mrs. Hanley. Nice to see you both again.

MORTIMER: I thought you might want to come with your lawyer, Dr. Cook?

COOK: You told me that this was an unofficial exchange of views, not a deposition. Am I right about that?

MORTIMER: Of course. You are right. This is not a deposition. No one is under oath and there is no recording going on. It's just a friendly get together. For me, it's a way to establish the best way to serve my client here, Mrs. Mason.

COOK: Of course.

MORTIMER: As you know, Mrs. Mason was injured by the use of Curital, prescribed by you for her sister, Mrs. Hanley? Is that correct?

COOK: Are you sure we are not being recorded? That sounds like a deposition question to me, Mr. Mortimer.

MORTIMER: No. Absolutely not. I just want this to be a frank discussion prior to proceeding any further in this case. As I was saying, did you prescribe Curital to Mr. Hanley?

COOK: Yes. I did.

MORTIMER: And, at least initially, you did not know that her sister, Mrs. Mason, was taking it.

COOK: That's correct.

MORTIMER: And you only subsequently learned that Mrs. Mason was taking the medication after her heart attack and stroke?

COOK: That's correct.

MORTIMER: And after that, you continued to prescribe the Cutical to Mr. Hanley who continued to give it to her sister. And you did that out of pure compassion for her difficult economic situation. Is that correct?

COOK: Yes, that's God's truth.

MORTIMER: As you know, doctor, providing a prescription under false pretenses is insurance fraud. In this case, the insurer is the federal government and that can get you into considerable difficulties.

COOK: Yes, I know. It could cost me my medical license. Or at least get me kicked out as a Medicare provider.

MORTIMER: But we are not interested in that aspect. We are only interested in you testifying, in perfect good faith, that Mrs. Mason was taking her sister's Curital prior to her heart attack and stroke. And that you learned that she had been taking them for at least six months prior to her illnesses.

COOK: You don't think someone will raise the question of her subsequent use of the medication?

MORTIMER: Why should they? And in any case, that doesn't interest me or my client. We only need to establish the fact that Mrs. Mason used Curital at least six months prior to her heart attack and stroke. What happens afterwards is unfortunate, but irrelevant to her case.

COOK: Do you really believe that? Everything will hinge on my credibility as a physician. And if it can be proven that I was dishonest in prescribing, that I committed fraud, than how can anyone believe anything I say about Mrs. Mason and her Curital?

MORTIMER: It's just a risk we will have to take.

COOK: We have to take?

MORITMER: My client and I.

COOK: And if I refuse to take that risk?

MORTIMER: Than I think I might just let the Medicare program know about your fraudulent prescription practices myself. Or perhaps the State Board of Medical Examiners might show some interest? Or the district attorney's office? Any one of them might be quite interested in how the public resources are being spent. What do you think?

COOK: (*To MORTIMER.*) It sounds like your black mailing me, Mr. Mortimer. Is that what this is? A shake down.

CHARLENE: Stop it!

MORTIMER: (*To CHARLENE.*) Stop what?

CHARLENE: Leave Dr. Cook alone!

MORTIMER: We cannot leave him alone and expect to get any compensation for your injuries. His testimony is the key to your case.

CHARLENE: I don't care. I smoked. I have diabetes. I insisted on taking that medication. I made my sister give it to me. Why shouldn't I be responsible?

MORTIMER: (*To CHARLENE.*) There is a proven link between the use of Curital and increased risk for heart attacks and strokes. The money is there. It's yours for the taking. All we need is Dr. Cook's testimony that you did, indeed, take the medication. The rest is irrelevant.

CHARLENE: And if his testimony puts Dr. Cook in danger?

MORTIMER: So what? If you can pay off your hospital bills and get some financial security? What difference does it make if that jeopardizes the doctor?

CHARLENE: And what if Dr. Cook loses his license? He's a good man and a good doctor. How is my hurting him make anything better. I don't think I can live with that.

MARGARET: (*To CHARLENE.*) Who cares what happens to Dr. Cook. You'll be rich. You can move to another city, another state. You can buy a condominium in Florida. Don't worry about what's going to happen to Dr. Cook.

CHARLENE: (*Turns to COOK.*) Did my smoking, hypertension and diabetes cause my stroke, Dr. Cook?

COOK: They certainly contributed.

CHARLENE: More than the Curital?

COOK: Mrs. Mason, Charlie, I've seen hundreds of smokers with diabetes who have had heart attacks and strokes long before Curtial was invented and they will be having them long after Curital is gone. Did Curital play a role in your heart attack and stroke? Maybe. Was it the leading factor? No! You've been your own worst enemy with your smoking and poor diabetic control. So help me, God.

MORTIMER: This is outrageous! This woman is trying to be compassionate with you and you insult her. You deserve to be denounced before the State Board of Medical Examiners.

CHARLENE: And blackmail? Is that something ethical lawyers usually do, Mr. Mortimer? Perhaps the State Bar Association would be interested in that?

MARGARET: (*To CHARLENE.*) You're insane! This attorney is trying to get you big bucks. Don't threaten him, for heaven's sake.

CHARLENE: Getting me big bucks? I think he's more interested in getting himself big bucks. At least Dr. Cook was trying to help me. Let's go, Maggie. I've had enough of this.

MARGARET: But Charlie.

CHARLENE: Maggie! Take me home. I'm tired. (*Gets up and tries to leave. Speaks to MARGARET.*) Are you going to help me or do I have to fall down in this lawyer's office and sue him?

MARGARET: (*Rushes to help CHARLENE.*) All right. All right. Let's go. Goodbye gentlemen.

COOK: (*Stands and goes over to help CHARLENE.*) Goodbye, Charlie. And thank you. I'll see you both in the office next month.

MARGARET: Over my dead body!

CHARLENE: I think you could arrange that, couldn't you, Dr. Cook?

COOK: (*To CHARLENE.*) No, Charlie, I'm afraid not. Our first obligation as a doctor is to do no harm. Primum non nocere.

CHARLENE: Amen.

(*MARGARET, CHARLENE and COOK leave the office. MORTIMER is left with pile of papers on his desk. MORTIMER tears up CHARLENE's papers.*)

MORTIMER: Good thing there's plenty more where that came from.

(*Lights dim to dark.*)

THE END

THE CLONING OF
ARTURO VAN KUNST

CAST OF CHARACTERS

DR. PIERRE MALVAUX: Scientist. A distinguished man in his late fifties.

DR. ARTURO VAN KUNST: Scientist. A distinguished man in his late fifties.

CRYSTAL CROYANT: Assistant to Dr. Van Kunst. An attractive women in her early thirties.

PAMELA VAN KUNST: Dr. Van Kunst's wife. A plain woman in her late fifties.

PABLO VAN KUNST: Arturo Van Kunst's son. A young man in his late twenties.

SETTING

Varies with the scenes as indicated.

SCENE I

(Presentation of an award to Professor VAN KUNST. There is a podium and both MALVAUX, who is the presenter, and VAN KUNST, who is the recipient, are dressed in academic regalia. MALVAUX stands behind the podium and VAN KUNST to the side. There is a "crowd" of spectators on a bench. Their backs are turned to the audience. The "crowd" is made up of the other members of the cast. They can wear simple paper, masks, perhaps held on sticks, to identify themselves as anonymous spectators.)

DR. MALVAUX: And it is with great pleasure that I present our distinguished guest and fellow colleague, recipient of the coveted Marshall Faibien Award for the Applied Sciences, Dr. Arturo Van Kunst. *(The crowd applauds. MALVAUX also applauds in VAN KUNST's direction. MALVAUX waits until the applause subside.)* Every one in this room knows Dr. Van Kunst's distinguished record. His work with polymerase chain reactions has resulted in numerous breakthroughs in viral identification which has revolutionized the whole field of virology. His work on amyloid plaque formation and enzyme dysfunction have opened new doors in research directed toward Alzheimer's Disease and the possibilities of new treatments for this most terrible of human diseases. And last, but certainly not least, in the domain of gene research, his pioneering studies on cloning have been admired and emulated in research facilities around the world. *(More applause.)* What is not as well known is that Dr. Van Kunst is an avid art collector who also paints. He has had his works accepted in juried shows both locally and in the Boston, Philadelphia and Atlanta areas. *(More applause. VAN KUNST smiles and bows politely in acknowledgment.)* In addition, his is a prolific writer, not only of innumerable scientific articles, but also several collections of remarkable short stories and plays, some of which have been produced locally. *(More applause.)* I would also be remiss if I did not mention Dr. Van Kunst's other artistic accomplishments. Believe it or not, Dr. Van Kunst plays the piano and also does ballroom dancing, both equally well. In fact, it was through dance lessons that he met his lovely wife, Pamela. *(More applause. PAMALA, who is in the "crowd," stands briefly and bows.)* In short, I would like to present the Marshall Faibien Award for the Applied Sciences to a truly outstanding scientist, a veritable Renaissance man, Dr. Arturo Van Kunst.

> *(VAN KUNST takes the prize and shakes hands with MALVAUX. VAN KUNST bows to the crowd that is applauding. They rise in a standing ovation. VAN KUNST and MALVAUX change places and VAN KUNST adjusts the microphone.)*

DR. VAN KUNST: Thank you for that gracious introduction I think it is traditional to give a short speech when receiving such an award. And since, in my wife's words, I am an incredible ham, I will not pass up the opportunity. *(Crowd laughs and applauds briefly.)* Dr. Malvaux was kind enough to allude to some of my scientific findings which have been largely expanded by the brilliant research of many others. These discoveries are, as always in science, just introductions of things to come. Already, in virology, we can not only count, but also modify viruses to inject DNA into other cells. Not only can we clone animals, we can also improve them by eliminating or adding genes. This opens opportunities for the treatment of cystic fibrosis, hemachromatosis, muscular dystrophy and many other genetic diseases which can now be identified and modified. Today's genetic material may be passed on, modified or unmodified, for generations to come. *(More applause.)* We realize, however, that the individual is not just genetic material, but a complex product of an interaction between the expression of his genes and his personal environment. *(Pauses.)* Therein lies the rub. Can we clone Einstein, Gandhi, or Van Cliburn? Yes, we probably can. But should we? In what environment can and should such individuals be raised? Some of us live in privileged environments, rich in art, music and literature, not to mention a roof over our heads and enough to eat. But many do not. It is my hope that each and every one of us will assume that the environment we create, especially in the domain of the arts, will be a fruitful one for the cultivation of genius, and not just its genetic reproduction. Each and every one of us has that moral imperative, the God given responsibility, to create a better, more beautiful world. We can not fail. For the future of the world depends of our efforts. Thank you. *(Applause. Everyone rises and crowds forward to shake VAN KUNST's hand.)*

(After the presentation, MALVAUX takes away the podium. The audience takes away the bench or chairs. VAN KUNST takes off the gown and gives it to PAMELA, who takes it away. VAN KUNST is dressed in a white laboratory coat. His assistant, CRYSTAL CROYANT, enters with a rack of test tubes or other scientific paraphernalia.)

SCENE II

DR. VAN KUNST: Well Crystal, what's the verdict?

CRYSTAL: Just as you predicted, Dr. Van Kunst. By adding some potassium, we increase the success rate from less that 10% to over 30%.

DR. VAN KUNST: Thirty? Is that all? Let's make it 50% or even 90%.

CRYSTAL: Thirty isn't bad at all. Malvaux's group hasn't broken 10% yet.

DR. VAN KUNST : Malvaux. Yes, Pierre Malvaux. He's bright, intrepid, careful, a good, but cautious man. His lab will get there eventually, but not soon enough. This may even get us a Nobel Prize one of these years. And poor Malvaux will be still dithering around with his 10%. Did you get the incubators?

CRYSTAL: Yes.

DR. VAN KUNST: And have you inquired as to the possibility of any volunteers?

CRYSTAL: That's another whole story.

DR. VAN KUNST: Don't tell me that the Institutional Review Board doesn't want to approve the project.

CRYSTAL: Worse than that. President Soigneux doesn't want any cloning research at all, and certainly no publicity of any kind. He says the university would suffer from any reference to human cloning. He understands the important scientific implications, but he says his job is fund raising and public relations, and any hint of research about this topic would be devastating.

DR. VAN KUNST: Here we stand of the threshold of a truly remarkable scientific achievement and Soigneux worries about groveling for pennies and placating an ignorant public.

CRYSTAL: You can't really blame him, can you? After that fiasco last year with the vaccinations and possible fetal malformations, he had to do some serious damage control with the big money crowd.

DR. VAN KUNST: Oh, I suppose I can understand. We need his financial support and he needs us. At least as long as we stay on the safe road. Such petty people. *(Picks up and examines one of the test tubes.)* And if we can't use any official volunteers, how about some unofficial ones?

CRYSTAL: That's pretty tricky, don't you think. Possibly illegal, certainly unethical?

DR. VAN KUNST: Very tricky indeed.

CRYSTAL: *(Looks skeptically at VAN KUNST.)* You don't have anyone in mind, do you?

DR. VAN KUNST: *(Looking at CRYSTAL.)* Twenty-five. Single. Life long dedication to the sciences. A natural risk taker. The soul of discretion.

CRYSTAL: *(Steps back.)* You don't mean me, do you?

DR. VAN KUNST: Why not? Minimal risk. Total confidentiality. A perfect understanding of the procedure. Why not you?

CRYSTAL: I'm very complimented, but I would like to politely refuse. And I hope you're not going to try to pressure me into it as my boss and research advisor.

DR. VAN KUNST: Oh really, I was only joking. I value your help and friendship more than you realize. It's just one of those flights of folly and imagination I'm so famous for, thinking outside of the box. Some people go for the moon and some people only make it to the corner store. Speaking of that, why don't you send out for some Chinese food? I'm starving and we still need to look at some of the data.

(They both walk off.)

(Lights dim to dark.)

SCENE III

(PABLO and PAMELA come on stage and help set up a dinner table with four chairs. VAN KUNST comes on when the table is set and sits down. Everyone waits for his signal to sit. They all laugh and begin a very animated conversation.)

PABLO: Then St. Peter asks her if she's ready to get drilled for wings and a halo and she answers "No, I'd rather go to hell." So he warns her that she'll roast in eternal flames and be ravished by devils day and night and she says "At least I already have all the holes I need for that."

DR. VAN KUNST: *(Does not laugh.)* I don't get it.

(PABLO AND PAMELA stop laughing.)

PABLO: She didn't want to have holes drilled for wings and a halo, Dad.

DR. VAN KUNST: Well, why not? It was just some temporary discomfort for the advantages of eternal bliss, why would she be so stupid and short sighted?

PABLO: Oh, Dad, what a sourpuss you can be.

DR. VAN KUNST: If this woman can't see the whole picture, than she deserves to go to hell and burn. If I were God, then I'd consider her a failure anyway.

PABLO: Like me?

DR. VAN KUNST: Of course not.

PABLO: Don't lie. I'm sure I'm a disappointment to you. Here I am at 27 and I haven't won a Nobel Prize or a Pulitzer or even been on the Best Seller List. My God! What a loser!

PAMELA: (*To PABLO.*) Please, your Dad didn't say that. You're not being fair. Your father is very proud of you?

PABLO: (*Leans forward.*) Well, are you? (*Long silence.*) Are you proud of me? Unmarried, undecorated, undistinguished and childless.

DR. VAN KUNST: Of course I'm proud of you. Don't you believe me? You're a successful adult, living on your own and doing your own thing.

(*Another long silence.*)

PABLO: Yes, I believe you. But it's hard to grow up in the shadow of such a remarkable father, don't you agree?

PAMELA: Yes, a Renaissance man, indeed. But as a wife it is just as difficult to live in the shadow of such greatness. I sometimes wonder what it would be like to have married a plumber who watches football and drinks cheap beer from the can. (*Turns to VAN KUNST.*) I always liked you from the very first time I saw you. You were tall, young, dashing and a terrific dancer. In fact, I turned to my friend, Gloria, and asked her how anyone in the world could get mad at a man like you. Now, of course, I know. But we're still married, still dancing and we've raised a successful son. And you are still painting, writing, playing the piano, going to your meetings and making brilliant discoveries. It's all very wonderful, but sometimes it's just too much for the rest of us. You know, Arturo, a little brilliance goes a long way. That being said, you are a very remarkable man.

PABLO: (*Raising his wine glass.*) To a remarkable man! Let's hear it for you, winner of the Faibien Award.

ALL: Here, here. (*Clink their glasses and drink to VAN KUNST.*)

DR. VAN KUNST: Thanks you for the support. Remarkable is nice, but have I really been that overwhelming to live with? (*To PAMELA.*) Have you really suffered so much by living with me?

PAMELA: I'm really okay with you, dear. After all these years, it's a bit second nature for me to put up with your excesses. But for Pablo, that's another story. Pablo lives in St. Louis. Do you think it's just chance that he live hundreds of miles away? *(There is no answer.)* Things are very civil among us all. Pablo calls at least once a week. We can still all sit down like this at the table for Thanksgiving. But there always seems to be this underlying strain between you and Pablo. It has to have been tough on him to grow up in the shadow of genius. I think he has suffered from a feeling that somehow he may not have quite lived up to your expectations. I can handle the feeling. But for Pablo? *(Looks at PABLO.)* That has had to be difficult for you.

DR. VAN KUNST: I have always done the best I could, as a parent, as a scientist, as an artist and musician. You can flagellate yourself as much as you want. But in the end, everyone does the best they can. I assume that is true of myself and of my son. *(Looks at PABLO.)* If you think I have failed in my duty as a parent, speak now.

PABLO: Or forever hold your peace. *(Bursts out laughing and PAMELA joins in, although VAN KUNST does not.)* Oh Dad, lighten. I appreciate my upbringing, no matter what a monster it has produced. *(Makes a distorted face and growling sound. Even Dr. VAN KUNST joins in the laughter. When the laughter dies down, PABLO continues.)* Now, to change the subject a little, what mind boggling experiments are you working on now, anyway?

DR. VAN KUNST: Thanks for asking. *(Nods in PABLO's direction.)* Dr. Croyant and I are working on the problem of human cloning.

PABLO: Human cloning? I thought that was illegal.

DR. VAN KUNST: Not exactly. Not yet, anyway. We can still work on existing stem cell colonies under strict guidelines. The interesting thing is that all cells are pluripotent.

PABLO: Pluripotent?

DR. VAN KUNST: Yes, pluripotent. That means that all cells contain all the genetic material to create a complete individual. The DNA sequences are there to form a complete individual. I could reproduce you, Pablo, completely from your DNA, which we could introduce into an embryonic cell. It's really very simple.

PABLO: Reproduce me! Heaven forbid. One of me is already too much, don't you think? (*Pulls his napkin over his head a mimics a girl's voice.*) I'm just too cute to be duplicated under any circumstances. (*Pauses and gets serious.*) Cloning may or may not be illegal, but is it ethical? Wouldn't you need a surrogate mother as well as an embryonic cell donor?

DR. VAN KUNST: Very perceptive. Yes, you would. But those are all just technical problems, not ethical ones.

PABLO: Technical problems? Finding a surrogate mother to carry a cloned embryo? Sounds creepy to me. We already have one of ourselves, why would anyone want to have two? Isn't one of me enough for a lifetime?

(*PABLO AND PAMELA laugh, VAN KUNST does not.*)

DR. VAN KUNST: What would be wrong with duplicating genetic material from a remarkable individual? Genetically, they would be the same, but that's all. The environment would make them completely different people, but perhaps more remarkable because they would be raised in an environment created for their particular genetic potential.

PABLO: Oh, that's great. When I'm 55 years old, I'd be looking at myself at 17. Now that's a weird and wonderful thought. (*Makes his voice low and raspy.*) Son, meet dad. Dad, meet son. You're looking good today. (*Changes voice.*) Just like I used to look and you look so good, too. (*Shakes his head in disbelief.*) No. That's just too weird, even for me.

DR. VAN KUNST: Weird? Why weird? Just unexpected. You could die knowing that your own biological self would be staring back at you, a promise for the future. The elusive goal of immortality. Genetic life without end.

PABLO: Amen! *(Makes the sign of the cross and bows his head and then looks up.)* All I can say is that you'd better leave that project alone. Leave it to someone else to be the first one this time. *(Pauses.)* Would you even seriously consider cloning human beings?

DR. VAN KUNST: Sure. Why not? Men are only held back by their own fears and prejudices. Columbus, Galileo, Copernicus, Einstein. Now they weren't afraid. They had visions and they pursued them to their logical conclusions.

PAMELA: You're scaring me. I've got goose bumps just listening to you talk.

DR. VAN KUNST: Then I think we need to dance a little to warm you up and burn off some of this wonderful dinner. *(Rises and summons PAMELA.)* Madame. *(VAN KUNST takes PAMELA. They circle around to the front.)* Let's dance!

> *(The couple begins to waltz to the theme from Dr. Zhivago. The music gets louder and louder and the couples spin as PABLO sits at the table and stares at the candles. The lights dim to dark.)*

SCENE IV

(Back in the lab. Minimal decor or none. Perhaps a table with some scientific equipment. VAN KUNST and CRYSTAL CROYANT are dressed in white lab coats.)

CRYSTAL: *(Crying.)* How was I to know?

DR. VAN KUNST: There, there. *(Patting CRYSTAL on the shoulder. Hands CRYSTAL a handkerchief.)* Let's think about this situation a little.

CRYSTAL: What's there to think about? My thesis has already been turned in. It's already in the hands of the committee members. And right in the middle are those passages from Dr. Malvaux's work. I didn't even use his name or put a footnote or anything. My God! I just ran out of time. I had to get it turned in or wait another full academic year. How was I to know the chairman would computer check every thesis this year? Those texts will jump right out. Pure, unadulterated plagiarism. I'm finished. This is the end of my professional career. *(Sobs.)*

DR. VAN KUNST: What if we can get your thesis withdrawn?

CRYSTAL: That's impossible.

DR. VAN KUNST: What if we get written permission from Dr. Malvaux for the use of the excerpts?

CRYSTAL: You know how he is. He doesn't have charitable bone in his body. He'd never do that.

DR. VAN KUNST: Why?

CRYSTAL: Because he's just a real stickler about crediting people. He sacrificed his own research assistant for unauthorized use of his written material. I'm sure he'd just love to do the same to me, working with his competitor. Anyway, I plagiarized him. That's all there is to it. He'll crucify me with pleasure. My career is finished.

DR. VAN KUNST: Maybe if we give him something he really needs and wants, like the cloning milieu formula?

CRYSTAL: Like what?

DR. VAN KUNST: Like our cloning milieu formula.

CRYSTAL: Dr. Van Kunst!

DR. VAN KUNST: Call me Arturo, please. We've certainly known each other long enough.

CRYSTAL: Arturo, that formula's taken us years to develop. We've sweated blood to come up with that thing.

DR. VAN KUNST: So?

CRYSTAL: You'd throw that away for me? Just to save my career?

DR. VAN KUNST: *(Puts his arm around CRYSTAL.)* Your friendship and support means more to me than any formula.

CRYSTAL: Even if it means sacrificing a possible Nobel Prize?

DR. VAN KUNST: What's a Nobel Prize anyway? It's just a piece of gold, another material possession. We're supposed to gather our treasures in heaven and not on earth anyway.

CRYSTAL: *(Wiping away the tears.)* I can't believe you'd do this for me. It would be like an undeserved miracle.

DR. VAN KUNST: Sometimes miracles do happen, you know.

CRYSTAL: *(Pulling away.)* You're not doing this so I'll be a surrogate mother for a cloning experiment, are you?

DR. VAN KUNST: Crystal, Crystal, that kind of decision must be yours and yours alone, without coercion, without pressure. I would not dream of linking the two. I may be devious, but I'm not evil. Besides, we don't even know if Malvaux would accept our proposition.

CRYSTAL: Accept it! He'd jump at the chance in a second.

DR. VAN KUNST: Perhaps you're right. But then again, you can never really understand human nature. We're all so complex and mysterious. *(Takes a test tube holder from CRYSTAL.)* Now, how about that latest series of clones?

CRYSTAL: *(Sighs.)* They're perfect Dr. Van . . . I mean Arturo. We almost got 100%. It's really unbelievable. The stem cells can be induced into blastocystes with no problem after they're transferred into the egg cell. It's incredible. We can increase the rate of successful implantation in female rats with just the addition of a simple hormonal preparations of a few days. Just a couple of shots, wait a few days, and there you go. Pregnant females with cloned embryos. Voilà!

DR. VAN KUNST: Voilà indeed. So easy and so complicated at the same time. It's really a miracle. Now, you go back to work and let me think about how I can go talk to Malvaux about our little proposition.

(Both leave. Lights dim to dark.)

SCENE V

(Cocktail party ambience. Vivaldi's "Winter" plays quietly in the background. Several of the other actors with masks stand in groups and chat. VAN KUNST and MALVAUX are stage center. They each hold a glass. There is the sound of conversations, and the Vivaldi in the beginning. Those sounds fade as VAN KUNST and MALVAUX begin to talk.)

DR. VAN KUNST: Malvaux, you devil you. So you're up to 10% success rate with the clones. That's good, very good.

MALVAUX: And you, if I'm not too curious? What is your current success rate?

DR. VAN KUNST: Ah, curiosity killed the cat. Do you really want to know?

MALVAUX: Yes, and I'm not feline. What about it? Can you tell me or is this some sort of state secret . . . for the Swedes, perhaps?

DR. VAN KUNST: Guess.

MALVAUX: Twenty-five percent?

DR. VAN KUNST: Higher.

MALVAUX: Thirty percent?

DR. VAN KUNST: Higher.

MALVAUX: *(Gasps.)* Fifty percent?

DR. VAN KUNST: *(Smiles and nods.)* Fifty percent or more.

MALVAUX: How did you do it? What's the secret?

DR. VAN KUNST: Wouldn't you like to know?

MALVAUX: Yes, quite frankly I would.

DR. VAN KUNST: Well. In fact, we made some rather simple modifications in the cloning milieu formulation. It took a lot of work on Crystal's part, you know Crystal Croyant, my assistant, but she plugged along and finally got it down right. It's incredible. From a miserable 10%, we're up to 55 or 60% successful extraction and almost 100% for implantation. It's extraordinary.

MALVAUX: And these simple modifications, I'm not going to know what they are, am I?

DR. VAN KUNST: Of course not. Unless . . . .

MALVAUX: Unless what? Do I have to sell my soul to the devil or something like that?

DR. VAN KUNST: *(Pulls MALVAUX a little closer.)* Not quite that dramatic. But we do have a little problem you might help us with.

MALVAUX: We?

DR. VAN KUNST: Yes, Crystal Croyant and I.

MALVAUX: What problem?

DR. VAN KUNST: Well, it really concerns my assistant, Crystal Croyant, the one who has done all this milieu modification research. You know her don't you?

MALVAUX: Yes, of course.

DR. VAN KUNST: It appears that she recently turned in her doctoral thesis to the review committee.

MALVAUX: So?

DR. VAN KUNST: She ran into a bit of unanticipated problem.

MALVAUX: Yes?

DR. VAN KUNST: She apparently included references from many of your published works, including some lengthy extracts of texts from you paper on pluripotent stem cell lines.

MALVAUX: So?

DR. VAN KUNST: So, in her haste to get the paper in before the deadline, she somewhat carelessly neglected to attribute the texts to you.

MALVAUX: *(Laughs.)* Neglected, eh? I bet the committee chairman ran his little plagiarism program again, the sly old fox. Caught another one, did he? Well, that will be the end of Ms. Croyant's career I suppose. One more promising female researcher, down the drain.

DR. VAN KUNST: Maybe.

MALVAUX: Maybe?

DR. VAN KUNST: We've known each other for many years. I think we can speak frankly. I thought that perhaps, in exchange for some privileged scientific information about cloning formulas, you might consider a letter to the committee chairman explaining to him your prior knowledge and authorization of the use of your texts. *(Pauses.)* It's just something to consider. You help us, we help you. No harm done, and everyone gets what they want and need.

MALVAUX: You say you're up to 50% success rate?

DR. VAN KUNST: Yes, 50% at least. Guaranteed.

MALVAUX: My God. That represents years of work. Maybe it even represents a Nobel Prize for you. Or at least another Faibien Award. Does Ms. Croyant's career mean that much to you? She's just another bright graduate student. There are thousands of them, you know. Is she really worth it?

DR. VAN KUNST: Let's say that I value her sense of loyalty and dedication.

MALVAUX: Getting a little on the side are we? I hope Pamela doesn't know.

DR. VAN KUNST: Get your scientific mind out of the gutter, please. No, I am not getting any the side. And Pamela doesn't have anything to worry about. Crystal Croyant and I have a strictly professional relationship.

MALVAUX: Ah, strictly professional, eh? That's what they all say. *(Pauses.)* Are you serious about this proposition?

DR. VAN KUNST: Dead serious.

MALVAUX: *(Grasping VAN KUNST's free hand.)* Then it's a deal. You'll get your letter for the thesis committee. I'll get the formula. And Ms. Croyant won't get the shaft. At least not that one?

> *(The both shake hands and laugh. Then each takes a big swig of his drink. Vivaldi and the other conversations rise in volume.)*

DR. VAN KUNST: *(Listening to the music.)* I love this part, don't you.

MALVAUX: Sublime. Absolutely sublime.

(The lights fade to dark and all exit.)

SCENE VI

(VAN KUNST and CRYSTAL are in a German style beer parlor. German or Czech polka music is playing, perhaps the "Clarinet Polka." There are tables with red and white checkered pattern and Chianti bottles with candles in them on the tables. Several other anonymous patrons are at one or two other tables. They wear their masks. VAN KUNST and CRYSTAL are dancing the polka. Everyone is laughing and talking loudly. After a few fast turns, VAN KUNST and CRYSTAL go to their table. They sit down to two brimming beer mugs.)

CRYSTAL: How do you find these places?

DR. VAN KUNST: *(Points to his nose.)* I have a nose for this kind of a place. Isn't it great. It's the only place in town with real Czech pilsner beer, and sauerkraut and dumplings as good as in Prague. *(The music continues softly.)* Do you hear that? That's our song.

CRYSTAL: Our song? What is it?

DR. VAN KUNST: *(Shrugs his shoulders.)* I don't know. It just sounds nice, don't you think?

CRYSTAL: *(Laughs.)* What a guy! Cultivated, humorous, a great scientist and wonderful dancer. What more could a woman ask for? Pamela is really a very lucky woman.

DR. VAN KUNST: Flattery will get you everywhere. *(Takes up his beer mug.)* Here's to you and your successful thesis! Congratulation, Dr. Crystal Croyant.

(CRYSTAL raises her glass. They drink, and then put down their mugs.)

CRYSTAL: I've never really thanked you for what you did for me.

DR. VAN KUNST: It was nothing.

CRYSTAL: No, it was really something. Nobody's ever stuck their neck out like that for me. I mean nobody. My own parents didn't even have the time or energy to come to my college graduation. Too busy, I suppose. But you have been someone who cared, someone willing to sacrifice for me.

DR. VAN KUNST: You're exaggerating.

CRYSTAL: No, I'm not. I'm dead serious. *(Pauses.)* And I have a surprise for you. I've also decided to go ahead with our project. *(Background music stops. Other patrons stop talking and freeze in their positions.)* I want to be a surrogate mother for a clone. Not any clone, but your clone.

DR. VAN KUNST: You can't be serious.

CRYSTAL: I'm dead serious.

DR. VAN KUNST: I refuse to have you link my helping you with that kind of sacrifice. They're not even in the same league.

CRYSTAL: I'm not linking them. And I am serious. In fact, I've already taken the hormonal preparation for the last seven days. My uterus will be ready. I'm ready. You should be too.

DR. VAN KUNST: I appreciate your gesture, but this is more that a science project. This is your body. This is a real baby, your baby, our baby.

CRYSTAL: Yes, our baby. It sounds so romantic in the abstract. Our baby, made without genetic mixing. Your baby, my womb, but our project. This is something more important than either your or me. There is no one else in the world that could or should do this. I'm not being stupid or silly or sentimental. This is in the same league as Copernicus, Galileo, and Columbus all mixed into one. It's a leap of faith and science and I'm ready to make it now, with you.

DR. VAN KUNST: No. I can't do such a thing.

CRYSTAL: Yes, you can. You must! For yourself, for posterity, for science and for me. You must.

DR. VAN KUNST: Can we think about it at least?

CRYSTAL: Yes, but only for three days. Then I'll be past the endometrial proliferative stage and the chances for implantation drop way off. You know as well as I do.

DR. VAN KUNST: *(Grabs CRYSTAL's arm.)* You don't know what this means to me. It's the culmination of a life's work. You just can't know what that means at your age.

CRYSTAL: Yes, I do know.

(A waltz begins to play. It can be the Czech waltz "Vitr." VAN KUNST takes CRYSTAL and they begin to waltz. The other couples can also get up and begin to waltz. The music gets louder, and then fades with the lights.)

SCENE VII

(In the background, CRYSTAL is on a gynecological table with her feet up in the stirrups. A white sheet covers her legs. VAN KUNST is at the foot of the table, working underneath. VAN KUNST is taking various medical tools and inserting them under the sheet. In the foreground, there is a conference table with MALVAUX and various other committee members. These members are other cast members who hold a mask in front of their faces.)

MALVAUX: But if we rule against doing any human cloning experiments, then we are tying our own hands from doing any important cloning research in the future.

COMMITTEE MEMBER 1: We really have no choice, Dr. Malvaux. This is not a scientific issue, it is a political and ethical issue. It's a real hot potato. Public opinion is viscerally opposed to any form of human cloning for whatever reason.

MALVAUX: But stem cells are human DNA. There's fundamentally no difference between doing that and cloning a human being. All the genetic information is there, you'd just have to implant it into an egg cell and put that in a human host. There's no difference, really between that and a Petri dish.

COMMITTEE MEMBER 2: No difference? Really, no difference between stem cells in Petri dishes and cloned babies in surrogate mothers. I tell you we're lucky to get away with the stem cells. Some people want to see that forbidden. Surely you're aware of the most recent legislation?

MALVAUX: I know the general public has visions of look alike clones raised for organ donation, but this is different. What about the child who needs a bone marrow transplant or the man with Parkinson's Disease, or patients with spinal cord injuries. Those people need cloning research. They can be the true beneficiaries. The research possibilities are limitless at this point.

COMMITTEE MEMBER 1: (*To MALVAUX.*) So are the problems. Do you know how many financial donors we would have left if they knew we even theoretically supported human cloning? Let's take the initiative here and now to come out against human cloning as a formal university policy. Do I hear a motion?

COMMITTEE MEMBER 2: So moved.

COMMITTEE MEMBER 1: And a second?

MALVAUX: (*Raises hand.*) I guess I can reluctantly second.

COMMITTEE MEMBER 1: The motion has been made and seconded. All in favor.

(*COMMITTEE MEMBERS 1 and 2 raise their hands.*)

COMMITTEE MEMBER 1: Abstentions?

(*MALVAUX raises his hand.*)

COMMITTEE MEMBER 1: Let the minutes show than the motion has been accepted with two votes in favor and one abstention. Do I hear a motion to adjourn?

(*COMMITTEE MEMBER 2 raises his hand.*)

COMMITTEE MEMBER 1: Then I believe that's all for today. Thank you, Dr. Malvaux and the other committee members, for coming. I'll notify the president of our decision.

(*COMMITTEE MEMBERS rise. In the background, VAN KUNST also rises and snaps off his surgical gloves. The lights shift to him.*)

DR. VAN KUNST: Well, Crystal, that's it. We'll know if it takes in the next few weeks. You've been very courageous. (*Goes around and squeezes CRYSTAL's hand.*) I won't forget this. We're making history today.

CHARLENE: (*Rises up a bit painfully.*) I believe you. I believe we are making history today. I would also hope we're advancing the cause of science.

DR. VAN KUNST: Of course we are.

CHARLENE: It's funny, but we've just done this extraordinary thing and I feel so unchanged, so ordinary. Even a little dirty.

DR. VAN KUNST: *(Laughs.)* What did you expect? Flashing lights, thunder, an angelic chorus? *(Taps CRYSTAL on the shoulder.)* This is more than a sordid affair. I'm not going to go out to a bar, light up a cigar and brag about my conquest to a colleague. This is science, amazing break-through science like no one has done before. It's like Columbus going off to the New World, like stepping on the moon for the first time.

CHARLENE: And a terrific advancement of scientific knowledge, I hope.

DR. VAN KUNST: Of course. A lot of science and a lot of very hard work.

CRYSTAL: Yes, hard work. *(Glances back at the examining table.)* Well, at least this part wasn't so bad. It was just lying on my back and getting probed a little. No worse than an OB-GYN visit.

DR. VAN KUNST: Do you feel used? Exploited?

CRYSTAL: No, just empty.

DR. VAN KUNST: I hope you're not empty. No, I would like you to be very *pleine* as the French say. Full up. Filled with something so extraordinary that both of our names will go down in scientific literature for the next millennium.

CRYSTAL: *(Smooths out her gown.)* I've got to go get dressed. *(Turns to VAN KUNST.)* And as for lasting a millennium, I can't help thinking of the Thousand Year Reich. That was supposed to last a thousand years, too, and see what happened there.

DR. VAN KUNST: I hope you don't see any comparisons. We're people of science, not politics. We are building on the foundations of a thousand years of scientific discoveries. We are just at the summit, looking out at infinite possibilities. Now, go get dressed. I'd like to take you out to that little Bohemian place. But no beer drinking this time. You've got precious cargo in there.

(Both leave the stage. Lights dim to dark.)

SCENE VIII

(Small, private party at VAN KUNST's home. It is their living room, prior to dinner. There's a sofa and a couple of arm chairs, perhaps Queen Anne style. There's a coffee table with a few books. An oriental rug sits under the table. Soft classical guitar music is playing.)

DR. VAN KUNST: *(Wearing a sport coat or suit jacket.)* Smells great!

PAMELA: Boeuf Bourguignon with glazed carrots and spring potatoes.

DR. VAN KUNST: And the wine?

PAMELA: A 1985 St. Emilion. A great year for Bordeaux, at least that's what you told me.

DR. VAN KUNST: I'm not sure Dr. Croyant can drink. I think she may be breast feeding.

PAMELA: *(Arranging flowers and some hors d'oeuvres.)* How old is the baby?

DR. VAN KUNST: Three months almost exactly to the day.

PAMELA: So precise?

DR. VAN KUNST: Just easy to remember. He was born on April 15th, tax day. That's a pretty easy date to remember.

PAMELA: And now we're July. July 14th, Bastille Day. This child certainly has a way with dates. By the way, who is the father?

DR. VAN KUNST: Some Latvian grad student.

PAMELA: Are they getting married?

DR. VAN KUNST: I doubt that. He's already back in Latvia if I understood correctly.

PAMELA: That's romantic.

DR. VAN KUNST: You never know about young people these days.

PAMELA: Crystal isn't that young. And I thought she was a bit more serious than that. *(Doorbell rings.)* That must be Dr. Malvaux and his wife.

MALVAUX: *(Enters and greets PAMELA with a friendly kiss.)* Sorry I'm late. My wife's ill. She sends her love, but there's no way she could tackle one of your famous gourmet dinners on a queasy stomach.

(Doorbell rings.)

CRYSTAL: *(Enters holding a baby carrier. Greets PAMELA, VAN KUNST and MALVAUX.)* Hi everyone. Hope I'm not late. Sandy needed to be changed right before we walked out the door, the little devil. *(Poses the baby carrier on the ground and takes a seat.)*

PAMELA: Would everyone like a little *aperitif.* We have some delightful Chardonnay and Arturo can whip us up a kir if you like.

MALVAUX: (*To PAMELA.*) You're the only person I know who uses the word *aperitif* in the right way and who knows what a kir is.

CRYSTAL: I'll just have a Perrier with a lemon slice, if you don't mind.

(VAN KUNST exits and the others chat while he's gone.)

PAMELA: (*To CRYSTAL.*) You must be exhausted . . . research, publications, motherhood, the usual household responsibilities. That's an awful lot to do for a single mother.

CRYSTAL: (*Looking down at the baby.*) Oh, it is sometimes a bit overwhelming. But Sandy's precious and he hardly ever cries. I've got this great Salvadoran woman who watches him during the day and also does some housework and cooking. She's an angel.

MALVAUX: An undocumented one?

PAMELA: *(To MALVAUX.)* Do you always have to be so controversial, Pierre?

CRYSTAL: For once, if you must know, she's perfectly legal. I think I've learned my lesson about that. (*Laughs a little and winks at MALVAUX.*)

(VAN KUNST returns and passes out the drinks.)

DR. VAN KUNST: *(Raises his glass.)* Let's hear it for Dr. Pierre Malvaux, this year's recipient of the coveted Faibien Award. I can't think of a more deserving scientist.

MALVAUX: *(Raises his glass.)* I can. And here's to the man who made it all possible and to his charming assistant who helped us both so immeasurably in our research.

(All drink.)

CRYSTAL: Just think of it. Two Faibien Award winners in the same room who still speak to one another. That's something extraordinary.

DR. VAN KUNST: *(To CRYSTAL.)* And perhaps a third in the making?

MALVAUX: Yes, yes. Why not? Our research has been so mutually beneficial. The results are there for the world to see. So let's let the world decide.

DR. VAN KUNST: Here! Here!

(They all drink again. PAMELA passes around the hors d'oeurves.)

MALVAUX: *(To PAMELA.)* Something smells wonderful. I suppose it's another great gourmet meal you whipped up in your spare time?

PAMELA: You're too kind. More kir?

MALVAUX: *(To CRYSTAL.)* What have you been publishing lately?

CRYSTAL: No publishing, just a lot of research for the time being.

MALVAUX: *(Points to the baby. Laughs)* That's not part of it, I suppose?

PAMELA: Pierre!

MALVAUX: Just joking. We did hear that your Latvian friend got hustled out of the United States pretty quickly. I guess they're getting a bit tighter about the student visas these days. Did he even have one?

DR. VAN KUNST: Have one what?

MALVAUX: A visa. A student visa.

CHARLENE: Of course he did.

PAMELA: What was his name?

CRYSTAL: Pavlov Sandovich.

PAMELA: Ah, Sandy. Of course.

MALVAUX: Let's take a look at this little Latvian.

CRYSTAL: He's sleeping, so just take a peak.

(CRYSTAL pulls back the cover and exposes the baby. VAN KUNST, MALVAUX and PAMELA all bend over to take a closer look. VAN KUNST and CRYSTAL smile. Both MALVAUX and PAMELA step back with looks of surprise.)

CRYSTAL: Isn't he just too precious?

PAMELA: Yes, yes. A beautiful baby. So much hair.

MALVAUX: When do you think Pavlov's coming back?

CHARLENE: Oh, I think he's permanently out of the picture. He had some obscure link to some extremist group back when Latvia was still part of the Soviet Union. I think I'm just going to have to shoulder the burden all alone. The precious little thing.

DR. VAN KUNST: Alone?

PAMELA: Well, with a little help from my friends. *(Nods to VAN KUNST.)*

(A rather long, awkward silence follows. VAN KUNST finally grabs his glass and raises it again.)

DR. VAN KUNST: Here! Here! To our true friends! And to the concept of mutual help.

(All raise their glasses except PAMELA. The lights dim to dark.)

SCENE IX

(The VAN KUNST bedroom. PAMELA is back at the dressing room table where she takes off her jewelry and make up. VAN KUNST takes off his jacket, shirt, etc.)

PAMELA: What do you really think of Crystal's Latvian boyfriend story?

DR. VAN KUNST: Nothing. That sort of thing happens all the time.

PAMELA: And the baby?

DR. VAN KUNST: Cute kid.

PAMELA: *(Stops combing her hair.)* Yes, a very cute kid. And I thought he looked a lot like you as a child. *(Turning to him.)* Is that your baby?

DR. VAN KUNST: Of course not! What a ridiculous idea!

PAMELA: I've looked at your face for thirty years. I've seen your baby albums. That child looks like you. Are you having an affair with Crystal?

DR. VAN KUNST: Absolutely not! I have never approached that woman sexually. I have never even touched her! We'll perhaps I have touched her by accident, but never in a deliberate, sexual way. We are research partners, friends, colleagues, fellow scientists and doctors. Please, get your mind out of the gutter.

PAMELA: That child looked exactly like you did. That has got to be your baby. If you want to divorce me and live with that woman, tell me now. Don't string me along like some fool socialite. I deserve better than that. *(Stands and confronts VAN KUNST.)* Swear to me it isn't yours. Swear to me now!

247

DR. VAN KUNST: I swear to you. I have never touched Dr. Croyant sexually. We have never slept together even once. I have never had sexual relations with that woman.

PAMELA: Who do you think you are, President Clinton? What do you mean exactly? *(Starts beating VAN KUNST on the chest.)* You liar. You dirty liar. Don't lie to me, damn it! *(Continues beating his chest.)*

DR. VAN KUNST: *(Grabbing her hands.)* You're hysterical. Calm yourself. I'm not lying.

PAMELA: *(Starts throwing things, tipping over furniture.)* Get out of here! Get out of this house! Go fuck your mistress and raise little Sandy. Sandy! What a joke. Call that baby Arturo Junior and be done with it. You filthy pig! Get out! Get out!

(PAMELA continues throwing objects as he backs away.)

(Lights dim to dark.)

SCENE X

(House in the country. A figure is sitting in a chair. It is SANDY, who wears a paper mask with the face of VAN KUNST. CRYSTAL, MALVAUX and VAN KUNST are standing the room in front of the seated figure.)

MALVAUX: Does he talk?

DR. VAN KUNST: Of course he talks. Sandy, say something to Dr. Malvaux. He's a good friend of your mother and me.

SANDY: Hello, Dr. Malvaux. My mother has spoken to me about you on many occasions. How are you today?

MALVAUX: I'm fine. Thanks you for asking. I don't think I caught your full name.

SANDY: Sandy Pavlov Croyant. I know you know my mother already. And this gentleman is her good friend, Dr. Van Kunst.

MALVAUX: (*To SANDY.*) How old are you? You seem very big and mature for your age.

SANDY: I'm only ten years old.

MALVAUX: (*Looks at CRYSTAL and VAN KUSNT in disbelief.*) Ten? That's impossible! (*To SANDY.*) I mean, you look considerably older than ten.

SANDY: (*To MALVAUX.*) I know I look older, but I have a disease called progeria which ages me prematurely. It's a very unusual genetic disease. Dr. Van Kunst explained it to me. My mom has let me read all about it. I think my body is already 50 even though I'm only ten.

(*MALVAUX looks at CRYSTAL and VAN KUNST who nod in agreement.*)

DR. VAN KUNST: We have always tried to be scrupulously honest with Sandy in so far as his progeria is concerned. It's the least we can do with such an intelligent boy.

CRYSTAL: That's right. He may be aging at an accelerated rate, but it has not affected his intelligence. (*Turns to SANDY.*) You're a very clever boy. Show Dr. Malvaux some of the things you can do.

SANDY: Dr. Van Kunst has taught me lots of subjects. He's even taught me how to dance. (*Begins to waltz around the stage all by himself, holding an imaginary partner.*) This is a waltz step. It came from Vienna many years ago. One-two-three, two-two-three, one-two-three, two-two-three. (*Switches to a polka step and continues to dance by himself.*) This is a polka step and it came from what is now the Czech Republic. One-two-three hop, two-two-three hop, one-two-three hop, two-two-three hop. *(Switches to a mazurka step and dances around.)* And this is a mazurka step. It originally came out of Poland. One-two hop, one-two hop, one-two-three, one-two hop, two-two hop, one-two-three.

DR. VAN KUNST: No, Sandy. That's not quite right. Let me show you. Come over here and be my partner. *(They assume a dance position.)* Now we both start out on our outside feet, you on your right and me on my left. Then we go down, back, hop, down, back, hop, and then six running steps. I pull you backwards. Ready?

> *(VAN KUNST hums. They begin to dance. It is a surreal scene with the two VAN KUNSTS, the original and his clone, SANDY, dancing a mazurka. Real mazurka music and they do a few turns. Both are smiling and laughing. The music fades.)*

DR. VAN KUNST: Good. Perfect. You're really a fine dancer.

MALVAUX: Just like your father.

SANDY: My father. Did you know my father? He came from Latvia.

MALVAUX: *(Stammers.)* No. I mean yes. I mean I used to know him a long time ago when he worked with your mother at Dr. Van Kunst's lab.

SANDY: My mom says he was a fine dancer. And she dances with me sometimes when she's feeling better.

MALVAUX: *(To Sandy.)* Have you ever been to school?

SANDY: Oh no, sir. Mother says I'm much too delicate for that. She's taught me entirely at home with the help of Dr. Van Kunst. I can do math up to geometry and I can talk in French, too. *Voulez-vous être mon copain, Monsieur* Malvaux?

DR. VAN KUNST: No, Sandy. *Copain* would be for someone your own age. It sort of means buddy. Better use the more formal *ami*.

250

SANDY: Voulez-*vous être mon ami, Monsieur* Malvaux?

MALVAUX: *Bien sûr que oui. Je aimerai bien être votre ami, si tu veux bien.*

SANDY: Not too fast, Dr. Malvaux. I'm only in French 2. *(Turning to VAN KUNST.)* Can we go outside and take a walk before it gets dark? It looks like great weather outside.

CRYSTAL: Yes, of course. But don't wander off from Dr. Van Kunst. And don't go to close to the subdivision down by the lake. You can get bad germs from the people down there.

SANDY: We won't. Bye for now.

(SANDY and VAN KUNST leave.)

MALVAUX: This is extraordinary. He's chronologically 10 and biologically 50. And he seems intelligent.

CRYSTAL: Yes, poor thing. He's aging more rapidly than we thought. Arturo and I have raised him up here where no one will bother us. In fact, the people down the hill think he's Arturo. They look almost identical now.

MALVAUX: Does Sandy realize what's happening?

CRYSTAL: What's happening?

MALVAUX: That he's Arturo's son, his clone.

CRYSTAL: No, he doesn't know that.

MALVAUX: How is it possible? Anyone with eyes could see the perfect resemblance.

CRYSTAL: *(CRYSTAL gestures around the room.)* No mirrors. No reflective surfaces of any kind. Sandy's never seen his own face.

MALVAUX: I thought I heard Arturo say that he wanted to be completely honest with Sandy. Didn't he say that?

CRYSTAL: Honest about his disease, the progeria. But neither of us could bring ourselves to tell him the truth about his status as a clone. It just seemed too hard for him to take. Especially with his accelerated aging.

MALVAUX: Does Pamela know about Sandy and what he is?

CRYSTAL: No, she finally took poor Arturo back after I dropped out of the picture and moved away. She never really understood what happened, but she suspected that we'd had an affair. He just kept denying if over and over again until I think she decided to believe it. After all, she only saw Sandy once as a baby. No, Pamela doesn't know a thing. You're the only one.

MALVAUX: How long does Sandy have to live?

CRYSTAL: (Sighs.) He's aging so fast; maybe three or four times the normal rate. It seems to be getting even worse with time. I don't know how long he can live. I just hope I can be here for him as he ages.

MALVAUX: Why shouldn't you be?

CRYSTAL: I've got my own health problems.

MALVAUX: Anything serious?

CRYSTAL: No, I don't think so. But I do worry about Sandy. Who would take care of him if I weren't available?

MALVAUX: Do you really think you did the right thing?

CRYSTAL: I don't know. Maybe if Sandy were normal. Or maybe if I didn't have to live in fear of being discovered, it would be better. I worry about it day and night. There just doesn't seem to be any answer.

At first I was sure I did the right thing, for science, for knowledge, for all those abstract reasons. But with Sandy really there and that terrible burden of knowledge, all those abstractions don't mean much. I think I just did it for myself and that's a terribly selfish thought.

MALVAUX: You did it for Arturo, too. Didn't you?

CRYSTAL: Yes, and for Arturo, too. But mostly for myself. All those hypothetical considerations don't mean much when you see your own child, even if it is a clone, aging before your eyes, unable to have a normal life, and with the terrible prospect of dying in the not too distant future. My God, sometimes I wish you would have accused me of plagiarism. It would have been the end of it right then and there. *(Cries.)*

MALVAUX : *(Tries to comfort CRYSTAL.)* I don't think anyone could have foreseen the outcome.

CRYSTAL: Maybe, but I think we have to be able to expect the unexpected. If we, the supposedly intelligent, the educated and the privileged can't project into the future, then who can? Who in the world can?

MALVAUX: I don't know. Perhaps you're right. Why don't we go out and walk with them. It might do you some good.

CRYSTAL: *(Turns to MALVAUX.)* Promise me that if anything ever happens and I can't take care of Sandy that you'll step in and help.

MALVAUX: I can't promise that. I have no idea what the future holds for any of us. Besides, I might be accused of being an accessory to a crime. Human cloning is a crime now, you know.

CRYSTAL: How could I not know? But that isn't the point. Arturo couldn't take him on and you are the only one with the scientific knowledge and the compassion to help us. I'm not asking for myself, I'm asking for Sandy and for Arturo.

MALVAUX: It's against my better judgment, but I will promise you. I'll do it for you and for Sandy. Arturo should have thought this whole thing through a bit before plunging ahead. I just hope it doesn't become a public scandal. The folks at the university and the committee in Stockholm hate scandals.

(They leave. The lights dim to dark.)

SCENE XI

(Another Thanksgiving at the VAN KUNST home. PABLO is there with PAMELA. VAN KUNST's chair is empty. The candles are lit and PABLO and PAMELA are eating and drinking.)

PABLO: Late again. Dad just can't seem to remember these important family holidays. Same old egotistical bastard.

PAMELA: Don't talk like that about him, even if it is sometimes true. After all, he is your father.

PABLO: It is true, Mom. He is an egotistical bastard. Not sometimes, but most of the time. No, all of the time. And he never admits he's been wrong. Christ, if he could have really done it, I think he would have made a clone of himself just to spite us. Imagine that for a moment. Two Arturos. *(Speaks to himself, changing positions slightly.)* Well how are you today, Arturo. Just fine. Thanks for asking, Arturo. Fine weather we're having, isn't it.

(Doorbell rings.)

PAMELA: *(Get's up to answer it.)* Who could that be on a Thanksgiving night? *(Goes over and opens the door. SANDY is there wearing his VAN KUNST mask. MALVAUX may play SANDY's role.)* For heaven's sake, dear, you don't have to ring the doorbell like a stranger. Did you lose your key or something? You're as late as can be. You missed dinner. We've been here for hours we just couldn't wait anymore.

254

PABLO: It's about time. Come and join us, finally. Yeah, you can finally say grace for our digestion. *(Bows his head and prays.)* Bless these gastric juices and the by-products of our gourmet dining experience. Amen.

SANDY: *(Stands still. Refuses to sit down. Looks around, bewildered.)* Is this the Van Kunst residence?

PABLO: Dad? Is there something wrong?

SANDY: *(Looks at him blankly.)* Dad?

PAMELA: *(Goes back to where SANDY is standing. PAMELA leads SANDY back to the table.)* You don't look well. Would you like something to drink?

SANDY: No, thank you. I came here to find Dr. Van Kunst.

PABLO: Is this a joke or something? What's a matter with you? Are you sick or having a stroke or something? *(Pauses.)* Maybe he's had a stroke. *(To SANDY.)* Are you having any other symptoms? Any headache, numbness, weakness? Answer, for heaven's sake. Dad, this isn't a joke, is it?

SANDY: *(Backing away alarmed.)* There must be a mistake. This must not be the right place. I took a taxi and he told me this was the place, the home of Dr. Arturo Van Kunst.

PAMELA: This isn't funny, Arturo. What's happening to you? Stop playing around with us.

SANDY: I am not Arturo. My name is Sandy Croyant. I'm looking for Dr. Arturo Van Kunst. My mother's sick and needs help and I don't know who else to ask.

PAMELA: Sandy? Sandy Croyant? You'd only be about 10 years old.

SANDY: I am Sandy Croyant. Sandy Pavlov Croyant. My mother is Crystal Croyant. We live out in West Chester and she's sick. I need to find Dr. Van Kunst so he can help her. Can you please help me find him? Please! My mother is very sick and I must find Dr. Van Kunst.

PAMELA: Oh my God! You are Sandy. Sandy Croyant. But you're . . . .

(PAMELA faints. PABLO rushes forward to help their mother. SANDY backs away from the commotion and runs back toward a large mirror which now illuminates in the background. SANDY stands transfixed in front of the mirror. The doorbell begins to ring again and again.)

PABLO: What in the hell's going on? Can someone tell me what's going on? Who the hell's at the door? *(Rises and goes to the door. VAN KUNST bursts in, disheveled and panting.)*

DR. VAN KUNST: Is Sandy here? I've got to find him now? Is Sandy here? His mother called and said he might have come here. *(Looks at his wife on the floor.)* What's going on? Pamela?

SANDY: *(Smashes the mirror with his fists. There's a shattering of glass and the tinkle of falling pieces. Swings around and advances to face VAN KUNST.)* I'm you! I'm you! *(Clutches VAN KUNST.)* You're my father! Why didn't you tell me? Why didn't you tell me the truth? I'm you, aren't I? I'm exactly you, only younger. What did you do to me? You bastard! You dirty old bastard! You made me and you made me look just like you and you never told me! *(Beats VAN KUNST's chest until he slows down and drops to the floor where he sobs.)*

(PABLO stares open-mouthed; he looks from VAN KUNST to SANDY and back again. PABLO also faints, taking an edge of the table cloth and the table's contents with him in a huge, noisy clatter. He lands on the floor next to PAMELA. Lights dim to dark.)

SCENE XII

(CRYSTAL and SANDY's home in West Chester. SANDY may be played by MALVAUX who wears the DR. VAN KUNST mask, now very old and wrinkled. SANDY is lying in bed. He is attached to oxygen. VAN KUNST, PAMELA, PABLO, and CRYSTAL are all present at the bedside. Some are seated, others standing.)

SANDY: I'm dying, aren't I?

CRYSTAL: *(To SANDY.)* Yes, you are.

SANDY: *(Looking at VAN KUNST who is seated at the bedside.)* It's not bad to die, I suppose, but it is bad to die before your own parents.

DR. VAN KUNST: Don't talk. You need to conserve your strength.

SANDY: Is it strange to see yourself die? I am you, and here I am, dying. And you are sitting at the bedside watching yourself die. That must be strange, isn't it?

DR. VAN KUNST: It's not strange. It's heart breaking.

SANDY: Are you really sad? I've been a lot of trouble to you. I'm sure your lives will be easier when I'm gone. I've been a lot of trouble.

DR. VAN KUNST: No, you haven't been any trouble.

SANDY: No, I guess I haven't been that much trouble. But I could have been. I could have picked up the phone and called a reporter or the police and then, here I am, your clone. I look just like you, Arturo. I mean really just like you. No one could deny the facts. I guess they could test the DNA to see if we matched. Oh, what a circus that would be. *(Pauses.)* I bet you both thought you'd get away with it and that I wouldn't ever figure out who I really was. Did you actually think I'd never figure it out?

CRYSTAL: (*To SANDY.*) I'm so sorry. I hoped you'd never find out, for all of us.

SANDY: But I did. I'm not stupid, you know, just old before my time. How is it to see yourself die? How does it feel deep down inside? Are you pleased? Are you happy it will be over?

DR. VAN KUNST: (*Bows his head a shakes it slowly.*) Don't torture me.

SANDY: Yes, it's time for me to go. I'm the product of your pride and now it's time for me to exit. I've proven it can be done, even if the world's scientific community will never know. I guess it's my fault this is turning out this way.

PABLO: None of this is your fault. You didn't make the decision to be created. The famous Dr. Van Kunst created life in his own image, his exact image. It's his fault. He had no right to do this. You could do anything to him now and he would deserve it.

SANDY: I should have gone to the newspaper and wrecked your life. The great Dr. Van Kunst, omnipotent giver and taker of life. No, creator of life. Not new life, but old life. Preserving his own genetic material forever and ever. Immortality. The quest of ages, finally realized. (*To VAN KUNST.*) Look at me now. Are you proud? Are you happy? Am I your triumph of medicine, your perpetuation of yourself? Your life without end, amen. (*Slips down in the bed.*) And you, Mother, my perverted Virgin Mary. I'm your unholy, immaculate conception. And now I'm dying before your eyes. What are you feeling? Mary's grief. Seeing her son crucified by forces out of her control, genetic forces stronger than both of you. Are you sad or are you just relieved the nightmare's over?

CRYSTAL: (*Weeping.*) I love you. I really do. I know you might not believe me.

SANDY: Love me! No, you loved Arturo. Twice. Once as that one. (*Pointing to VAN KUNST.*) And once as me. Double the pleasure, double the fun. Just like the chewing gum commercial. My God, it's too good.

CRYSTAL: Please don't torture me any more. I only want to know if you can forgive me for what I did.

SANDY: *(Sitting up a little. Pauses.)* No, I can't.

PABLO: *(To SANDY.)* What do you want them to do? What do you want us to do? What can we do for you?

SANDY: I could ask you to be the brother that I never really had. I could ask you to keep me immortalized in your heart and in the hearts of your children for generations to come. But that would be ridiculous, wouldn't it? *(Pauses a while and thinks.)* How about something simple, something peaceful and beautiful for a change? Why don't you to sing for me.

PABLO: Sing? Sing what?

SANDY: Amazing Grace.

PABLO, PAMELA and CRYSTAL: *(Try to sing Amazing Grace with stifled sobs and broken voices. SANDY joins them, but his voice weakens and he slumps over.)* Amazing grace, how sweet the sound, that saved a wretch like me. I once was lost, but now I'm found, was blind, but now I see.

> *(SANDY dies. The others weep. Lights fade to black. MALVAUX, who was playing SANDY, now takes off his mask and steps to stage forward to give a final monologue.)*

MALVAUX: So that's the story. Dr. Arturo Van Kunst, great scientist, patron of the arts, writer, artist, dancer, cloned himself. And instead of achieving some miraculous biological immortality, his son proceeded him in a gruesome, premature death. Yes, Sandy died and Dr. Van Kunst had to watch himself die. *(Pauses.)* The great scientist remained a broken, tormented man. He lived beyond his son, but not by much.

He died a few months later of so-called natural causes. Crystal Croyant left science altogether. She never fulfilled, as her uncharitable colleagues stated, the promise of her youth. Pamela eventually remarried a much less remarkable, but pleasant and considerate man of plebeian interests. Pablo has gone about his life, not overly distinguished, but generally a happy and productive citizen. *(Pauses again.)* And as for me? Well, I've won more distinguished scientific prizes than ever. Some people say that the Swedes are even considering me for a Nobel Prize for my work on cloning. But I'll never be able to match Arturo's triumph. Yes, the great Dr. Arturo Van Kunst cloned himself. Now that's really something to think about, something to dream about.

(MALVAUX walks off. There is a projection on the back of the stage of multiple VAN KUNSTS. Lights dim to dark. Close curtain.)

THE END

A QUESTION OF VALUES

DISCLAIMER: Any resemblance to the living or dead is strictly fortuitous.

CAST OF CHARACTERS

SISTER ETERNA: CEO of St. Ursuline's Hospital. A neat woman in her mid-fifties.

DR. HOWARD KRASLOVICH: Internist and board member of the Red River Hospital. A well-dressed man in his mid-fifties or sixties with graying hair.

CHARLES IVANHOE: CEO of MegaHealth Corporation. An expensively dressed man in his late 40's.

CATHY WINTHROP: CEO of Red River Hospital. A well-dressed woman in her midforties.

TRACY GLISSANT: Consulting attorney for Red River Hospital, may be a man or woman. Dressed in a conservative dark suit.

BERRY EPINEUX: Executive Director of the Red River Foundation. Mid-fifties, executive type.

SETTING

Varies with the scene.

SCENE I

(KRASLOVICH walks forward into a pool of light. In the obscure background is a conference table with chairs. EPINEUX and ETERNA are standing next to the table in the darkness. KRASLOVICH speaks directly to the audience.)

DR. KRASLOVICH: So, that was it. I was supposed to resign from the Red River Foundation Board and the other board members could all sigh a collective sigh of relief. This would be the last chapter of my participation in this noble experiment. Or, should I fight tooth and nail to keep my place on the board? But for what? For whom? For myself? For the town? For the common good?

SR. ETERNA: *(Wanders over from the background darkness. Puts her hand KRASLOVICH's shoulder.)* Many and varied are the paths to destruction and great are the number that follows therein. But straight and narrow is the path to salvation and few are the number that follows it.

DR. KRASLOVICH: Thank you, Sister Eterna. I always appreciate your words of advice. But what I need to know is if I should fight those bastards on the Foundation Board or not? I don't even know if I should bother.

SR. ETERNA: If you don't want to fight, then don't. You can be a good old boy and take the easy road. But be sure that you can live with yourself afterward if you do. Let me paraphrase the saintly Thomas More. When the other board members go to heaven for living according to their consciences and you go to hell for not living according to yours, do you think they'll come with you for any reason?

DR. KRASLOVICH: *(Sighs)* I understand your point.

(The lights go up. There is an empty conference table and chairs upstage.

EPINEUX is standing next to the table. KRASLOVICH walks toward him.)

DR. KRASLOVICH: *(To EPINEUX.)* I know this may prove as hard on you as it is for me, but you're going to have to vote me off the board if you want to get rid of me. I am not resigning voluntarily.

EPINEUX: I'm sorry to hear that. But if that's the way you want it, that's the way it's going to be. Let me call the other members of the Board. Ladies! Gentlemen! Can we get back to work here, please?

(*The other members of the cast enter. They are the other Red River Foundation Board members. KRASLOVICH sits at one end of the table and EPINEUX sits at the other. ETERNA, GLISSANT, WINTHROP and IVANHOE are seated in between.*)

EPINEUX: For our next order of business, I would like to propose the removal of Dr. Kraslovich from the Foundation Board. I know that this may be a difficult, or even traumatic, vote for some of you, but circumstances necessitate this unpleasant proposal. Do I hear a motion and a second? Mrs. Glissant?

GLISSANT: I move that Dr. Kraslovich be immediately removed from his position as a member of the Red River Foundation Board of directors.

WINTHROP: I second the motion.

EPINEUX: The motion has been moved and seconded. Do I hear any discussion?

(*KRASLOVICH raises his hand.*)

EPINEUX: Dr. Kraslovich.

DR. KRASLOVICH: I have known most of you for many years, both personally and professionally. Despite the recent malicious rumors that have been circulating, I believe that my lifelong contributions to this community, from both a medical and non-medical standpoint, speak for themselves. I have never been opposed to any positive initiatives in this town, whether they are in health, education, the arts, or economic development. Why then has it come to this? Why am I on the verge of being voted off the Foundation Board? (*Pauses.*) It has come to this because I have dared to question the morality of the decision to sell our not-for-profit community hospital to a for-profit organization. Yes, I have dared to question the morality of that decision and how it was made. *(Pauses)* Is that a crime? Is soul searching so alien and undesirable that it cannot be tolerated in an organization dedicated to the good of the community? Is this board so closed to introspection that I must be removed to prevent it?

EPINEUX: *(To KRASLOVICH.)* The decision to sell the hospital and create the Foundation has already been made long ago. Questioning that decision now simply puts the whole Foundation mission into jeopardy.

DR. KRASLOVICH: How? How does a question of fundamental morality put your mission, or any mission, in jeopardy?

EPINEUX: Because we cannot afford the luxury of second guessing our own creation. If that worm of doubt enters the fruit, then the whole fruit will be corrupted.

DR. KRASLOVICH: Isn't the fruit already corrupted?

EPINEUX: *(To KRASLOVICH.)* Look at these decent men and woman. *(Waves his hands toward the other board members seated around the table.)* They are the very flower of this society, the pinnacle of virtue. Don't you dare stand here and accuse them of moral dishonesty. It's destructive and it's wrong. You are not their judge, regardless of how superior you may think you are.

DR. KRASLOVICH: No, I am not their judge. Each person here must look into his or her own heart and answer the fundamental question of whether they have made the right decisions for the right reasons. *(Pauses.)* Disregarding all the Foundation's glossy publications and self-congratulatory bill boards, we must ask the question of why we are here. Can you answer that question, please? *(To WINTHROP.)* Cathy?

WINTHROP: For the good of the community.

IVANHOE: For our children's future.

SR. ETERNA: For the greater glory of God.

DR. KRASLOVICH: (*To EPINEUX.*) And you?

MR. EPINEUX: For all those reasons and also to create a charitable foundation which will outlive us all. In other words, to establish a vicarious sort of immortality.

DR. KRASLOVICH: (*Points to the various board members as he speaks.*) For the good of the community, our children's future, the greater glory of God, to create an everlasting foundation. (*Pauses again and nods.*) With all do respect, I believe you're each here for yourselves.

ALL: No, Not me. Not us.

DR. KRASLOVICH: You are here for what you perceive to be your personal best interest. And if your personal self interest happens to correspond with the good of the community, or your children's future, or the greater glory of God, then so much the better. Some good may actually occur from the money created by the hospital's sale and the subsequent formation of the Foundation. But don't try to fool yourselves or anyone else. This Foundation is an exercise in fundamental self-interest. (*To ETERNA.*) Sister, I'm sure you understand. I've heard you express similar notions in the past, haven't I?

SR. ETERNA: Perhaps, but times change and circumstances change and I must look out for the collective good of the community and our religious order.

EPINEUX: (*To KRASLOVICH.*) Your ideas are very interesting. But now the question is whether our fundamental best interests and yours happen to coincide. I believe that most, if not all, of the other board members agree that they do not. Is there any other discussion? (*EPINEUX looks around. Everyone shakes their head.*) Then the motion to remove Dr. Kraslovich from the board has been moved and seconded. All in favor or his removal raise your hand. (*WINTHROP, IVANHOE and GLISSANT all raise their hands.)* All opposed? *(KRASLOVICH raises his hand.)* Abstentions? *(ETERNA raises her hand.)* Then let it be recorded that by a vote of three for, one against and one abstention, Dr. Howard Kraslovich has been formally removed from the Red River Foundation Board. *(EPINEUX pounds the table very loudly with a gavel.)* Thank you all. This meeting is adjourned.

> *(KRASLOVICH rises up and moves to the front center of the stage. He is bathed in a solitary pool of light. The other board members rise and leave the stage in different directions. KRASLOVICH advances forward and the curtain closes. He and the others give their monologues from in front of the curtain in a single pool of light.)*

DR. KRASLOVICH: So that's how I ended my involvement in the Red River Foundation. They officially declared me a persona non grata, an enemy to their noble cause. I had gone from a valued member of the team to a dangerous outcast. So how did I make this remarkable transition? Stay with me awhile and find out. But first, let me allow some of the principal characters in this drama to introduce themselves. *(Walks off stage.)*

> *(Each subsequent person comes to give their introductory remarks to the audience in the same pool of light.)*

SR. ETERNA: *(Prays with her hands clasped and her head bowed.)* Your kingdom come, your will be done, on earth as it is in heaven. Amen. *(Makes the sign of the cross.)* Hello. I'm Sister Eterna, CEO of St. Ursuline's Hospital and a proud member of our religious order, the Sisters of Perpetual Succor. That's succor, not sucker as some people pronounce it. *(Smoothes out her tailored suit and continues.)* Who would have thought? From the heart of Avoyelles Parish to the head of corporate headquarters. Now that's what I'd call a miraculous ascension. *(Pauses.)* At first I thought I'd be emptying bedpans and spoon feeding Alzheimer's patients. Or perhaps working in the Congo in the AIDS clinic at Kinshasa. But no, I eventually got my MBA in hospital administration at Notre Dame and became CEO of a series of ever important and ever larger Catholic hospitals run by our order. Now

I don't think only about the mission, but I'm obliged to think about the margin as well, the profit margin, of course. Always remember that there is no mission without a margin. I repeat. No mission without a margin. Catchy, isn't it. This is how I address my fellow nuns and lay collaborators. *(Starts to strut back and forth on the stage with a particularly military air, tapping a pencil or a ruler against the palm of her hand.)* We are the stewards of our hospital and community resources! Each wasted disposable glove, each wasted bedpan, each unnecessary day in the hospital all put the edifice of the hospital . . . . no, the mighty edifice of the holy, apostolic Catholic church itself in jeopardy! Do you want to be the one who pulls down the glorious edifice of Christ's church? Eh, ladies? Not I, say each of you! Yet when you encourage that patient's family to take an extra complimentary meal, when you provide an extra towel or blanket, when you let that patient stay in bed instead of getting up and out, you put the margin in peril. You jeopardize the whole structure. You imperil the glorious healing mission based on the ministry of our Lord Jesus Christ! *(Reaches a crescendo of passion and then stops. Bows to her imaginary audience and the real one.)* And so it goes. Everyday is a struggle to balance revenues and costs. The insurance companies, the federal government, the state insurance plan, the HMO, they all squeeze and manipulate while we cut this corner and that. There are tough decisions to be made. But we will make them! We will make them all for the greater glory of God! *(Walks off.)*

DR. KRASLOVICH: *(Walks on.)* Decisions. Decisions. They're odd, you know. Sometimes they creep up on you when you least suspect them. Sometimes you try and use all your intelligence and skill to focus on the big ones and they just sneak up on you before you know it. I'm Dr. Howard Kraslovich, as you already know. I'm an internist and CEO of a distinguished medical group in town. It's a touch, tricky job, but our clinic has managed to plug along for decades now, imperfect, but prosperous. I sometimes wonder who will follow me as the next clinic CEO. I guess it really doesn't matter, does it? Not in the long run. I'll retire or die and the clinic will keep on going. It makes you wonder what difference we really make, doesn't it? *(Pauses and looks around.)* Sometimes I think I should be devoting more time to clinic management and less to seeing my own personal patients. After all, running a multimillion dollar clinic could be a full time job. But I just can't bring myself to sacrifice the clinical part of medicine. I really do like my patients, at least most of them. And I think they really do appreciate me as a person and a doctor. That sense of trust and appreciation is something precious, something that takes years to develop. No one should fault me for trying to do both administrative work and clinical work. Frankly, I think I've got the best of both worlds. Plus, I'm a valued member of the executive board of Red River Hospital. That's a weighty role as well. Very weighty indeed . . . to the tune of a several hundred million dollars a year or more. That's real money, you know. And isn't that what it's all about in the end? Money? *(Walks off.)*

IVANHOE: (*Enters from off stage.*) I'm Mr. Charles Ivanhoe, CEO of MegaHealth Corporation, a very for profit and very profitable organization. I'm here to talk to you about health care. Health care! The last great unexploited industry in the nation. Can you believe the economic potential? The healthcare industry represents over 16% of our gross national product. Do you understand what that means? Billions of dollars spent for an industry that no one can do without. Cars? You can always walk? Clothes? You could wear the same old rags everyday if you wanted. Houses? Who really needs a million dollar mansion with an indoor pool and Jacuzzi? But health care? *(Pauses.)* When you're sick, you need a doctor. When you're really sick, you need a doctor and a hospital. Then there's the x-rays, the lab tests, the medications. My God! The more you consume, the richer we get. It's heaven, fiscal heaven! And who knows where it will end? Will health care expenditures rise to 25% of the gross national product? Thirty percent? Why not? There's unlimited demand and almost unlimited resources. My God! What economic potential! *(Confidentially to the audience.)* We've already begun, you know. We began by snapping up a few non-profit hospital systems here and there that were teetering on the edge of fiscal doom. And *voilà*! Now they're cash cows and the nucleus of a health care empire that stretches from coast to coast and even overseas. At this point, instead of financial disasters, we're looking for institutional plums with excellent balance sheets and great economic potential. Our investors love us. Wall Street loves us. Those mutual fund managers love us. They can all smell a good thing when they've got it. The cash keeps flowing in . . . from Wall Street, from Medicare, from Medicaid, from the vast army of third party players who just keep shelling out the money and bemoaning the lack of fiscal discipline while they pass on the increased premiums to the public. What a deal! What a life! This is a great country, isn't it? (*Exits, rubbing his hands and gesticulating in wild triumph.*)

WINTHROP: (*Walks on in an elegant, lady-like step. Speaks with a mild Southern accent.*) Hello. I'm Cathy Winthrop. I'm Sister Eterna's counterpart at the Red River Hospital. It's been a fabulous ride for me, from a small town nursing home administrator to the CEO of a distinguished community hospital. Don't think it's been easy. I was the first person in our family to get a college degree, and in healthcare administration no less. It's been very tough. I have had to be tougher than men, smarter than men. I have managed to reach this point by sheer force of will. It has cost me a rather unsavory divorce. My husband could not stand living with such a successful woman, at least that's what I thought. He called it irreconcilable differences. Yeah, irreconcilable with his very large ego and very small penis. I think his secretary pretty much got what she deserved. Yes, I lost my husband, but I've never regretted it. I only regret not losing this Southern accent. It's such a pity. I think I could even make it big in Atlanta, or Dallas, or even New York if it weren't for this residual Southern twang. Now that's a real pity. (*Leaves the stage.*)

GLISSANT: (*Strides on with a haughty step.*) Questions of value. Questions of morality. So tedious and unnecessary. I'm Tracy Glissant, Red River Hospital attorney. Of course I have my other clients, but the hospital is a real horn of plenty. My heavens, someone always suing them: patients, insurance carriers, employees. It's endless. I never get bored and I certainly don't run out of pay checks. The diversity of cases is amazing and the fees are wonderful, always on time. Who cares which side wins because I always get paid. I tell Mrs. Winthrop, Cathy to me, that we have a beautiful mutually beneficial relationship. Win or lose, I win. She worries about all this litigation, but I tell her and the other hospital board members to keep focused on the goal. What goal? Settlement, of course. Sometimes I hear words like justice and honor, right and wrong. It gives me a headache. Just remember one word, I tell them . . . settlement. For us, it also means a juicy contingency fee. You see, it's always a win-win situation for the legal profession. And it couldn't happen to a nicer person . . . ME! (*Points to herself, then bows to the crowd and leaves.*)

EPINEUX: (*Walks in with a military step.*) Hello. I'm Berry Epineux. You've seen me in action already. I'm the Executive Director of the Red River Foundation Board and a full time employee of the Foundation. God bless the Foundation, the offspring of the hospital sale to MegaHealth Corporation. My role is to preserve and protect the Foundation from all its enemies, both internal and external. It would also be nice if we had a positive impact on the community. That's our goal, after all. But in a hundred years, who will know or remember any of this. (*Makes a wide gesture with his arms.*) I have an academic formation in Administration of Charitable Boards. It would be a personal tragedy to see this worthy Foundation not attain its lofty goals, especially since my self esteem and salary depend on it. Efficient administration is my goal. The uplifting of the community is only a happy by-product. With as much money as this Foundation possesses, my job security will be assured until retirement. Why shouldn't my job be exceptionally well reimbursed? After all, it is a worthy organization and heaven help anyone who jeopardizes my mission, or my salary. (*Strides off stage with a military march.*)

SCENE II

(*The previous introductions took place in front of the curtain which now opens to reveal the St. Ursuline's Hospital Winter Ball. A banner to that effect stretches over the stage. Tinsel streamers and strings of tiny, white lights create a festive ambience. Tango melodies play in the background.*)

SR. ETERNA: (*Greets the guests.*) Dr. Kraslovich! So good to see you! Welcome to the winter ball.

DR. KRASLOVICH: (*Dressed in a tuxedo.*) Nice to be here, Sister. Looks like a great turnout.

(There can be an imaginary crowd on panels with silhouettes or other techniques.)

SR. ETERNA: And your lovely wife, Doctor?

DR. KRASLOVICH: She's visiting our boys in Atlanta for the weekend.

SR. ETERNA: *(Pulls the doctor aside a little.)* Could I speak with you a few minutes in private?

DR. KRASLOVICH: Of course. Any time, Sister.

SR. ETERNA: Call me Eterna, please.

DR. KRASLOVICH: Of course, if you'll call me Howard.

SR. ETERNA: Howard, of course. We recognize the great contribution your clinic makes to the hospital and we are looking for ways to solidify our relationship. To firm it up, so to speak. *(Leans very close to the doctor, who backs away.)* We would like to have your clinic into some sort of limited partnership with our hospital, something more exclusive.

DR. KRASLOVICH: Exclusive of Red River Hospital, your competitor, I assume.

SR. ETERNA: Perhaps.

DR. KRASLOVICH: You know that our clinic has always had doctors working at both hospitals, both Red River and St. Ursuline's. St. Ursuline's Hospital is very important to us, but so is the Red River Hospital. After all, they are both non-profit institutions which serve the best interests of the community as a whole. And that's what we're really interested in, the health care of the community as a whole, isn't it?

SR. ETERNA: Of course, Doctor. Howard, I mean. Would you care to dance?

DR. KRASLOVICH: I'm not very good at dancing.

SR. ETERNA: No matter. Neither am I. They were not too keen on dancing at the convent.

(KRASLOVICH *clutches ETERNA and they do a sensual, sophisticated tango with several figures.*)

SR. ETERNA: I didn't know you could dance like that.

DR. KRASLOVICH: You either, for that matter. You do a mean tango. What else do you do that I never suspected?

SR. ETERNA: I'm full of tricks. Good ones, of course.

DR. KRASLOVICH: So it seems.

SR. ETERNA: What would it take to interest you and your medical group in a new doctor's building adjacent to our hospital? We could advance the money for the construction or build it ourselves and lease it back to you at very favorable rates.

DR. KRASLOVICH: That's way too much togetherness for us, Sister. We're just fine where we are, independent from both of the hospitals and somewhere in between.

SR. ETERNA: In between? Geographically, perhaps, but I wouldn't exactly say that your role on the Red River Hospital Board makes you exactly impartial. St. Ursuline's has never had the privilege of having you on their board, not that I can remember.

DR. KRASLOVICH: No, they haven't. But I don't remember ever being asked either.

SR. ETERNA: No, that's true, but things could change.

DR. KRASLOVICH: Things are always changing, and that's part of the problem with life. Just when you think you've got it all figured out, things change around you.

SR. ETERNA: Yes, of course. But if you just stay focused on the mission, then everything will be all right. Remember, my good Doctor, seek ye first the kingdom of heaven, and all things will come to you.

DR. KRASLOVICH: Perhaps you're right. And it's a fascinating thought, but I'm afraid I'll have to ponder it later. I have to be going now, Sister. I've got another social engagement tonight, a dinner at the Café on the Courtableau.

SR. ETERNA Sounds chic.

DR. KRASLOVICH: Just business, I'm afraid.

SR. ETERNA: Give my regards to your wife when she gets back.

DR. KRASLOVICH: Will do. Thanks so much for the party.

SR. ETERNA: And give that building proposal some thought, would you? Our closer association might just be a match made in heaven.

SCENE III

(KRASLOVICH steps forward. The banner for the winter ball and the decorations disappear. A panel with turn-of-the-century script announces the "Café on the Courtableau." There is a table of well-dressed guests including IVANHOE, WINTHROP, and GLISSANT.)

IVANHOE: *(Rises to greet KRASLOVICH.)* Dr. Kraslovich, I believe. I'm Charles Ivanhoe, CEO of MegaHealth Corporation. Call me Charlie, please.

DR. KRASLOVICH: Yes, I'm Doctor Kraslovich. Nice to meet you.

IVANHOE: Kraslovich? That's a Slavic name, isn't it?

DR. KRASLOVICH: Yes. It's Croatian, in fact. But that's several generations ago. My family came over to Louisiana as oyster men originally. Thank heaven for good old American upward social mobility. Otherwise I might still be raking up oysters in Cameron Parish.

IVANHOE: I'll drink to that. A toast to American upward social mobility!

(Everyone raises a glass and drinks.)

DR. KRASLOVICH *(Takes a seat.)* I'm not too late, am I?

(A waltz musette music plays discreetly in the background. It is more suggestive of Paris than Louisiana.)

IVANHOE: No, no. You're just on time. *(Introduces the other guests.)* You know Mrs. Winthrop, of course and Mrs. Glissant.

DR. KRASLOVICH: Of course. Hello Cathy. Hello Tracy.

IVANHOE: I believe you are all aware of why we are here. Our team has studied the accounts of the Red River Hospital and we believe that a sale or merger would be beneficial for both your hospital and MegaHealth Corporation. Since you have traditionally been a not-for-profit hospital, a sale would necessitate the creation of a foundation, the Red River Foundation, for example. The funds generated by the sale would constitute a true philanthropic windfall for the community. Imagine it: public health initiatives, educational grants, vaccinations programs, wellness programs, art funding, and much, much more. The opportunities are unlimited and the funding would all come from interest on the foundation's assets. It's a once in a lifetime opportunity, ladies and gentlemen. I am sure you see the possibilities for yourselves as well as for the hospital and the community as a whole.

WINTHROP: As current CEO of the Red River Hospital, I do not have a voting role on the board. As you all know, the hospital, while fiscally very sound, remains very vulnerable in this period of mergers and downsizing. We all realize that the current market conditions favor economies of scale. Our religious competitors at St. Ursuline's have amassed considerable economic reserves and we are left to our own devices. This sale to MegaHealth Corporation represents a heaven sent opportunity to assure the solvency of the Red River Hospital for decades to come. And then there is the added benefit of the creation of a well-funded, world-class foundation which would continue as a compliment to the other charitable works of the hospital. What a unique opportunity. I agree with Mr. Ivanhoe completely and support the concept of a sale of Red River Hospital to MegaHealth Corporation.

DR. KRASLOVICH: (*To WINTHROP.*) Two questions? The first question is whether we can legally sell a non-profit hospital to a publicly traded for-profit corporation? The second is whether the current financial state of the hospital is so precarious that it really dictates a sale at this time?

WINTHROP: Dr. Kraslovich, Howard. Let me answer the second question first. Due to our recent series of acquisitions of outlying community hospitals and physician practices, we have over a hundred million in outstanding debt. MegaHealth Corporation is willing to assume that debt, plus provide 250 million for the creation of the Red River Foundation as payment for the equity in our current structure.

DR. KRASLOVICH: Two hundred and fifty million! That means they will pay 350 million for the whole thing. Is that true?

IVANHOE: Yes! Let me answer that for my friend, Mrs. Winthrop. Yes, Red River Hospital does have debt, but your accounts receivable are solid. You have significant market share. And we are convinced we can both make a profit and sustain the growth and development that your board, of which you are an important member and current CEO have so successfully achieved.

DR. KRASLOVICH: (*To WINTHROP.*) And what about the other question? Is it legal? Can we sell a not-for-profit community hospital without consulting the community?

WINTHROP: I'll let Mrs. Glissant, the attorney for the hospital, answer that question.

GLISSANT: Hello Howard. How are your wife and children?

DR. KRASLOVICH: Doing very well, Tracy. Thank you, and yours?

GLISSANT: Good. My youngest is having her second child in March. Thank you for asking. Now let me get to the heart of the subject. I have carefully studied the original hospital charter as well as subsequent modifications. It is my professional opinion that the hospital board can legally sell the hospital under the conditions offered by MegaHealth Corporation. It's as simple as that. The hospital board can act with complete autonomy. There need not be any vote of the general medical staff. In fact, including the staff in the discussion may significantly complicate the proceedings. Any other questions?

DR. KRASLOVICH: I have a third question. If, in fact, this is both technically and legally feasible, is such a sale morally correct?

WINTHROP: (*To KRASLOVICH.*) What do you mean exactly?

DR. KRASLOVICH: I mean, we are converting a not-for-profit community-based institution into a for-profit publicly owned one. And those profits will no longer remain in the community. They will be siphoned out to investors all over the country. Is the good that comes out of the sale commensurate with the loss of resources and the loss of local, community control?

IVANHOE: Control, control. Good heavens, Dr. Kraslovich, Howard, I mean. It sounds as if we have an antagonist, adversarial relationship. There is nothing further from the truth. We will be synergistic, not antagonistic. Brothers in pursuit of health care, not Cain and Abel. The advantages of scale and the glorious impact of a foundation will largely offset any loss of control. Besides, this is a 50/50 deal, a shared control and what's more, if the board isn't convinced after a trial period, you can always buy us out and end the deal, pure and simple. The sale will be totally reversible after a trial period.

DR. KRASLOVICH: Really? You mean we will be able to buy you out of the sale?

IVANHOE: Of course, you have my word.

DR. KRASLOVICH: But can we make a decision of this magnitude without consulting the medical staff or the community?

WINTHROP: You've lived in this community for years. You know the complexity of the issues. You know the simplicity of the general public and the terrible nit-picking of the medical staff. Every time we try some innovation, there are always countless negative comments and needless complications from the doctors of the medical staff. Don't you think that's a formula for disaster? Imagine the debates. Imagine the wrangling. Imagine the misconceptions and potential hostility and turmoil.

DR. KRASLOVICH: But . . . .

WINTHROP: (*To KRASLOVICH.*) No buts about it. I know you're a fine doctor, but you sometimes like to complicate things unnecessarily. Remember, keep it simple, stupid. That's K-I-S-S for short. (*The background music is playing a little louder.*) Care for a little waltz tonight. I've heard you're quite the dancer.

IVANHOE: I think we should all dance.

> (*WINTHROP takes KRASLOVICH. IVANHOE takes GLISSANT and they all laugh and dance a wonderful waltz musette. After the dance, they return to the table for a bottle of champagne.*)

WINTHROP: This calls for champagne.

IVANHOE: A toast to the Red River MegaHealth Hospital.

GLISSANT: Here! Here!

DR. KRASLOVICH: *(Somewhat reluctantly)* To our health. Santé.

WINTHROP: The whole board meets next Tuesday. But with Dr. Kraslovich's support and Mrs. Glissant's legal analysis, it should be a done deal. Another glass, everyone! To the sale of the Red River Hospital to MegaHealth Corporation!

ALL: To the sale!

SCENE IV

(Stage goes dark. The "Café on the Courtableau" is replaced by the very flashy "Avoyelles Casino." There are a few slot machines, if possible, although they can be represented by a slide projection. There is a background casino noise which is suggestive, but not loud enough to drown out the dialogue. ETERNA is working the slot machine as she waits for IVANHOE to arrive.)

SR. ETERNA: Mr. Ivanhoe! *(Gestures to IVANHOE.)* Over here! *(Gets off the stool and goes to greet IVANHOE.)* So glad you could meet me here today.

IVANHOE: No problem, Sister. It's a pleasure.

SR. ETERNA: Please, call me Eterna.

MR. IVANHOE: Call me Charles.

SR. ETERNA: Okay, Charles. Have a seat. *(Gestures to one of the high stools in front of the slots. Points to one.)* Do you gamble?

IVANHOE: Of course. But I thought it might be forbidden for you ladies to gamble.

SR. ETERNA: No, not at all. After all, evil is in the intent, not just in the deed.

IVANHOE: Speaking of intent, what is your intent concerning our offer to purchase St. Ursuline's?

SR. ETERNA: My personal intent, or that of the Sisters of Perpetual Succor?

MR. IVANHOE: The sisters, of course.

SR. ETERNA: *(Pulls on the slot a couple more times. Bangs the machine with her fist.)* Damn thing! Oh, excuse me. Well, we did meet in the home convent in San Bernardino last week. We discussed your offer very seriously. As you must know, the sale of the entire Sisters of Perpetual Succor medical system to MegaHealth Corporation represents a momentous proposition. The discussion proved to be most interesting and very passionate, even by religious standards. There were a few important questions raised, however.

IVANHOE: Such as?

SR. ETERNA: Would the sisters retain any control over the health care facilities or just the charitable foundation created by the sale?

IVANHOE: In your particular case, the sisters would retain control only over your new foundation. In that way, you would be relieved of the drudgery of running the hospitals and you could just concentrate on doing good works. All that administrative burden would be lifted from your frail, but very capable shoulders.

SR. ETERNA: Ah, my shoulders are frail, but my fellow sisters help me carry the burden, and Christ carries us all, of course.

IVANHOE: Amen. *(Bows his head and closes his eyes briefly.)*

SR. ETERNA: Thank you. *(Pauses.)* Now, the other question involves our competitor across town, the Red River Health System. We were interested in knowing if you had made a similar purchase offer to them. And, if so, what would be the anti-trust implications if MegaHealth Corporation owned both hospital systems in a single market area?

IVANHOE: You ladies certainly don't miss a beat, do you?

SR. ETERNA: No, we don't. Not if we can help it.

IVANHOE: Well, the truth is that we have not yet made a similar offer to Red River. If we were able to purchase both hospital systems, we would have to divest one or the other to a disinterested third party. Frankly, that would prove both financially onerous and logistically difficult.

SR. ETERNA: *(Pulls on her slot machine.)* Three Cherries! I've won! I won! *(There is a clinging of coins falling from the machine. ETERNA scoops out her winnings into a plastic bucket.)* I love the old style machines, don't you? Nothing like the clatter of coins and the dirt on your fingers. Look at all that!

IVANHOE: *(Casually interested)* How much?

SR. ETERNA: About 20 dollars in nickels. Not bad for a two dollar investment.

IVANHOE: You're a lucky lady. When can we expect an answer about our purchase proposal?

SR. ETERNA: All things in due time. It's something we really have to pray about. After all, our hospital system is an expression of the healing ministry of Jesus Christ. That's not the sort of thing you sell lightly, even if a charitable foundation is formed in the process. There's something a little Judas Iscariot about it, don't you think? Selling out to a for-profit? *(Some Cajun music begins to play. It can be a Cajun jitterbug. ETERNA stops to listen.)* Do you dance?

IVANHOE: A little.

SR. ETERNA: It's a Cajun jitterbug. Not too hard. *(Grabs him.)* Just move your right foot forward and back, then give me a spin every once in awhile.

(They dance. IVANHOE spins ETERNA.)

SR. ETERNA: Yes! Yes, that's it. You're a great dancer, Charles.

IVANHOE: Flattery will get you everywhere, Eterna.

(They continue to dance as the lights fade on the Avoyelles Casino.)

SCENE V

(ETERNA's office. There is a large crucifix suspended or sitting on the desk. A stained glass window is suspended as well and lit from behind. SR. ETERNA works with some papers on the desk. KRASLOVICH enters.)

SR. ETERNA: Howard, come in, sit down. I wasn't expecting you.

DR. KRASLOVICH: Are you free for a couple of minutes, Sister?

SR. ETERNA: For you, any time. Sit down.

DR. KRASLOVICH: I heard that MegaHealth made an offer to buy you out. You refused Ivanhoe's offer didn't you?

SR. ETERNA: Yes, we did refuse it. It was tempting, very tempting. But, in the end, we refused.

DR. KRASLOVICH: *(Pauses, sighs)* Have you heard the latest?

SR. ETERNA: What are you talking about?

DR. KRASLOVICH: The medical staff and the local Ecumenical Convention are filing a lawsuit against the Red River Hospital Board members who voted to sell the hospital and create the Foundation.

SR. ETERNA: Can they?

DR. KRASLOVICH: Sure, anyone can sue. But it's hard to believe they could raise the money to pay the lawyers. Some doctors are involved and are furious about the whole transaction. They claim we changed the hospital charter and illegally sold the hospital without medical staff or community input.

SR. ETERNA: Is it true?

DR. KRASLOVICH: Yes and no. We did sell it without any medical staff or community input. That's true. But we didn't have to change the hospital charter or medical bylaws to do it. Even if the absence of input is true, we were completely within our legal rights. They don't have a legal leg to stand on. The hospital board could dispose of the hospital in any way it pleased. At least that's what Mrs. Glissant, the hospital lawyer, tells us and she's one of the best. It's just messy and unpleasant. *(Pauses again.)* Why did you refuse Ivanhoe's offer to buy St. Ursuline's?

SR. ETERNA: We felt that health care was still our mission, Christ's mission of healing. And that we were unwilling to give that up for the luxury of only managing a charitable foundation, regardless of how large.

DR. KRASLOVICH: It's amazing the amount of hostility our new Foundation has generated. Who would believe it? It's giving away millions of dollars for health care, education and the arts and somehow it's being viewed an evil by-product of an immoral sale by some members of the community, especially some of my physician colleagues. They say the Foundation is the new 900 pound gorilla of the local charitable world, crushing all the other organizations in its footsteps. *(Pauses.)* Was it a mistake to sell out?

SR. ETERNA: *(Shrugs her shoulders.)* We didn't do it. We asked around. We prayed. *(Makes a praying gesture, and then crosses herself and bows her head briefly.)* Some other non-profits told us that the creation of a foundation was just a lure, a trick to get you to sell the hospital. Maybe it is. Maybe it isn't. But you can certainly still do good with the money.

(Choral music drifts in from the nearby convent. It's a woman's chorus singing sacred music of some sort, perhaps in Latin.)

DR. KRASLOVICH: Was it your mission statement that kept you from selling you hospital system to MegaHealth? Is that what kept you on your chosen course?

SR. ETERNA: Mission statement. Yes, we do have a great one, you know. It's all full of idealism, virtue, love and beneficence. And Christianity, of course. *(Pauses.)* It's odd. I recently went to a meeting . . . a business course. The professor laughed aloud at the idea of mission statements. He said they were used by hypocrites to manipulate fools. Isn't that interesting? He said that when we evoke "the mission" or "the church," even "God," we are just evoking abstractions. He said that no one could or should even respond to such appeals. *(Stands and begins to walk around.)* When I ask the employees to give up their raises or forgo their time off "for the sake of the mission," it's really just something I'm asking them do for me. I'm the real beneficiary. If they like me personally, if they believe in me personally, then they might comply. But for "the Church" or "the hospital?" It's tough to get people to make sacrifices for such abstractions. They might do it for the Pope because he's someone real, tangible, credible. But not for some institution they hardly understand and certainly not for pure altruism. When we ask people to go the extra mile, they must have the perception that it benefits them. And they must want to help the individual asking for their help. They might do it for Christ if they have some very personal conception of him, although I suspect that would be the exception and not the rule. *(Pauses again, returning to her desk.)* It's odd, but I seem to have lost a little of my faith that day. That conference I went to had the strange effect of deflating my missionary zeal. Poof! *(Makes a rapid outward gestures with her arms.)* Like a balloon when it's punctured. Strange, isn't it?

DR. KRASLOVICH: I think I understand. Or maybe I just don't want to understand, at least not yet. I really wanted to do the right thing by creating the Foundation. How could I predict that our noble initiative would rip apart the community and get me sued to boot? How did you know?

SR. ETERNA: Know what?

DR. KRASLOVICH: Know to refuse Ivanhoe's offer.

SR. ETERNA: *(Shrugs her shoulders.)* It would be nice to tell you that our decision was some mysterious sixth sense, or perhaps divine intervention. But that simply wouldn't be the truth. I guess we were just lucky.

DR. KRASLOVICH: You know that Ivanhoe lied about the buy back clause? They never had any intention of letting us buy back the hospital. It was a marriage made in hell, and the road was paved with good intentions.

SR. ETERNA: The road to hell is always paved with good intentions.

DR. KRASLOVICH: Now Ivanhoe's out of MegaHealth. From what I hear, he may be in federal prison for Medicare fraud. Winthrop's skipped town, but not before collecting a big bonus from MegaHealth. And Glissant is keeping a very low profile as she invests her considerable contingency fee from the hospital sale. Our Foundation is under attack. And I'm being sued personally for my role in the decision making.

SR. ETERNA: And the hospital is doing fine, I suppose.

DR. KRASLOVICH: I don't even know about that. All I know is that they're always talking about their damn profit margin. What does this cost? How much does that cost? What will reduce the length of stay? How can this or that procedure be better reimbursed? My God, it's the economics of health care. If I hear the words profit margin once more, I'll puke.

SR. ETERNA: Once the Sisters of Perpetual Succor were considered the evil outside influence in this community. We were supposedly controlled from San Bernardino or the Vatican or from wherever. You remember that, don't you? Everyone said that the Papist were going to take over.

285

DR. KRASLOVICH: Sure, I remember. Now MegaHealth Corporation is the evil outside influence. They're the profit margin masters and the sisters are the saintly masters of the mission. Nice turnaround.

SR. ETERNA: My good doctor, my good friend. Remember there is no mission without a margin whether it is at St. Ursuline's or Red River Hospital.

(*The sound of the choral music has increased. It is in 3/4, or waltz time, "Let There Be Peace on Earth, and Let It Begin with Me." ETERNA comes around from the desk and offers her hand to KRASLOVICH.*)

SR. ETERNA: Perhaps a dance will cheer you up a bit. It's a slow waltz step, very sacred, of course.

DR. KRASLOVICH: I don't feel much like dancing.

SR. ETERNA: Come on now, indulge me. Don't be such a sour-puss.

(*ETERNA takes KRASLOVICH in dance position. They dance around as the music increases in volume and tempo until they are spinning around in a fast, elegant waltz. They circle around and dance off stage as the lights dim to dark. The curtain closes.*)

SCENE VI

(*KRASLOVICH steps forward in front of the curtain into a circle of light and begins speaking.*)

DR. KRASLOVICH: (*Sighs and shrugs his shoulders.*) They all disappeared. Ivanhoe's supposedly in jail somewhere. After those accusations of Medicare fraud, he just had to go. MegaHealth Corporation let him drop like a hot, infected potato. What did he care? He may lose a few million, but he probably has a hundred million stashed away in the Bahamas. As for our distinguished hospital

CEO, Mrs. Cathy Winthrop, she took off almost as soon as the sale was finalized. Evil tongues in the community say that she pocketed a few hundred thousand in bonuses before she took off for greener, friendlier pastures. I guess impropriety would be hard to prove under the circumstances. After all, she was only doing her job. I wonder how she feels now? Selling out her own hospital, then disappearing like a thief into the night. I even heard she took a job at a Catholic hospital. Maybe prayer will help her out. *(Pauses again and looks around.)* Mrs. Glissant, our distinguished consultant attorney is still around. I hear she's going to be president of the state bar association. Now that's something to think about. *(Pauses again.)* All that talk about a lawsuit against the hospital board, it just fizzled out. Frankly, I suspect no one really wanted to take on the multimillion dollar foundation with their almost unlimited cash reserves for legal defense. It's odd, but when I learned the lawsuit project had been dropped, you would have thought I would have felt good. But no, I really didn't. I even felt disappointed in a perverse sort of way. *(Pauses.)* And then there's me, another survivor. I'm still practicing medicine. I'm still on the hospital board and I'm still on the Red River Foundation Board as well. Working on the Foundation Board is tough, you know. Mr. Epineux is one mean task master. He has an extensive background in charitable boards. He's also got a six figure salary as Executive Director, and access to a lot of money. On the Board, we agonize over how to give away the millions of dollars spun off from the sale of the hospital. Giving money away is much more difficult than I ever imagined. There's education, health initiatives, the arts, economic development, community outreach projects by the dozens. And what's amazing is that they are all good projects. Imagine that. Every organization that asks for money is doing good. And you would think that giving money to all these fine people would give me that warm, fuzzy feeling inside. But it doesn't. All I do is keep thinking about the sale of the hospital to MegaHealth and wondering if it was the right thing to do. *(Pauses again and sighs.)* Can great good spring from great evil? Can the Red River Foundation buy back the good will of the community and, if so, at what price? I just can't get it out of my mind. Each time I look at one of those glossy Foundation publications or see one of those huge Foundation billboards extolling some recent project, I wonder again: At what price, good will? The saddest part is that I can't even shut it off at night. I wake up in a sweat from the same nightmare. Mr. Epineux is squeezing the life out of me while he laughs. I try to take a deep breath, but he holds me so tightly, I can't get any air. I struggle and kick, but he keeps on laughing until I feel the life drain out of me. Then I wake up, drenched in sweat. It's horrible. Why on earth would I have a nightmare like that when working with an organization that's a dream come true for the community?

SCENE VII

(The curtain opens and reveals an elegantly set dinner table with an animated party going on. The guest includes ETERNA, IVANHOE, WINTHROP, GLISSANT and EPINEUX, President of the Red River Foundation. EPINEUX rises and signals to KRASLOVICH to join them.)

EPINEUX: Come in, Doctor. The dinner's getting cold. *(Pulls out a chair and seats KRASLOVICH.)* You look shocked to see us all here together tonight. It's just a gathering of old friends.

DR. KRASLOVICH: Well, frankly I am a bit shocked. I expected you, as President of the Foundation to be here, but I really didn't expect to see any of the others here tonight.

SR. ETERNA: *(To KRASLOVICH.)* I'm delighted to see you. *(Goes over and they exchange a friendly hug.)*

DR. KRASLOVICH: Sister, it's always a pleasure. *(Turns to face IVANHOE.)*

IVANHOE: Surprised to see me? I guess you thought I might be in jail, didn't you?

DR. KRASLOVICH: Perhaps not in jail, but at least not here. I thought you had fallen from favor.

IVANHOE: Ah yes, my fall from grace at MegaHealth Corporation. Maybe I did, but I sure took a few big wigs down with me. (*Laughs loudly and continues in a conspiratorial tone.*) And I do have a little nest egg hidden out of harm's way.

WINTHROP: (*To KRASLOVICH.*) Howard, dear friend. I wouldn't miss the opportunity of seeing you again, even if I did move out of town rather precipitously without even leaving you a forwarding address.

DR. KRASLOVICH: (To WINTHROP.) Of course, a pleasure to see you, too.

EPINEUX: As Executive Director of the Red River Foundation and President of the Board, I'd like to propose a toast. (*Raises his glass and all the others to too. KRASLOVICH raises his glass only slightly.*) To the painful birth of a magnificent organization, the Red River Foundation.

ALL: Here, here! To the Foundation!

DR. KRASLOVICH: (*Keeps his glass noticeably low. Turns to IVANHOE.*) I really am surprised to see you here. Did you plan this evening like you planned everything else that has already happened?

IVANHOE: My dear doctor, of course I planned this evening, just like I planned the formation of the Foundation, with a little help from my friends. Our team at MegaHealth already tried this technique in other parts of the country with people a lot more sophisticated than you folks here, no insult intended. It worked elsewhere and it worked here. Why should you be any different? After all, everyone everywhere has their price, n'est-ce pas, Cathy? (*Turns to WINTHROP and gives her a little pinch.*) Some business people, just like some whores, are more expensive than others.

MRS. WINTHROP: Oh really, Charles, do you always have to be so blunt?

MR. IVANHOE: Blunt? I can also be soft and penetrating, too. You should know that better than anyone, shouldn't you?

WINTHROP: Oh, shut up, you greedy pervert!

GLISSANT: Come! Come! We're all friends here. Can't we maintain a little civility?

IVANHOE: (*To GLISSANT.*) Civility, you talk about civility. Why, you screwed your own community, got a big legal commission, and then went on to sit on the Board of the Foundation where you can rake in the legal fees from them and from MegaHealth. Talk about civility. You can prostitute yourself from both sides and still be giving a blow job at the same time. Now that's a talent. I don't know about civility. (*Laughs very loudly.*)

GLISSANT: (*To IVANHOE.*) You can laugh now. But the federal government will have a field day with you and none of your high priced Eastern lawyers will be able to keep you out of prison either.

IVANHOE: (*To GLISSANT.*) High priced? You certainly should know a thing or two about that, Tracy. Your East Coast colleagues have something to learn from you on that score. Wow! You were as expensive as they come, my dear, and I have seen some pricey tarts.

SR. ETERNA: Now, now, you two. Let's let bygones be bygones. We've all moved or changed in some way, hopefully for the better. I've personally moved to an even higher level in the administration of the Sisters of Perpetual Succor. Now I practically run the whole show. My philosophy is one of forgiveness. Look at Cathy. We forgave her and now she's even working for one of our hospitals . . . in another state of course. (*ETERNA puts her hand on WINTHROP's hand.*) I think Cathy has seen the error of her ways and opened up to a more charitable, loving approach to health care administration. Haven't you?

WINTHROP: Yes, Sister, I have. (*Leans over to ETERNA and they exchange a friendly kiss.*) Now I know the meaning of warm, loving relationships in the context of Christian values of charity and the healing ministry of Jesus Christ.

(ETERNA crosses herself, then both women give each other a long, very sensual hug.)

IVANHOE: *(Laughs loudly.)* *(To WINTHROP.)* What bullshit! Cathy, you'd go to bed with anyone if you got the right price, even if it were the Pope himself.

SR. ETERNA: *(To IVANHOE.)* Be quiet! I'm sure you know the story of Christ and the adulteress.

IVANHOE: Sure I do, but the difference is that she presumably stopped screwing people after Christ told her to go and sin no more.

ETERNA: *(To IVANHOE.)* Don't be vulgar, Charles! Taking Christ's name in vain is a sin and I'm sure you're not interested in adding to your anticipated time in purgatory.

IVANHOE: *(Laughs.)* Well, if you can call a minimum security white-collar prison purgatory, I guess I'll take my chances.

GLISSANT : *(To KRASLOVICH.)* You've been awfully quiet. Aren't you proud of the work of the Foundation? It's been a real success story.

DR. KRASLOVICH: Yes, I'm impressed. The Foundation has done some very important work. But I can't get the feeling of betrayal out of my mind.

EPINEUX: Betrayal!

DR. KRASLOVICH: *(To EPINEUX.)* Yes, Berry, betrayal. You're President of the Foundation. You seem to be fully committed to its success. You don't seem to have any lingering afterthoughts or hesitation. Why?

MR. EPINEUX: Afterthoughts? Hesitations? Of course not. Our Foundation is an absolute good, and it's here for good as well. *(Pauses)* That sound's catchy doesn't it? Here for good. Perhaps we can use it in some publicity.

DR. KRASLOVICH: But can good be spawned from evil? Does the end justify the means?

EPINEUX: Evil? What are you talking about?

DR. KRASLOVICH: Well, perhaps not evil, but a questionable, or maybe just a debatable decision.

EPINEUX: (*To KRASLOVICH.*) Debatable? Questionable? What's questionable or debatable about funding adult education, nursing, economic development, the arts, health initiatives all around this area? Let me ask you this, who in their right mind would not support those projects?

DR. KRASLOVICH: Of course those are good and noble activities. But MegaHealth takes 20% profits out of this area and ships them off to its share holders all over the world.

MR. IVANHOE: So?

DR. KRASLOVICH: All that hospital profit leaves the community, doesn't it? That philosophy of satisfying the shareholders changes the character of the institution, doesn't it?

IVANHOE: Of course it does! And if it were up to me, I would take 30% profits out of this dump. Screw the community!

GLISSANT: (*To IVANHOE.*) I believe that you're already in quite a bit of trouble. Do you really want to aggravate your case?

IVANHOE: My case is one for economic development, unbridled capitalism, that magnificent greed that made this country great. And those forces will continue to operate, even in this little backwater town. Your stupid little Red River Hospital is nothing but a profit center. Nothing more. Nothing less. Even Sister Eterna left this town for greener pastures, spiritually speaking, of course. (*Turns to ETERNA.*) Isn't that so, Sister.

SR. ETERNA: I only follow God's will. *(Taps WINTHROP's hand as she speaks.)* And Cathy's following his will, too. Isn't that so, my dear?

(ETERNA and WINTHROP exchange another lingering kiss.)

WINTHROP: *(To ETERNA.)* Yes, it is true. *(Brushes back the hair on ETERNA's head with a loving gesture.)*

IVANHOE: Oh, please. Do we have to excuse you ladies to go out for a love fest or what?

GLISSANT: *(To IVANHOE.)* That's close to slander and it's blasphemy to boot. Stop while you're just a little bit ahead, you sleaze.

IVANHOE: Me, a sleaze! Well you're a hypocrite! You're just luckier, or maybe smarter, than I am, you legal sidewinder. You've got your hand so far into the cookie jar that it would take the good Dr. Kraslovich forceps to extract it.

MR. EPINEUX: *(Taps on a glass to draw attention.)* Gentlemen, ladies. Please. Calm down. I represent the Foundation and only two of you are board members, *(Turns to GLISSANT and KRASLOVICH.)* As for Mrs. Glissant, I think we can be certain of your loyalty to the Foundation. But as for Dr. Kraslovich, Howard, it seems to me that you are vacillating. Is that true?

DR. KRASLOVICH: I . . . I don't really know. It just feel bad sometimes. I feel . . . dirty somehow.

(The other members of the party, except EPINEUX, rise one by one and slowly turn their chairs backwards and sit down. Only EPINEUX is left facing the doctor.)

EPINEUX: *(To KRASLOVICH.)* As members of the Foundation Board, we understand the importance of different opinions and diversity of view points, but we can not tolerate doubt about the underlying integrity of our mission.

SR. ETERNA: *(Turns briefly to face the audience)* Mission! Mission! There is no mission without a margin!

WINTHROP: Mission! There is no mission without money!

GLISSANT and IVANHOE: *(Also turn briefly to face the audience)* Money! Money! Money! Money IS the mission. Money is OUR mission!

> (IVANHOE *stands and takes GLISSANT by one hand and WINTHROP by the other toform a trio. To the music of "Love Makes the World Go Round," IVANHOE spins the ladies around. Then WINTHROP goes under the arch formed by IVANHOE and GLISSANT. Then GLISSANT does the same with the arch formed by IVANHOE and WINTHROP. As they turn, they sing.)*

"Cash makes the world go round,

Cash makes the world go round.

Love may be good for dummies,

But cash makes the world go round."

SR. ETERNA: *(Laughs and claps at their antics.)* Wonderful! So witty!

> *(The music stops and the dancers return to their seats to catch their breath.)*

EPINEUX: *(Pulls KRASLOVICH stage forward.)* If your views are so irreconcilable with our own, perhaps you should withdraw from the Foundation Board?

DR. KRASLOVICH: Withdraw?

EPINEUX: Yes, withdraw or you can be voted out. What would you prefer?

SR. ETERNA: *(Spins around with her arms held out.)* This is entirely too tense. I think we need to continue with a little dancing to decrease the tension. What do you say, ladies and gentlemen? Form a line and let's do a little "Cotton Eyed Joe."

DR. KRASLOVICH: I'm really not in a mood for dancing, Sister. These people are about to boot me off the Board. Do you think dancing is really appropriate under the circumstances?

SR. ETERNA: Oh, for heaven's sake, do I always have to force you to have a little fun? *(Grabs KRASLOVICH and pulls him over to the others.)* Now, let's form a line. Come on now, Howard. Don't be a stick in the mud. *(Pulls KRASLOVICH over.)* Now put your hands out and grab the person's hand who is two down from you. *(They form a front basket hold.)* That's right. Now cross your right foot in front, and then kick it out. And one-two-three forward. Good. Now, with the left. Cross, kick and one-two-three. Perfect. Let's try it with music!

(Cotton Eyed Joe begins and the actors begin to dance. They do several turns, pivoting round the stage. One by one, the dances drop off until only KRASLOVICH remains on one side of the stage while the others are clustered off to the other side.)

SCENE VIII

DR. KRASLOVICH: So, that was the beginning of the end. Mr. Epineux pronounced the first accusation of irreconcilable philosophical differences between the Foundation Board and myself. Then the rumor mill started to spin. Faster and faster. Louder and louder.

WINTHROP: Did you hear that Dr. Kraslovich opposes childhood vaccination? It's incredible, isn't it? Why, he doesn't approve of any of the Foundation's health care initiatives in the rural parishes at all. That's where the biggest medical need exists and the highest percentage of uninsured and under-insured patients. Can you imagine! And a doctor no less.

OTHERS: No! You don't say!

GLISSANT: Did you know that Dr. Kraslovich opposes the construction of the new arts center? I heard he said that this town didn't need a new theater, but that it needed more monster truck rallies and barbecue cooking contests since we didn't have any cultural needs.

OTHERS: No! You don't say!

IVANHOE: Did you hear that Dr. Kraslovich opposes economic development in the community? I heard he didn't want the downtown development district because it would only benefit the blacks. Can you believe he made such racist remarks? He even wants to dissolve the Foundation and give the money back to the rich doctors.

OTHERS: No! You don't say!

SR. ETERNA: But why? Why would he oppose downtown development?

GLISSANT: (*To ETERNA.*) Sister, the fact is that he doesn't want progress. He wants the place to be like it was before. He wants the rich, old families, and the doctors to control everything. It's positively selfish and destructive. I would say that his attitude is really immoral.

SR. ETERNA: But why? What motivation could he have to oppose such positive initiatives?

GLISSANT: Power. He wants all the power for himself. He wants all the power so he can control the money and the hospital. That's all I can figure. It's just so incredibly greedy.

IVANHOE: Did you hear that Dr. Kraslovich wants to take away the adult education money, and the Head Start program money, and the technical education funds out of the Foundation budget? Can you believe it; he's opposed to all education? He just wants everyone here to remain ignorant and poor so the educated few, such as himself, can control everything and continue to exploit the rest.

OTHERS: No! You don't say!

WINTHROP: Has the doctor lost his mind completely? Could it be early senility? Has anyone suggested a psychiatric evaluation?

EPINEUX: Who knows? It does sound crazy, doesn't it? Who would want to go to a doctor like that? He must lack all sense of judgment, medical and otherwise. I wonder if he should even be allowed to practice medicine. Who would go to a doctor like that? *(Turning to WINTHROP.)* Would you?

WINTHROP: Heavens no! I still have some sense of judgment.

EPINEUX: *(Turns to GLISSANT.)* Would you?

GLISSANT: Hell no! I think he should be reported to the Board of Medical Examiners to suspend his license. That would get rid of him.

SR. ETERNA: Please, some charity. Dr. Kraslovich is a good man, a good doctor. I've known him for years.

EPINEUX: *(To ETERNA.)* He's changed since you've been away from town. That's all I can say. He used to have sound judgment and be a team player. But that's all finished. Every since the sale of the hospital, something evil happened to him. He's a source of doubt and dissension.

WINTHROP: Could it be drugs or alcohol? Perhaps he's an impaired physician?

GLISSANT: Or a mid-life crisis? Or, worse yet, Alzheimer's? Perhaps we ought to get a court mandated psychiatric evaluation. I know a judge who could help us out. He owes me a favor or two.

EPINEUX: My question is why doesn't he just retire? At the least, he should have the decency to get off the Red River Foundation Board. Why would anyone want someone like that sabotaging their efforts to benefit the community?

GLISSANT: He definitely needs to be removed. If it's not a legal issue, than it's a moral imperative. He's become destructive, unstable. It can't be good for the Foundation or for the many present and future projects that depend on clear thinking. His presence is a threat to those projects.

SR. ETERNA: And to the community as a whole, for that matter. We must always think of the greater good, however painful that may be sometimes. Christ sacrificed himself for the greater good. And I'm sure Dr. Kraslovich will be willing to do the same.

EPINEUX: Exactly. So I take it we all agree. Dr. Kraslovich must be removed from the Foundation Board. He has got to go.

ALL: Yes, we agree.

EPINEUX: Then I can take him that message from the Board?

ALL: Yes!

> (EPINEUX walks over to KRASLOVICH. The circle of light which illuminated the other group now fades to black. The two men are now in the only circle of light.)

EPINEUX: Howard, we know this will be hard on you, but I think it is in the best interest of everyone.

DR. KRASLOVICH: Everyone, or just you personally?

EPINEUX: Please don't make this any harder than it has to be. Your removal from the board, either voluntarily or not, is for the best.

DR. KRASLOVICH: The best, eh? Whose best? Your best or mine?

EPINEUX: Are you going to spare us the embarrassment of a formal vote, or are you going to offer your resignation? Either way, you will leave the Foundation Board.

(The stage darkens and the curtains close. KRASLOVICH walks forward into a pool of light. Meanwhile, the stage is cleared behind the curtains.)

DR. KRASLOVICH: Well, you know the rest of the story. They voted me out. I went from being an honored member of the team to a dangerous subversive. Do I look subversive? I don't think so. (*Turns around and looks at himself.*) You'll be glad to hear that the Foundation has done very well without me. The remaining members of the Board had no problems finding another outstanding, civic-minded community citizen to replace me. It was a financial planner, I believe, who just happens to manage the large accounts of several Board Members. Such a coincidence. (*Pauses.*) They have gone on to fund excellent projects in health, the arts, education, and economic development. Yet they have never answered the question of whether the end justifies the means. Are positive social programs possible when they money comes from such a dubious source as the sale of a not-for-profit hospital? And perhaps that is a question for much more subtle philosophical minds than theirs or mine. I have not been able to answer that question, but I do feel that I have acted according to my conscience. For that, perhaps I may well go to heaven, if heaven indeed exists.

(The curtains open and the Sousa march, "Stars and Stripes Forever," starts to play very loudly. The other actors dance onto the stage. They skip and hold hands while they dance in a joyful serpentine movement. The first and last actors wave their hands as they circle around the doctor who watches them. The last one in line is ETERNA, who drops off to take the doctor. She and KRASLOVICH dance a rapid Scottish step (two polka steps followed by four fast pivoting steps) to the same music as the others circle around them skipping. The other actors skip off the stage and KRASLOVICH and ETERNA follow, still dancing the Scottish step. The lights dim to dark and the actors do NOT re-enter the stage for a bow. The last strains of "Stars and Stripes Forever" end abruptly as the musical refrain ends.)

THE END

HANGING BY A THREAD

CAST OF CHARACTERS

CARL HAMPTON: Helen Hampton's son. Middle aged man in his fifties or sixties. Well-dressed and well-spoken.

BETTY HAMPTON: Helen Hampton's daughter. Middle aged women in her fifties or sixties. More frumpy appearance.

HELEN HAMPTON: Mother. Old lady in her eighties or nineties. She wears a hospital gown and has a feeding tube sticking out of her stomach, which she plays with from time to time.

FRED HAMPTON: Helen's deceased husband. Old man in his seventies or eighties. Very frumpy, despite a suit. Speaks with a nasal drawl, which can be vaguely country.

DORIS: Home health and hospice nurse. Young woman in her late twenties or thirties. Not an educated speech pattern.

DR. FRANKLIN: Hampton family physician. Middle aged man in his late fifties or sixties. Dressed in a white lab coat, not scrubs. He always wears a tie. He never wears his stethoscope around his neck.

The characters may be any race or combination of races according to the director's discretion.

SETTING

Varies with the scene. There do not have to be complicated set changes, since the scenes can be all on the stage and simply be indicated with the lighting.

SCENE I

(The stage is nearly empty. There is a large hospital bed in the center with a bedside stand. Mrs. HELEN HAMPTON is lying there. There are various tubes coming out from the bed: a Foley catheter with urine in it, a gastrostomy tube, and oxygen. An intravenous pole is holding a bag of cream—colored tube feeding. The oxygen tube is attached to a green tank at the bedside. A spotlight shines on the bed and illuminates the scene. There are also two simple chairs, one on each side of the bed, but CARL and BETTY are not using them for the moment. The two siblings are standing and arguing with one another at the foot of the bed while HELEN lies motionless with her eyes closed.)

CARL: I won't do it anymore!

BETTY: The heck you won't!

CARL: No, I'm done with all this. What are we doing here? Look at her. She's already half dead. We're keeping her alive with tubes and fluids, something you insisted on I might add. And we've spent hours and hours, not to mention thousands of dollars, to keep mother here artificially alive in her own home. For what? For whom? It's a disgrace!

BETTY: You ungrateful little spoiled brat! Mother slaved over us. She raised us when our good-for-nothing dad was out gallivanting around. You had asthma so bad she had to stay up nights to sit at your bedside with a nebulizer. Now you would deny her a few hours of your precious time and a few dollars from your inheritance. What an ungrateful, nasty, lazy slacker. There's no other word for it.

CARL: Are you done?

BETTY: No! I'm not done. You just want mother to die so you can buy that beachfront cottage, or that Lexus SUV, or retire a few months earlier from your cushy job.

CARL: I'm sorry, but I won't feel guilty anymore. I don't know why you do, but I don't. Not any more. And as far as the hypothetical inheritance goes, there's not going to be anything left. And I don't care. Give it away to charity if you like. It would do more good than this. *(Gestures to the bed with the tubes.)*

BETTY: Charity begins at home, in case you've forgotten.

(HELEN moans and moves a little.)

BETTY: Now see what you've done. She's awake and in pain and it's your fault.

CARL: *(Walks over and adjusts the pillow.)* She's suffering because you want her to, and I don't know why. I'd like to help her get some peace.

BETTY: Hypocrite! Leave! Go back to your yuppie wife and kids and your high paying job that mom helped you get by slaving to put you through college. I'll take care of Mother even if it kills me. She's not going to be abandoned and she's not going to any nursing home to rot away like a piece of meat. Not while I'm alive.

CARL: That's a cheap shot about college and the job. You know I worked hard to get where I am. Don't cheapen it because you're unemployed by choice. Who's taking advantage of whom, anyway? Besides, you're not eating, you're not sleeping and you're worrying yourself to death. If you don't start taking better care of yourself, then it becomes my problem anyway, doesn't it? Do you want to die before mom does?

BETTY: I'd rather die taking care of my own mother than live one day thinking I did not do my duty.

CARL: Duty? To whom? To mother? To yourself? To dad? To God?

BETTY: I don't know. *(Sits down in the bedside chair on her side of the bed and takes HELEN's hand.)* I just know I couldn't live with myself if I didn't do this. I know it in my heart. Maybe that's where you and I are different.

CARL: What? I don't have a heart? *(Pauses. Looks at HELEN.)* No, I guess I don't. Not for this. *(Looks at BETYY.)* Why don't you hire someone to sit here with her? Or let me hire some people, day and night if you like?

BETTY: Don't bother spending your hard earned money just to soothe your guilty conscience. Just leave. I'll be fine. Go!

CARL: Guilty conscience! Someone feels guilty here, but it's not me. *(Looks at HELEN in the bed. Shakes his head.)* I'm going. But I'll be back. We're not done with this discussion.

BETTY: Yes we are. Right now. Get out! Get out of here. *(Goes to CARL and pushes him backwards.)* Get out of here! You're not helping her and you're sure not helping me.

CARL: *(Grabs BETTY by her wrists and holds her.)* Stop it. Stop screaming. And stop pushing me around. You could get away with that when we were kids, big sister, but not now. Not any more.

BETTY: *(Continues screaming.)* Get out! Get out!

CARL: *(Releases BETTY and steps back.)* I'm going. But it's not over. What you're doing here is wrong. Wrong for mother. Wrong for me. And wrong for you. In your heart of hearts, you know I'm right, too.

BETTY: *(Covers her ears and screams to cover the sound of CARL's voice.)* Get out and stay out! Leave us alone!

CARL: *(Turns and walks away.)* I'll be back. She's not going away and I'm not going away either. Not yet, anyway.

(CARL exits. BETTY waits in silence. BETTY goes over to sit in one of the chairs by HELEN's bedside where she slumps over on the bed and falls asleep.)

SCENE II

(Music starts to play, rather loudly. It's Scott Joplin's "Maple Leaf Rag." BETTY continues to sleep, but HELEN, dressed in a gown and with white socks, jumps out of bed and dances. She does the Charleston step in an animated way. She looks very much alive and well. After a few minutes of her solo, the music fades and she walks stage forward. The light follows her and leaves BETTY and the bed in semi-obscurity.)

HELEN: That was a heck of song. Fred and I used to go dancing down at the Crystal Club before he started messing around. They had this big, crystal ball that hung down from the ceiling and spun around. It flashed lights all over the place. People were smoking and drinking and dancing. It was wonderful, magical. And Fred was such a good dancer. He could do the foxtrot, rumba, cha-cha-cha, tango, and even the waltz and polka. My, that man could dance. He always told me that a man who could dance was more precious to a woman than a diamond ring. And that there were ten women who wanted to dance for every man who could. He liked those odds very much. *(Looks around off stage and yells.)* Come on, Fred! Come on in and say hello to the folks. Where is that man?

FRED: *(Dressed in a rumpled dark suit and tie, FRED comes on stage. Looks around at the stage and the audience.)* I'm coming. You don't have shout to raise the dead.

HELEN: *(Takes FRED's hand, and then embraces him. They exchange a kiss and a short hug.)* Raise the dead. Now that's a good one. You've been dead and gone ten years and you still look good. The suit looks great, Fred. It's from Berkshire's, isn't it. A little wrinkled, but not too bad.

FRED: Yeah. *(Turns around.)* Everyone thought I looked great in it.

HELEN: Especially Margaret Foreman. That little hussy!

FRED: Now, now. That was a long time ago. She's long dead, too. Don't you ever forget anything?

HELEN: Some things a woman can't forget, or forgive. I never understood how you could do something like that while you had a wife and two children at home?

FRED: Don't get riled up. It's not a question of wives or children, it's just human nature.

HELEN: Animal nature is more like it.

FRED: Margaret flattered me. She made me feel special, attractive.

HELEN: And I didn't make you feel special and attractive?

FRED: Sure, but not in the same way. Margaret loved to laugh. She never wanted a deep, meaningful relationship, only a little fun.

HELEN: And we never had fun? Not even dancing?

FRED: You're a much better dancer. Poor Margaret couldn't put one foot in front of the other.

HELEN: So what was the attraction?

FRED: I'm just a superficial person. No depth of feeling, no philosophical streak, no philanthropic aspirations. And Margaret thought that was fine. She and I were comfortable together, uninspired and uninspiring, just what you always held against me. I still loved you, but I felt like I was never quite living up to your expectations, even when I brought home the check.

HELEN: I was your wife, for heaven's sake. You weren't paying me off. I raised your children and washed your clothes, and slept with you. What difference did it make that I wanted more for you than you wanted for yourself? Is that crime? Did I deserve infidelity for that? Especially from that woman?

FRED: No, it was not a crime. But it was hard on me too, that's all. I could put up with the bad job, the long hours, the mediocre pay, but the weight of your expectations just got to me after awhile. I know you meant well, but so did Margaret, in her own way.

HELEN: Don't talk to me about that little two-timer.

FRED: Can't you just try to forgive and forget?

HELEN: Not infidelity! Not as long as I'm still alive.

FRED: *(Looks over at the empty bed with the tubes hanging out.)* Looks like you're not doing a very good job of it.

HELEN: I'm in a sort of coma, but I'm still hanging in there.

FRED: Yeah, by a thread. *(Walks closer to the bed and picks up the feeding tube.)* This stuff keeps you alive?

HELEN: Yes, tube feeding, and Betty's single minded will power.

FRED: She was always a strong willed child. Like you.

HELEN: Strong willed. Yes, but what good did it do me?

FRED: Don't be so hard on yourself. You kept the family together against all odds. I certainly didn't help much, did I?

HELEN: You did what you could, I suppose.

FRED: Just not up to your expectations.

HELEN: No.

FRED: And is Betty living up to your expectations now? She sacrificed her accounting job and social life in Austin just to stay here next to you. That's pretty noble, isn't it?

HELEN: *(Looks at BETTY, who is still slumped over the bed in sleep.)* I suppose so. It's just that I would like her to have some happiness, too. She's sacrificing herself for me.

FRED: I still think it's pretty darn noble of her, isn't it?

HELEN: Noble, yes, but maybe not the best thing for her or for me. I don't know. I just don't know anymore. Things seemed so simple and straight forward before. But now, lying in that bed. Unable to talk or clean myself or eat on my own. Is it really so obvious?

FRED: I dunno. That's all too complicated and philosophical for me. Wanna dance?

HELEN: *(Looks at herself and at FRED.)* You really think I'm dressed for a ball?

FRED: You're just perfect. You're wearing a gown, aren't you?

HELEN: Yeah, a crummy hospital gown, with my rear end showing behind.

FRED: *(Takes a look.)* I kinda like it that way. Come on, let's dance. *(Takes HELEN's hand in dance position.)*

(The "Blue Danube Waltz" comes on with its familiar tune. FRED bows. HELEN curtsies. When the musical introduction ends, the couple twirls around the stage a few times. The music fades. Mother goes back to bed and attaches her oxygen. Only the oxygen tube needs to be replaced on HELEN's face. The other tubes, for feeding and the Foley catheter, simply lead into the bed. HELEN just needs to pull the covers back over herself. FRED walks backwards off stage. FRED waves to HELEN as he leaves and she waves back.)

SCENE III

(DORIS, the home health nurse, walks on to the stage. DORIS pulls apart some imagined curtains to let in the light. The lights focus on the bed. BETTY wakes up and shakes her head while DORIS checks the various tubes.)

DORIS: Rise and shine sleepy head.

BETTY: *(Rubs her head and straightens her hair and clothes.)* Doris? You're here already? *(Looking at her watch)* What time is it, anyway?

DORIS: It's already 7:30, Miss Betty. *(Continues to check the tubes and looks under the covers at HELEN. Checks HELEN's heels and buttocks for breakdown.)* Now, let's take a look, Mrs. Hampton. Any breakdown? No. Nothing at all. Everything looks good and pink. *(Checks in the adult diaper.)* Ah oh, there's a little accident. We got to get you cleaned up, young lady.

(DORIS goes through the motions of removing the diaper, wiping off the buttocks and cleaning the bed. She rolls HELEN over on her side, then rolls up the bottom sheet on one side, then rolls the patient back and takes out the old sheet. The process is reversed to put on a new sheet. And the diaper is replaced.)

BETTY: You can call her Helen or Miss Helen if you like. You certainly know her well enough.

DORIS: No, Miss Betty, I was taught by my parents to always address my elders by their proper name. And you and I both know that Mrs. Hampton is older than me. *(Empties the urine bag into a graduated container.)* About 1,500 milliliters of urine in the last twenty-four hours. That's not bad at all.

BETTY: *(Takes a book from the bedside table.)* It's less than yesterday by about 300 milliliters.

DORIS: That sound's right. But that's only a small difference. She's still got a great urine output. You only worry if it really drops off.

BETTY: What should her urine output be?

DORIS: At least twenty cc's an hour.

BETTY: *(Jots that down in her little book.)* That's good to know. It's precise, something I can verify and keep track of.

DORIS: My gosh, Miss Betty. If you keep on like this, you'll become a regular nurse.

BETTY: *(Finally stands and helps DORIS adjust HELEN's sheets.)* Doris?

DORIS: Yes, Miss Betty?

BETTY: My brother thinks we ought to stop the tube feeding. He thinks it's cruel to keep mother alive like this. What do you think?

DORIS: *(Stops and looks at BETTY.)* I can't answer that question. That's something that the patient and the family have to decide.

BETTY: And if she were your mother?

DORIS: I really can't answer that question.

BETTY: Why?

DORIS: You can't take care of someone and decide what's best for them at the same time. You need some distance.

BETTY: Why? I would think you know more about the problem.

DORIS: That's just it. I'd be too close to the problem. You gotta have that distance. How could I decide what's best when I get all choked up about everything? It would be my mama, not just my patient. Do you understand what I'm trying say? It's complicated.

BETTY: I see. *(Looks back at HELEN with her tubes.)* But how can I know if I'm doing the right thing?

DORIS: I dunno. *(Changes the pillow case and adjusts the pillow.)* My cousin had a little boy with cerebral palsy. Poor little thing. He was just as cute and bright as could be, but he had this twisted up and deformed body. Such a pity. He couldn't sit up. He could talk, but it was all slurred and funny sounding. The doctors knew he was smart. He just had a bad body from brain damage at birth. *(Stops working.)* My cousin took care of that boy at home until he was nearly 15 years old. He lived a lot longer than the doctors thought he would. Then he died of pneumonia. He just couldn't cough right. At the funeral, my cousin cried and cried like her heart would break even though the preacher told us all he was in a better place with Jesus. The preacher said the boy would get a new body, a perfect body, a spiritual body. But my cousin just cried and kept crying for weeks. She said she would never get over it. And that it just wasn't natural to have to bury your own children. During all the time she was taking care of that boy, her husband left her. Then her two other kids grew up and moved as far away as they could get. They loved their brother in their own way, but he took all of their mother's time and energy. She loved them all, but there's only so many hours in a day to spread around. Now she's alone. She doesn't even know what to do. It's like some part of her died with that little boy and that part didn't make it to Jesus.

BETTY: Do you admire her for taking care of her little boy like that?

DORIS: I dunno. One part of me admired her for her dedication and all, and another part of me felt sorry for her husband and the other kids. I wondered why she would devote that much love and effort to a little boy who was going to die when the rest of the family needed her too? Fifteen years is an awful long time. A lifetime. Too long for me, Miss Betty.

BETTY: Do you think my mother is going to live another fifteen years?

312

DORIS: Never can tell. I see some folks like this in the nursing home who've had their tube feedings for ten years. *(Looks at HELEN.)* What did your mother want you to do?

BETTY: That's the problem. I don't know. We never talked about it. We did a lot of arguing back when I was younger. Then I went away to school. Then I was busy at work. Too busy, I guess. Too busy for myself, too busy for mom. Then, and all of sudden, she had this stroke. My brother said she'd have wanted to go peacefully, but I made the decision to have Dr. Franklin put in the feeding tube. I didn't want her to starve to death for heaven's sake.

DORIS: It's tough to see someone die from starvation. The worst case I ever saw was this old man who could still talk a little. But he couldn't swallow. So the family decided to put in a feeding tube, then they decided it was a mistake and wouldn't use it. That old guy kept saying he was hungry and thirsty, so we put Coke down the tube. No food, just Coke. He dwindled away real slow. And up to the end he keeps talking about being hungry with this tube sticking out of his stomach. I felt real bad about that one.

BETTY: Did he suffer?

DORIS: Not that I can tell. He just faded away. It was sad. That was a nice family and you could tell they all took it hard. They loved him, but they just couldn't figure out what to do.

BETTY: *(Checks the book again.)* This is only her first bowel movement in two days. Can we get something from Dr. Franklin? I think she should have at least one BM everyday.

DORIS: Not too loose. If you get diarrhea and the skin breaks down, that can be horrible, too. I saw this one paraplegic with a bedsore in his buttocks that was the size of dinner plate and went right down to his spine.

BETTY: No, we don't want that. But we need something for her bowels anyway.

DORIS: Right, Miss Betty. I'll ask.

BETTY: And what about physical therapy?

DORIS: I think she's too far gone for that, but I'll ask Dr. Franklin. They can evaluate her. I'll call the office and let him know. And you can ask him any other questions when you see him in the office.

BETTY: Thanks, I really do appreciate your help.

(Lights dim to dark.)

SCENE IV

(The two chairs are pulled forward by the actors. This is the doctor's office. The bed with HELEN remains, but she is in the semi-darkness. DR. FRANKLIN, dressed in a white lab coat and a tie, comes over to greet BETTY.)

DR. FRANKLIN: Nice to see you, Miss Hampton. Have a seat.

BETTY: Thank you. Please call me Betty.

(They both sit in the chairs they have pulled up from the bedside.)

DR. FRANKLIN: How can I help you today?

BETTY: It's mother. She's not looking very well lately. I'm concerned about her bowel movements, her urine output, and her bladder catheter.

DR. FRANKLIN: What about her catheter?

BETTY: Don't you think that the catheter can cause a urinary tract infection?

DR. FRANKLIN: Yes, of course it can, but if you pull it out, she will certainly be incontinent and that can cause awful bedsores.

BETTY: What about her lungs?

DR. FRANKLIN: She can't cough anymore, so her secretions just stay there and build up. Patients in her condition get bronchitis or pneumonia very easily. It's their leading cause of death.

BETTY: And her bowel movements?

DR. FRANKLIN: Too much or too little?

BETTY: Both. Sometimes she has diarrhea and sometimes she's constipated. We just can't seem to get it right.

DR. FRANKLIN: That's common with patients who are getting tube feedings.

BETTY: Do you think she's doing all right?

DR. FRANKLIN: She's doing as well as can be expected for someone in her condition. How are you doing?

BETTY: I'm okay.

DR. FRANKLIN: You look tired.

BETTY: I'm not. I'm really not tired at all.

DR. FRANKLIN: How many hours of sleep are you getting?

BETTY: Enough! And this isn't about me anyway. It's about mother, isn't it?

DR. FRANKLIN: Of course, but you don't want to get sick. If you do, who will take care of your mother?

BETTY: Not my brother. That's for sure.

DR. FRANKLIN: Why do you say that?

BETTY: Because he's washed his hands of the problem. He finds time for his wife, his kids, his job and his charitable boards, but not for his own mother. He just wants to lead his own selfish life and let mother die in some stinking nursing home. Can you believe such ingratitude?

DR. FRANKLIN: Perhaps he's not as strong as you.

BETTY: Strong? No, he's not. He's weak and spineless and heartless and usually full of crap, if you want to know the truth.

DR. FRANKLIN: That's harsh.

BETTY: Harsh? What would you say if your sibling left you to make all the decisions and do all the work?

DR. FRANKLIN: Has he really done that? Or do you just disagree with his conclusions?

BETTY: *(Pauses and sighs.)* I don't know.

DR. FRANKLIN: Maybe you ought to give him a chance. It can't be easy for him either.

BETTY: Easy? Who's got the cushy job and the gorgeous, devoted spouse, and the brilliant, well-mannered children? He's a spoiled brat. And I'm the one doing everything for mother.

DR. FRANKLIN: Perhaps you're being too hard on yourself and your brother?

BETTY: Mother's worth it. She raised us almost single handed. Dad spent most of the time away with his job. And that's before he started . . . . *(Trails off without completing the sentence.)* Then he up and died when I was only twelve. After that, mother did it all. She worked, kept house, helped with homework and never missed a softball game. She slaved so Carl and I could go the university. She's a saint. That's all. She's a saint. And saints don't deserve to be abandoned like old, sick dogs that can't hold their urine anymore. Dad let her down, Carl wants to let her down, but I'm not going to. *(Looks at DR. FRANKLIN.)* Do you think she's suffering?

DR. FRANKLIN: I don't think so.

BETTY: Do you think she feels pain?

DR. FRANKLIN: I think she can feel pain, but probably not recognize it as such like we do.

BETTY: How can you tell for sure?

DR. FRANKLIN: There's no way to be absolutely sure. Medicine is sometimes as much of an art as a science.

BETTY: I would hate it if she were having pain. I would hate myself for causing it.

DR. FRANKLIN: Why would you hate yourself?

BETTY: I caused mother so much pain for so long. I said such hateful things to her. It would kill me if I were just doing all of this for my own selfish reasons. Do you think I'm selfish?

DR. FRANKLIN: No, I don't think you're selfish. I think you hurt to see your mother like this. I think your head may tell you some things while your heart tells you something else. I think you need to put them in harmony.

BETTY: Put them in harmony. It sounds easy, but it's not. *(Pauses and sighs.)* Can she hear us when we talk around her?

DR. FRANKLIN: I don't know for sure. Perhaps she can. But I doubt whether she understands what's she's hearing. Too much brain damage for that.

BETTY: Can we still get her something for her bowels?

DR. FRANKLIN: Of course. I'll talk to Doris about it. But you have to promise me to get some rest. Promise?

BETTY: I'll try.

SCENE V

(The stage darkens and the light shifts to HELEN's bed. BETTY and DR. FRANKLIN pull their chairs back to the bedside and leave the stage. HELEN sits up and throws off the covers as she disconnects her oxygen mask. The other tubes stay in the bed.)

HELEN: Hear them? My gosh. With all that complaining and bellyaching, who couldn't hear them? *(Looks around, then steps forward toward the audience.)* Yes, I worked. I helped with homework. I did the heavy chores. And yes, I attended my share of soccer games and soft ball tournaments. And don't forget those endless social studies projects. Boy, did we do some really great projects, Carl and I. It was a pleasure to work with him. Such a pleasant boy, intelligent, clever with his hands, inquisitive and very tender with me. *(Pauses.)* Now Betty. She was something else. Wild, rebellious, even a bit violent at times. Once she buried all her Barbie dolls in the back yard. I never did figure that one out. When she reached adolescence, I thought an atomic bomb went off inside of her. She wouldn't talk to me. She only yelled. She told me she hated me and that she wanted to run away and never come home. I heard all her insults and it broke my heart, it did. She calmed down when she went away to college. Now look at her. Have you ever seen a more devoted daughter? *(Looks over at BETTY.)* Funny thing was that she adored her father . . . the louse. She got this idea into her head about how he was some sort of henpecked martyr. Martyr, my eye! He did more than fill orders when he traveled. I stayed at home and worked while he gallivanted around. Good heavens. *(Pauses.)* And Betty just adored him. He could be sweet with her, too. Like the time he took her to see Peter Pan, the musical. After the play, they went to one of these fancy pastry shops on Powell Street and ate éclairs while sipping tea. Tea! Fred hated tea and he hated the theater, too. Maybe she knew all along he was just doing it for her, but she never told me so. No, no. *(Pause)* She would always ask when he was coming home. And if she could wait up a little longer to see him at night. Or could she call him at his hotel. Yeah, sure, as if I knew what number to reach him or when he really intended on coming home, if ever. Oh well. I guess he paid for his crimes. Death is a pretty high price, although I was told he died painlessly. The coroner said he had a heart defect, a bad rhythm, or something like that. His heart just went too fast, then stopped and he ran his car smack dab into a concrete overpass piling. A bad heart, eh? I could have told the coroner that. *(Pauses and shakes her head.)* And that was that. He was dead. The problem was that Betty blamed me for his death. Somehow, she thought I was responsible for his dying, for not loving him enough, the devil. *(Shaking her head in silence.)* She finally got the real picture. After she went to college, she started asking questions. One spring break, she just asked me point blank if Fred had been cheating on me. I still don't know exactly how she got wind of it. Maybe a friend at college told her something. I know I didn't have to tell her anything, but I did. I wanted to. As I was telling her, I looked at Betty's face and I could almost see her image of her father transforming from martyr to monster. *(Looks at the audience.)* Hey, she wanted to know! And I wanted to set the record straight about Fred. *(Looks around the stage.)* Speaking of Fred, I wonder where he is now. *(Yells offstage.)* Fred! Fred! Where the heck are you? Come over here right now! *(FRED makes his way on stage.)* Now what kind of mischief are you up to now?

FRED: *(Adjusts his pants and pulls up the zipper.)* I'm coming. I'm coming. Good heaven's, woman, you just think I've got nothing to do but wait for you to call me day or night.

HELEN: You haven't changed a bit, have you? Can you stop thinking about yourself and your own pleasure and think about your family for once? Have you seen what Betty looks like lately?

FRED: Yes, she looks pretty ragged. Do you think she's getting enough sleep?

HELEN: No.

FRED: Won't Carl help her a little?

HELEN: Yes, but why should he? He's got a wife, kids, a good job. He already volunteers on a half a dozen charitable boards, United Way, the symphony, the art museum. What would he accomplish sitting and worrying over an old, shell of woman who just won't die?

FRED: *(Looks up and down at HELEN.)* For an old, shell of a woman, you look pretty good to me. *(Pinches HELEN and she pulls away.)*

HELEN: Stop it, you old lecher! We're talking about Betty.

FRED: She'll be okay. She's a strong girl, a smart girl. Like you.

HELEN: But she's all worn out.

FRED: You're the one who's worn out, not Betty.

HELEN: What will she do when I'm gone?

FRED: Betty will grieve. You'll leave a void in her life, but she'll fill it.

HELEN: Yeah, like you. You filled a lot of voids.

FRED: Maybe. But I never considered myself indispensable. Betty will get over it. She might even reconcile with Carl and transfer some of that time and attention to her nephews and nieces.

HELEN: Fat chance!

FRED: You never know. Why don't you give her some credit? She just might forgive and forget whatever real or imagined sin Carl's committing against you.

HELEN: Forgive and forget? That stuff again? *(Pauses, then steps forward and adjusts FRED's tie.)*

FRED: Why did you tell Betty about Margaret Foreman and the others? You didn't have to.

HELEN: *(Steps back, obviously taken off guard by the question.)* She wanted to know what you were really like, that's all.

FRED: Was it so wrong to let her believe I was a decent man who worked hard and supported the family he loved?

HELEN: *(With some anger in her voice.)* The truth! She wanted the truth and I gave it to her. There's nothing wrong with that either.

FRED: You poisoned a young woman's mind against the memory of her own father because you were mad at me. Isn't that really it?

HELEN: You sanctimonious hypocrite! I didn't poison anyone. You poisoned me with your fooling around.

FRED: You could have left her in blissful ignorance. I was dead already. What harm could it have done?

HELEN: Because I was angry at you. I was so angry I wanted Betty to know . . . everything. I waited until she was old enough and she asked. She wanted to know. She asked and I told her, that's all.

FRED: Did she really want to know? Or did you just want to punish me, even in death?

HELEN: You're a real work of art, Fred Hampton. You can still twist things all around, can't you? You can make me look like the bad one even when you were guilty of sleeping around. Don't tell me you're superficial, because it's not true. You're deep and you're devious.

(A lively ballroom mazurka starts to play.)

FRED: That's a mazurka. Remember that one? We used to dance it at the vintage dance balls down in Lafayette. Great dance. *(Extends his arms out.)* For old times sake?

HELEN: *(Shakes her head, but takes FRED's arms.)* You old devil. You can be a real charmer when you want to be. I know why Betty and I loved you so much.

(The couple dances a spirited mazurka with long, traveling steps. They make several turns around the floor until FRED deposits HELEN back in her bed. FRED dances off alone and HELEN puts herself back in bed and pulls the top sheet over and adjusts the oxygen.)

SCENE VI

(BETTY comes in and sits at the bedside. BETTY takes her notation book and makes a few entries. DORIS comes in after knocking on an imaginary door.)

DORIS: Anyone home?

BETTY: Yes, we're here. Come on in.

DORIS: How are you doing today?

BETTY: Okay.

DORIS: And how's our young lady?

BETTY: She's fine.

DORIS: *(Takes the temperature. Checks the tubes, listens to the heart and abdomen, and then jots a few notes her book.)* Can I sit down?

BETTY: Sure, have a seat. *(Checking her book.)* Mother's at thirty-five cc's per hour urine output. That's good isn't it?

DORIS: Right on target.

BETTY: She had two soft BM's since yesterday.

DORIS: That's good.

(Knock at the door. CARL enters. He holds some adult diapers.)

DORIS: How are you doing?

CARL: Fine. Thanks for asking. How's mother?

DORIS: She's doing as well as can be expected.

BETTY: Why do you bother asking, anyway? I thought you didn't want to be troubled with mother anymore.

CARL: Don't be ridiculous.

BETTY: *(Stands up to confront CARL.)* I may be ridiculous, but at least I'm compassionate.

CARL: Compassionate?

(CARL looks over at DORIS and then pulls BETTY downstage, where they are arguing loudly enough to be heard by both the audience and DORIS.)

CARL: Keeping a proud, independent woman like a vegetable in the garden. You call that compassion? What kind of life it this? What sort of twisted ideas run through your guilty head, anyway?

BETTY: Guilty! You little, spoiled brat. Mother always did prefer you, but I'm the one who's sticking with her now, not you. Go on! Get out of here! Leave us alone. Run out on her like dad did. Get out!

CARL: You twisted bitch!

BETTY: You selfish, low-life bastard!

CARL: Yeah? So if I'm a bastard, who was the father? And what does that make our saintly mother? Think a little before you open your big stupid mouth!

DORIS: Shhhh! Could you two tone it down a notch?

CARL and BETTY: *(Both turning to face DORIS who is still seated with her book in hand.)* NO!

CARL: *(Turns on DORIS.)* You're just part of the problem. You're an accessory to the crime with Dr. Franklin and my sister. What is this? A perverted science experiment to see how long you can keep some old lady alive? Is that it?

BETTY: You leave her alone, you monster. Doris is an angel.

CARL: Some angel. An angel of death, making sure the poor victims are totally used up, destroyed, just like you'll be if you keep going like you are. Where's the quality of life here for Mother, or for you? What are we doing? Are you doing this for Mother or for yourself?

BETTY: Mother, of course.

CARL: Really? Isn't part of this about making up for living away in Austin all these years? We were both busy. We both had lives. Was that a crime?

BETTY: Maybe it was a crime. Maybe our priorities were all mixed up.

CARL: And if they were all backwards? *(Takes the feeding tube with his hand.)* Does keeping Mother alive with this make up for it?

BETTY: Maybe it does.

CARL: Not in my mind, it doesn't. Think quality here. Think about it.

BETTY: This is all I do think about, damn it. You might think this is easy on me, but it's not. This is killing me, too. I suffer with mother. Every moan, ever grimace, every spasm shoots through me like a hot poker. I feel helpless and that's killing me, too.

CARL: I know.

DORIS: *(To CARL.)* Perhaps you ought to go in and talk with Dr. Franklin. He might address some of your concerns.

BETTY: Yes, go ahead and see Dr. Franklin. And now you can leave. I don't need any more soul searching to add to my misery. You're torturing me. Can you just try and be part of the solution and not just another part of the problem?

CARL: I'm going, but remember that you might be part of the problem, too. *(To DORIS.)* And I will be seeing Dr. Franklin. If you won't stop this nightmare, perhaps I'll have to do it by myself.

BETTY: Stop your threats and leave, please. You're not helping.

CARL: I'm trying the only way I can.

BETTY: So am I.

(The lights dim and CARL takes the two chairs and pulls them stage forward.)

SCENE VII

(DR. FRANKLIN's office. The two chairs are now pulled up to the forward stage. CARL is seated in the chair on stage right. FRANKLIN, dressed in his tie and white lab coat, comes and extends his hand to CARL.)

DR. FRANKLIN: Nice to see you Mr. Hampton. Doris told me you might be in.

CARL: Nice to meet you. Call me Carl.

DR. FRANKLIN: What can I do for you?

CARL: It's about my mother. Let me get to the point. She's got no quality of life. And I can't stand to see her that way. We're prolonging her suffering for what I consider our own selfish reasons. Do we have to go on with all these feedings? Is it some sort of legal thing?

DR. FRANKLIN: No, it's not a legal problem and we don't have to continue.

CARL: Then why are we? I hate to be blunt, but are you making money off this? Do you own the home health service or something?

DR. FRANKLIN: Despite what you may think, and what you suggested to Doris, this is not some inhuman science experiment as you called it. Although I do earn a fee for supervising your mother's care, that is not my motivation. I think you know that you are being unfair.

CARL: I'm sorry. I'm just upset and this is getting on my nerves.

DR. FRANKLIN: I know you and your sister are both under a lot of stress, but Betty wants me to continue the feedings. If that were not the case, we could convert your mother to comfort care status, get her switched to hospice, and stop the feedings. She'd dwindle away and die peacefully.

326

CARL: Would that hurt? Would she suffer?

DR. FRANKLIN: No, we think in terms of ourselves. But she has brain damage. She'd just dwindle away.

CARL: Starving to death?

DR. FRANKLIN: It's not painful. Nature will take its course in someone who can no longer eat on their own.

CARL: Can we do it? Stop the feeding?

DR. FRANKLIN: Anytime, but you and your sister must agree. You can't have one person in the family fighting with another. It's not worth having that kind of disruption and conflict. Your mother would surely not have wanted to be the source of a bitter controversy between her own children. And you don't want a legacy of bitterness to poison your relationship with your sister.

CARL: That's already poisoned. I don't know from what, but Betty's bitter and full of guilt and I really don't know why. You are right about Mother, she certainly would not want us fighting. She never did. *(Looks at FRANKLIN.)* She really wanted us to get along. As kids, we did, you know. We had a lot of fun together. Then something happened as we got older. The more I succeeded my own life, the more Betty seemed to resent me.

DR. FRANKLIN: That often happens with siblings. But Betyy does seem to sincerely care about your mother.

CARL: Care? I don't know who she thinks she's really caring for? It's like she can't let go of something deep inside. *(Pauses.)* Am I some sort of monster to want nature to take its course with my mother?

DR. FRANKLIN: I don't think so. But death is so final. No one knows what, if anything, lies beyond. It's odd, but I've seen believers and non-believers approach death either with dread or total serenity. Their religious feelings didn't seem to matter much.

CARL: And what do you believe?

DR. FRANKLIN: It doesn't matter what I believe. This is a family decision.

CARL: But it does. Here you have all this power in your hands, in your pen. You can send some patients to life and some to death with a stroke of your pen. Such power must be intoxicating.

DR. FRANKLIN: It's a huge responsibility. It's an enormous weight. I had this old man one time and I was trying to help the daughter decide whether to put him on a breathing machine or not. He was lying there on the bed between us and I'm trying to convince the daughter not to be overly aggressive. And he's dying right in the bed between us.

CARL: What did she do?

DR. FRANKLIN: She decided to intubate her father and, against my better judgment, we did it. *(Pauses.)* Two months later he walked out of the hospital, and now three years later I still see him in the office as an outpatient. And every time I see him, I think about what I tried to do. I tried to convince his daughter to let him die. And she refused. And she was right.

CARL: You can't be God. You can't foresee the future.

DR. FRANKLIN: No, I can't foresee the future. But I still have the power of life and death over people. It's an awesome power. And I do feel like God sometimes. And sometimes it takes a Betty to drag me back to earth.

CARL: So you think that mother is going to wake up and walk around someday?

DR. FRANKLIN: No, not in her case, I don't. But I do make mistakes, as much as I would like to avoid them.

CARL: Strive not to be as gods, for mortal aims befit moral men. The Greeks wrote that over 2500 years ago.

DR. FRANKLIN: Wise men, those Greeks.

CARL: Would you talk to my sister?

DR. FRANKLIN: Why don't you both come back next week? Tuesday at 10:30? Would that be okay?

CARL: We'll both be here even if I have to drag Betty in.

DR. FRANKLIN: She needs to come voluntarily. This needs to be a family decision. No fighting.

(Each man picks up his chair and places it back at the bedside. Then they leave by opposite sides of the stage.)

SCENE VIII

(HELEN hops out of the bed and scurries to center stage.)

HELEN: Things are certainly heating up, aren't they? Dr. Franklin is right. I hate to see those kids fight. When they were young children, they were inseparable. They played for hours in the yard, building forts, and castles, whatever. I don't know what happened. *(Pause.)* Maybe it was my fault? Maybe Betty felt left out when I spent so much time with Carl? You can't hide that sort of thing from children, you know. You try to love them all equally. But you can't help having your favorite. It's just human nature. During her high school years, Betty said she hated me and wouldn't ever come back home once she left. *(Pauses.)* Then I started to get three phone calls a week from college. Mama could you do this and Mama could you send that. *(Pauses.)* It's funny how kids are different. Carl went off to college and stayed months at a time without calling. I had to blackmail him into calling at least once a month. My darling little boy, he just drifted away gradually. I guess it's natural, but it still breaks your heart when it's happening. Now, look at them, fighting like cats and dogs over a no good lump of rotten meat. If I could, I'd get up and spank both of them. *(Pauses.)* Well, maybe just give them a little swat. And then I'd hug them both so hard it would make their ribs ache. Just once. One more time. *(Sighs and looks around.)* Now where's that Fred gone to when I need him? Fred! Fred Hampton!

FRED: *(Comes in from offstage.)* Calm down, dear. You're going to bring down the house with all that yelling.

HELEN: Bring down the house. *(Looks around her.)* Some house.

FRED: It was a good house. We had some great times in this house.

HELEN: A good house, eh? Broken water pipes. Termites. A leaking roof. All those weekends here alone with the kids, just trying to figure out how to make ends meet.

FRED: Sure, there was that, but what about those great birthday parties. Remember that one when I dressed up in a dinosaur suit. And you made a dinosaur cake with green frosting. It was wild, and the kids loved it. *(Pokes at HELEN.)* It was fun. Admit it. We had some real fun.

HELEN: Yes we did.

FRED: Or remember that trip to the city to see the opera, Carmen. Good heavens, I don't know how you ever got me to go to an opera.

HELEN: It was our tenth wedding anniversary.

FRED: Oh yeah, I forgot.

HELEN: You always forgot. But that time I wouldn't let you forget.

FRED: That time, I'm glad you didn't. Remember that dinner at the Four Seasons, the meal that cost a whole week's salary. Man it was good. Fresh asparagus soup with crab. Venison and wild cranberries. And that amazing dessert tray. And don't forget that wonderful cabernet sauvignon. *(Rubs his hands and smiles.)* Remember all those waiters hovering around. They even put your napkins back on your lap when you got finished going to the bathroom. What a hoot!

HELEN: And the opera. It was beautiful. Admit it.

FRED: Okay. I'll admit it. I was sure I'd hate it all, but the music swept me away, just like you did so many years ago. In the end, when Carmen refuses to submit to Don José and he kills her, I cried. I actually cried. I thought of you the whole time, so proud, so defiant, and so independent, even to the bitter end.

HELEN: And you were my Don José, all right, killing me with your infidelity and indifference.

FRED: Unfaithful, perhaps. Indifferent? Never! I was always in awe of you, Helen. Overwhelmed then and still now. *(Pauses.)*

HELEN: Wouldn't it be nice to see that opera again. Come on. Grab your chair. Let's go to see Carmen, just the two of us.

FRED: You're kidding.

HELEN: No. *(Goes and gets the chairs and sets them downstage facing obliquely toward the audience.)* Remember the scene with Carmen in prison. She was there and she was singing to Don José about the inn under the ramparts. She's beautiful, irresistible. And she can't stand to be locked up in prison. Not with her free spirit.

> *(HELEN sits FRED in the chair and stands boldly in front of him. The music begins, loud and beautiful. HELEN mimes Carmen's beautiful song, in French "Près des remparts de Seville . . . ." etc. Beckons to Fred. That particular music is a*

slow, seductive waltz and the couple turns as the music continues, and then fades. HELEN gets back in bed. She waves to FRED as he walks offstage.)

SCENE IX

(BETTY and CARL readjust the two chairs to create Dr. FRANKLIN's office. BETTY sits down, but CARL remains standing in back of her chair.)

BETTY: So how are your children doing?

CARL: Fine, thanks for asking.

BETTY: Is your youngest still at Yale?

CARL: Actually at Princeton.

BETTY: Yes, of course. It's so hard to keep all those prestigious Eastern schools straight. And still in the Glee Club?

CARL: Yes.

BETTY: Did you see him in the school's big production again this year?

CARL: Yes, we did, and it was a wonderful performance. They did Broadway hits. *(Sighs and looks at BETTY.)* Are you really interested?

BETTY: I'm trying to be civil. That's all. Just civil.

(An uncomfortable pause.)

CARL: Have you seen the Impressionist exhibit at the museum?

BETTY: No, I've had other things on my mind.

CARL: I could take over for you here for a few hours and let you go check out the exhibit?

BETTY: A few hours from your busy schedule telling rich people how to invest their money?

CARL: Yes, and I'd be glad to do it. It's a great exhibit and you need to get your mind off mother.

BETTY: I'm sure it's a wonderful exhibit. You were always sensitive to the visual arts. At least you're sensitive to something.

CARL: I'm trying, too. So please work with me here.

BETTY: I am working, too, for both of us.

(CARL begins to say something, but stops.)

DR. FRANKLIN: *(Dressed in his usual professional best, enters with an energetic step.)* Betty, Carl, nice to see you both. Sorry about the delay.

BETTY: No problem. We were just catching up. Nice to see you.

CARL: *(Shakes hands with FRANKLIN.)* Nice to see you again, doctor.

DR. FRANKLIN: *(Sits down in the free chair and faces BETTY and CARL.)* Can I get you a chair, Carl?

CARL: No, thanks. I'll stand. I've been sitting all day.

DR. FRANKLIN: I know you're here to talk about your mother.

(CARL and BETTY nod in agreement.)

DR. FRANKLIN: As you see yourselves, she has not shown any signs of improvement over the last months since we put in the feeding tube. In fact, I find her less responsive, even to painful stimuli.

BETTY: (*To FRANKLIN.*) Painful stimuli? Are you hurting her?

DR. FRANKLIN: No, of course not. Doris just gives her a small pinch over the breast bone. Usually that will cause the patient to draw up their arms. In your mother's case, she moves them outward. That's a very primitive reflex and indicates loss of most cortical function.

CARL: What does that mean?

DR. FRANKLIN: That her brain stem is functioning, so she keeps breathing and her heart and guts still work, but she can't think or feel anymore like you or I.

BETTY: Will she ever get better?

DR. FRANKLIN: No, she won't. What you see is what you get.

BETTY: I've read about these cases where someone's been in a coma for years and then wakes up and asks for a Coke. Why not mother?

DR. FRANKLIN: (*After a long silence.*) She's not going to wake up. She is not going to get better. She will get pneumonia or a urinary tract infection or a bad bed sore or heaven knows what other complication. Every patient in her clinical condition gets deathly ill, it just depends on when. Then, they ultimately expire.

BETTY: When?

DR. FRANKLIN: I don't know. Weeks? Months? Years?

CARL: This could go on for years?

DR. FRANKLIN: With excellent medical care, yes.

CARL: (*To BETTY.*) We can't do that to her. We can't let her sit there and rot.

BETTY: We? You speak for both us now? *(To FRANKLIN.)* If she were your mother, what would you do?

DR. FRANKLIN: *(To BETTY.)* Doctors should never treat their own family. I can't answer that question any more than Doris could when you asked her.

BETTY: She told you about our conversation?

DR. FRANKLIN: Yes, of course. As the treating physician, the nurses and nursing aides always inform me of the patient's health and of the family's concerns as well. It's normal.

BETTY: So if you can't treat your own mother, what if she were a perfect stranger?

DR. FRANKLIN: I'd stop the feedings, put her under hospice care, and continue making her as comfortable as medically possible. Betty, I see dozens of these patients in the nursing homes. They get started on tube feedings and then they may live for years. Their muscles contract and waste away so the patients get all twisted up and deformed. They can't talk. They can't move. But they can feel pain. It breaks my heart to see people like that month after month, year after year. We're all getting older. Someday there won't be enough nursing home beds to hold us all if it keeps going like this. *(Pauses.)* Now at least we have hospice. And they only give comfort care. They don't force feedings. They don't send the patients back and forth to the hospital. Doris works for hospice, too, you know. She could continue to help your mother die with dignity.

BETTY: Die with dignity? That's still death, isn't it?

DR. FRANKLIN: Yes, it is still death.

BETTY: And what gives you or Carl and me the right to choose between life and death for my mother?

DR. FRANKLIN: Because your mother can't decide anymore.

BETTY: So doesn't that make us all the more responsible? Shouldn't we be all the more certain that we are not just snuffing out a life because it is inconvenient, or expensive, or just unnecessary?

CARL: Betty, please. Get off your moral high horse and look at the reality down here. Mother's a vegetable, not a person. She's a plant that we're giving food and water to so she continues to survive for our own selfish ends.

BETTY: Selfish! Who's selfish here? You, the one who can't see mother suffer? Or me, who has the courage and conviction to stand by her in her most vulnerable hour?

CARL: Don't be ridiculous. Why are you doing this? Dr. Franklin and I are trying to help end this useless suffering.

BETTY: Stop it! Stop spouting this drivel! You're trying to kill her because . . . . *(Stops.)*

DR. FRANKLIN: *(To BETTY.)* Killing is forbidden by the Hippocratic Oath. But letting nature take its course is not.

BETTY: Nature! What's natural about starvation? What's natural about euthanasia? What's natural abut two men ganging up on a helpless, old woman and snuffing out her life?

DR. FRANKLIN: *(To BETTY.)* Please get a hold of yourself. No one is talking about euthanasia here.

BETTY: *(Yells at FRANKLIN.)* God! You're just playing God and you're so full of yourself that you don't even see it.

DR. FRANKLIN: Perhaps, but God shows mercy and compassion in the face of suffering. At least I hope he does.

BETTY: Do you? Is killing old ladies showing compassion?

CARL: Shut up! You're insulting the doctor and you're insulting me.

BETTY: You! I haven't even started on you. You're nothing more than the sorcerer's apprentice. You don't even have the balls to take the decision. You need to hide behind Dr. God here. Yes, you're his archangel lapdog. His ball-less little lap dog.

CARL: And you have the balls, eh? Is that it? Is that why you're still an unmarried old maid, or maybe a closet dike. Is that more like it?

BETTY: Shut up! Shut your mouth!

(BETTY lunges at CARL and begins to pound his chest. CARL does not resist, but keeps his hands and his sides.)

BETTY: You nasty, little bastard!

(BETTY continues to pound CARL, but her blows become weaker and weaker. Finally, BETTY stops and CARL puts his arms around her.)

CARL: Look at yourself. You're worn out. You're mentally and physically exhausted. I can't stand to lose mother and you at the same time. You're the only family I have and I do care about you. I want you to be happy. I'm sorry about what I just said.

BETTY: *(Backs up a little and looks at CARL.)* I don't want to lose mother either.

CARL: She'll still be there. In your heart and in my heart. *(Points to his head and heart.)*

BETTY: *(Manages a weak laugh.)* You always had a knack for such sentimental drivel.

CARL: And you have the hardest head of anyone I know, except perhaps mom.

BETTY: As hard as your heart?

CARL: You're head's harder by far.

DR. FRANKLIN: *(Had backed away during the confrontation, but now approaches BETTY and CARL.)* I'm sorry to push things along, but have you reached some sort of decision here?

BETTY: *(Turns to CARL.)* Can we make a decision now?

CARL: It's our decision, not Dr. Franklin's and not Mother's.

BETTY: Am I really being so selfish, so sanctimonious, and so unreasonable to want her to live?

CARL: No, you're not selfish, nor sanctimonious, nor unreasonable, big sister. I just think you're wrong.

BETTY: *(Laughs despite herself.)* My head tells me one thing, but my heart tells me another.

CARL: Don't listen! Hitler said: Seek me with your heart, not with your head and look how that worked out.

BETTY: Thanks for your erudition and the flattering comparison. You're really something else.

DR. FRANKLIN: Does this mean we continue with only comfort measures for your mother?

CARL: Betty? Can we agree?

BETTY: I'm tired. I guess I'm ready to see it end.

CARL: How do we know it will end? Maybe when one door closes, another opens.

BETTY: Maybe. *(Turns to FRANKLIN.)* Comfort care only.

DR. FRANKLIN: Comfort care only. No food. No water. No antibiotics.

CARL: At home or in a nursing home?

BETTY: No! No nursing home, please!

DR. FRANKLIN: Nurses can provide hospice services in the nursing home.

BETTY: No! No nursing home. I can bend, but that would break me. (*To CARL.*) I promised her she's never go into a nursing home.

CARL: She's already gone away. Her mind's gone and her body's going. Nursing home, home, what difference does it make at this point?

BETTY: It makes a difference to me. I'd like to continue treating her at home. Please let me have that concession. It won't affect either of you. Let me at least have that small concession.

CARL: That's so hard on you. It's wearing you out. It's a 24 hour a day job.

BETTY: That's okay. I know the consequences and I'm willing to accept them. Please let me keep her at home.

CARL: *(To FRANKLIN.)* It's okay with me to continue treating her at home if Betty insists. She knows what she's getting into and she knows what it's doing to her. I respect Betty for that, even if I don't agree.

DR. FRANKLIN: You'll both have to sign a DNR, a Do Not Resuscitate form.

BETTY: No resuscitation?

DR. FRANKLIN: No chest compressions or intubation when she stops breathing and her heart stops. We just keep her comfortable.

BETTY: She won't suffer, will she?

DR. FRANKLIN: No, I promise. She does not have to suffer and she will not.

BETTY: Please, give me your word. I can't stand the thought of her suffering.

DR. FRANKLIN: You have my word. She will not suffer.

(CARL takes BETTY's hand. She looks up at him and places her other hand on his. They look at one another for a moment. Then FRANKLIN and BETTY take their chairs and replace them beside HELEN's bedside. FRANKLIN, BETTY and CARL walk offstage. The light settles on HELEN's bed.)

SCENE X

HELEN: *(Hops out of bed.)* Now, isn't that a pretty picture. Screaming. Yelling. Insults. Tears. Yes, a very touching picture, indeed. And that doctor. What a sanctimonious hypocrite. I'm sure he's just tired of the whole business, except for the Medicare payments, of course. Betty sometimes hits the nail right on the head. Dr. Franklin thinks he is God. Dr. God. *(Imitates the doctor's intonations.)* You have my word. She won't suffer. *(Goes back to her own voice.)* Ha! What the heck does he know about my feelings? How does he know for sure, anyway? I have already suffered: strokes, a heart attack, gall bladder disease, arthritis. And the worst of all . . . . *(Pauses and looks around at the audience.)* Wanna guess? Of course! Having those two bundles of joy nearly ripping my body apart. Goodness gracious, I thought I would die. I never ever experienced that level of pain before or since. Betty, the first one's always worst, left me with a vaginal tear the size of a football field. At least if felt like that. Talk about pain and suffering! And Carl wasn't much better. That darn Ob-Gyn told me the second baby would be a piece of cake. Some cake! Carl decided to come out feet first and I was five minutes from having a caesarean. Oh, how I did scream.

(Shakes her head and looks around the audience.) Nowadays they give you ladies an epidural or just go ahead and do a caesarean for the heck of it. No pain, no suffering. Just a little inconvenience, scheduled for the best time of the week for the patient and the doctor. Back then . . . wow! *(Pauses and mimes holding a child in her arms.)* But what joy, too. I remember holding Betty in my arms, just after she was born. Such a tiny, wet, red, ugly looking thing. But so beautiful, too. And she cried and she cried and it broke my heart to hear her. I was so sad for her and so glad for her at the same time. Fred was there, too. He hung over me and he cried like a baby. There we were, all three of us crying at the same time. Even the doctor smiled and told us we were a lovely family with a beautiful baby. *(Pauses.)* When Carl came a couple of years later, he hardly ever cried as a baby. I would creep up at night and look in the crib, just to make sure he was still breathing. He'd wake up sometimes and just look at me with his big eyes and his baby smile. So cute, both of them. Now just look at those two, both college graduates in their fifties with good jobs and careers. Carl has his family, a nice wife and beautiful children. Well, actually young men and women now, already in college. How the time passes. *(Pause.)* So now they want to starve me to death. Me, the one who breast fed them both until my nipples almost fell out. That Carl nursed until he was almost one year old, and then went straight to solid food. Could they really starve me to death? Should they? Dr. Franklin said it doesn't hurt. And he says he wouldn't let me suffer. Maybe he's right. Maybe he knows what he's talking about. Maybe it is my time to go. Look at Betty, worn out with worry and fighting with Carl and everyone else. You saw her with that little book, marking down my pee and my poops. The poor girl. She's worn out and needs some rest too. Poor little thing. I need to take her in my arms and give her a warm hug. *(Extends out her arms in a gesture of comfort.)* There, there, Betty. You're tired and worn out. I know you're afraid to let me go, but you can do it. I think we've all suffered enough. I love you. I'll miss you. I won't forget you or Carl.

FRED: *(Approaches from behind and taps HELEN on her shoulder).* Over here, Helen.

HELEN: *(Spins around and shakes her finger.)* Oh you! Just like a bad penny.

FRED: You can hug me if you want to hug someone.

HELEN: You good for nothing vagabond.

FRED: Good for nothing, eh? Well I can remember some very good times. And part of me was good for something. We did have two children, didn't we? Remember?

HELEN: Oh, stop it!

FRED: No, I'm not stopping it. *(Pinches her.)*

HELEN: *(Struggles and giggles.)* Stop it, I said.

FRED: *(Stops pinching her and looks pensive.)* What do you think Betty and Carl are going to do?

HELEN: I don't know. *(Pauses and looks away, then back towards FRED.)* It can't be easy for them. How can you let someone die, especially your own mama? I can tell they're suffering, too. Betty wants so much to do the right thing. And Carl wants to please his mother, just like he always did. It's odd. They're grown-up people and they are just as confused and vulnerable as they were when they were little children. All this is hurting them. I know it is.

FRED: Then let go.

HELEN: I really want to. But then again, I don't. I'm just scared.

FRED: It's okay to die. I did, and look at me. *(Spins around with his arms extended out.)*

HELEN: So what's it like?

FRED: Look at your body, old and wrinkled and incontinent.

HELEN: *(Looks down at herself and shakes her head.)* Yeah, it's a sad sight.

FRED: Now imagine yourself new and whole. No pain. No hunger. No anxiety. Just peace.

HELEN: Can we still be friends?

FRED: Not friends, *(Pauses)* lovers. We can love each other so completely that it surpasses all understanding.

HELEN: Pretty philosophical for a superficial guy.

FRED: *(Smiles)* Thanks. I've been studying up in my spare time and I've had a lot of it.

HELEN: There's still something so final, so irreversible about death. I'm afraid.

FRED: Don't be.

HELEN: You went quick-like. Just one big bang and you were gone.

FRED: Yes, but that doesn't make any difference. *(Pauses.)* I miss you. I really miss you and want to care for you like I never could back then. You need that. You need affection and warmth. You deserve it.

HELEN: Warmth and affection? In the grave?

FRED: No, here, all around.

> *(FRED looks at HELEN a few moments and then takes her hand and leads her around. They do a very slow Czech circle dance, called "Louky." It has a haunting, melancholy melody and slow, graceful steps. Part of the dance is done as an open couple and part as a closed couple. FRED leads HELEN back to the bed. HELEN hesitates and shakes her head, but CARL insists. CARL gently sits her down and glides offstage as HELEN settles herself back in bed.)*

SCENE XI

(HELEN's in bed. BETTY is sitting on one side while CARL is sitting on the other. DORIS takes down the tube feeding and takes it away. Then DORIS comes back and stands in back of BETTY's chair.)

BETTY: So what do we do now?

DORIS: We wait.

CARL: How long?

DORIS: I don't know. No one knows.

BETTY: Can the doctor tell us?

DORIS: No. He says he's always wrong. He explained this to one family that when he says the patient will die in a few days, the person dies in a couple of hours. Or worse yet, they go on and on for weeks. So he never says anything about when patients are going to die anymore.

CARL: And what about you, what do you think?

DORIS: I think we should wait. It's only a matter of time. Nature will take its course.

(CARL and BETTY sit in the chairs while DORIS stands near the head of the bed. The lights go off for a few seconds, and then come on. All three have changed positions slightly, but obviously. This is repeated three times to evoke the passage of time. BETTY can be reading a book one time, then writing in her bedside notepad, or looking off into space. CARL can be daydreaming, then reading a magazine, or doing some paperwork. After the third time, the lights stay on and FRANKLIN enters, dressed as usual.)

DR. FRANKLIN: Hello Betty, hello Carl, hello Doris. *(Waves to DORIS who waves back. Goes over to the bed and takes HELEN's pulse. Listens to her heart and lungs.)*

BETTY: Any change?

DR. FRANKLIN: Her breathing's shallower and it's irregular now.

BETTY: What does that mean?

DR. FRANKLIN: It usually means that her brain stem function is slowing and that she will not live much longer. *(To DORIS.)* Does she still have the pain patch on?

DORIS: Yes, a fifty milligram patch.

BETTY: Is that too much? It won't stop her breathing, will it?

DR. FRANKLIN: No, it's perfect. *(To BETTY.)* Are you getting enough sleep?

CARL: *(Answers for BETTY)* Not really. She refused to leave the bedside.

BETTY: Yes, I'm fine.

CARL: I try to get her to leave, but she just won't. She's as stubborn as mother.

BETTY: I'm not stubborn; I'm just not going to abandon her. Dad did, but I'm not. Not this time.

CARL: *(To BETTY.)* Dad did the best he could. We're all just doing the best we can.

BETTY: *(Sighs)* I know you're right. But mom's best was so much better than us all combined.

DR. FRANKLIN: *(To HELEN)* A remarkable woman.

BETTY: You'd better believe it. *(Takes HELEN's hand.)* I'm here for you, mother. I'll stay here. I'm not tired. I just want to be here. That's okay, isn't it?

CARL: *(To BETTY.)* She can't hear you.

DR. FRANKLIN: She probably can hear us. But she can't understand the words. *(Advances toward HELEN. Touches her neck. Lifts the lids and looks at the pupils. Takes out his stethoscope and listens to the chest. Replaces the stethoscope in his lab coat pocket with a slow, deliberate gesture.)* She's gone. I'm sorry.

BETTY: Gone where?

DR. FRANKLIN: She's dead.

> *(BETTY looks surprised and then kisses HELEN's hand. CARL turns his back to the bed. Neither CARL nor BETTY cries. CARL stands with his hands crossed. DORIS advances and pulls the sheet over HELEN's face.)*

DR. FRANLIN. Have you chosen a funeral home?

BETTY: Ardoin's.

DORIS: I'll call Ardoin's and the coroner's office.

DR. FRANKLIN: Thanks. *(To BETTY and CARL.)* If either of you need anything, please call me.

> *(FRANKLIN walks off stage. CARL follows him without turning back to face his HELEN or BETTY. BETTY starts to move in CARL's direction, but stops and turns around. DORIS puts her hand on BETTY's shoulder and the two women walk off stage in the opposite direction from FRANKLIN and CARL.)*

SCENE XII

(The lights come back. HELEN's bed is illuminated. HELEN sits up, climbs out of bed, and starts spinning around the stage in graceful circles.)

HELEN: Gone! Gone! Gone! What are they all talking about? *(Spins around and holds her hands up.)* Gone! Gone! Gone! *(Laughs.)* I'm free! Free at last. No pain. No hunger. No stiffness. Free from that worn out piece of crap body, that stinking carcass. What a change! I'm not gone, I'm here. *(Looks around the empty stage and then looks at the audience.)* Betty and Carl have already left. I wanted to say goodbye at least. And thank them for all these months of torment and trouble. Such needless pain and suffering. *(Tilts her head to one side and thinks a moment.)* Maybe it was necessary somehow. I've read that pain is the breaking of the shell that encloses our understanding. Maybe it's true, but I think that understanding sometimes comes with too high a price tag. Then again, who am I to decide? *(Shakes her head.)* Too much thinking. Fred's right. Being superficial is the best. *(Twirls around again.)* Whee! Just look at me now. *(Again looks at the audience and addresses them in a calmer tone. Twirls around slowly and then stops and looks around the stage. Her face betrays anxiety. Shivers.)* I don't think this is a very warm place. In fact, it's pretty darn cold and lonely. *(Wanders around looking lost and frightened.)* Fred! Fred! Oh, for heaven's sake, where is that man when you need him? He promised to be here and now I'm all alone as usual. Where is that man?

FRED: *(Walks in from offstage. He is dressed in a white tuxedo, if one is available, if not he can wear snow-white pajamas.)* Now calm down.

HELEN: *(Sighs with relief.)* Finally. What am I supposed to do now?

FRED: First, are you ready to leave?

HELEN: Of course I'm ready.

FRED: And to forgive and forget?

HELEN: *(Frowns, looks back at the bed, then sighs.)* Yes, I suppose so.

FRED: Even Margaret, the hussy?

HELEN: *(Pauses.)* Yes.

FRED: And me?

HELEN: *(Pauses again and smiles.)* Yes, even you.

FRED: That's good. I like the "forgive and forget" part.

HELEN: It's more than you deserve, but I'm not doing it for you or for Margaret Foreman.

FRED: And for whom are you doing it, may I ask?

HELEN: For myself, of course.

FRED: *(Nods his head in agreement and then extends his hand.)* Mrs. Hampton. May I have the honor?

HELEN: Of course, Mr. Hampton. I think our job here is done. It's time to go. *(Takes FRED's hand and holds it up in front of them.)*

> *(The music which begins is a stately Quaker hymn, "Simple Gifts" from Aaron Copeland's Appalachian Spring dance suite. The couple parades around the stage. He has his arm outstretched and her hand is resting on his. They march around once in a regal way and exit. Lights dim to dark and the curtain, if there is one, closes.)*

THE END

CHILDREN'S PLAYS

OLD MAN KNOWITALL
AND THE THREE GOLDEN HAIRS

(BASED ON A CZECH FOLK TALE)

CAST OF CHARACTERS

NARRATOR

KING

WOODMAN

WOODMAN'S WIFE

FIRST OLD WOMAN

SECOND OLD WOMAN

THIRD OLD WOMAN

FISHERMAN

QUEEN

BOATMAN

MAN BY THE MAGIC TREE

MAN BY THE MAGIC WELL

KNOWITALL'S WIFE

KNOWITALL (THE SUN)

NARRATOR: Once upon a time there was a king in a distant land who loved to hunt. He had gone far into the forest and was lost when he came across the hut of woodsman and his wife. He knocked on the door and the woodsman answered.

WOODSMAN: Who is it?

KING: I am a hunter who has lost his way. Could I stay in your home tonight? Tomorrow I will find my way home.

WOODSMAN: Yes, certainly. But my wife has just had a baby and we will be unable to entertain you at this time. Please come in and share our humble cottage.

> (*The KING enters and sees the WOODMAN'S WIFE with the new born baby. The WOODMAN'S WIFE places the child in a cradle.*)

WOODMAN'S WIFE: I'm afraid you must share the room with our new born child. But he seems to be a good baby and I hope he will not cry. Please lie down here on a blanket and make yourself as comfortable as possible.

NARRATOR: The King lies down and the couple leaves. The King goes to sleep, but wakes when three old women come in and bend over the cradle. He pretends to be asleep, but he is really listening.

FIRST OLD WOMAN: This child will know many dangers.

SECOND OLD WOMAN: Yes, but he will survive them all and live happily to a very old age.

THIRD OLD WOMAN: He will grow up to marry the daughter of the King who is now sleeping in this house.

> (*They circle around the cradle, casting their spells, then leave. The KING sits up when the OLD WOMEN leave and faces the audience.*)

KING: This son of a wood cutter cannot grow up to marry my daughter, the princess. She is only a few days old and must marry a prince when her time comes. This baby must die. I will take him and throw him into the river where he will drown. (*Picks up the cradle and steals out of the hut. Leaves a few golden coins in the hut as an afterthought.*) This money should help them overcome their grief.

NARRATOR: The wicked King threw the cradle into the river, but the child did not die. A fisherman found the cradle and he and his wife raised the child as their own. They called him "Ondin" after the waves that brought him to their hut. Twenty years passed, and the baby grew up into a fine and handsome young man. By chance, the King happened to be hunting in that part of the country and stopped to get a drink of water at the fisherman's hut. It was Ondin who brought him the water. The sight of the handsome youth startled the King.

KING: (*To the FISHERMAN.*) Is that young man your son?

FISHERMAN: Yes and no. We have raised him like our son, but I really fished him and his cradle out of the river twenty years ago. He is a handsome youth, isn't he?

KING: (*To the audience.*) This must be the same boy I threw into the river so many years ago. He did not die. But he must not live to marry my daughter. I will send him to the palace with a note saying that he must be killed as soon as he arrives because he is a dangerous traitor.

KING: (*To the FISHERMAN.*) Call your son. I need him to take an urgent message to the palace to give to the Queen. (*Scribbles a note on a paper and gives it to ONDIN.*) Take this message to the Queen in the palace and make sure you do not read it or give it to anyone else.

ONDIN: Yes, Your Majesty.

NARRATOR: Ondin set off for the palace. But while crossing the woods he became hopelessly lost. He finally came across a little house in the middle of the woods. The owner of the house was none other than the third old woman who had predicted his marriage to the King's daughter.

ONDIN: (*Knocks on the door.*) Hello. Anyone home?

OLD WOMAN: Yes, young man. Can I help you?

ONDIN: I am lost and night is coming. Can I stay in your house until dawn? Then I can find my way to the palace. I have an important message for the Queen.

OLD WOMAN: Please, come in and rest. Lie down and sleep before you set off tomorrow. I have a comfortable corner here for you.

NARRATOR: Ondin went to sleep. But while he slept, the old enchantress took the message and changed it with a new one.

(*OLD WOMAN takes the message, reads it, and exchanges it for another.*)

NARRATOR: In the morning, Ondin woke up, but the house and the old lady were both gone. He continued his trip to the palace.

(*ONDIN enters the palace and is escorted to the QUEEN. Next to her is her lovely daughter, the PRINCESS.*)

ONDIN: Your Highness, the King has sent me with this urgent message.

QUEEN: (*Opens and reads*) "It is my command that my daughter marry the young man who bears this message today. This must be completed urgently, before my return to the palace." (*Turns to the PRINCESS.*) You must be married today to this young man. It is your father's command. Let's make the necessary preparations now.

(*All leave the stage*)

NARRATOR: A few days later the King comes back to the palace. He is surprised to see the young man still alive and holding his daughter's hand.

KING: And what is this?

QUEEN: This is your new son-in-law.

KING: What? How did this happen?

QUEEN: We received your message that they were to be married before you returned to the palace.

KING: (*Turning to ONDIN.*) Did you stop anywhere before coming to the palace?

ONDIN: Yes, I stayed at the hut of a very old lady. But it was so strange because in the morning she and her house had disappeared.

NARRATOR: The King recognized the words of the old woman who had predicted the marriage of his daughter to the baby Ondin. But he vowed that he would still be rid of his new son-in-law one way or the other.

KING: You may be married, but I still want you to bring me a gift for my daughter. I want nothing less than three hairs from the head of Old Man Knowitall.

ONDIN: Who is he? And how will I find him?

KING: That's your problem. (*The KING leaves with the QUEEN and the PRINCESS.*)

NARRATOR: Poor Ondin really didn't know where to go, but he started off bravely and after many days came to a great lake. At the edge sat a man with a boat who passed people from one shore to the other.

ONDIN: Hello. I'm looking for Old Man Knowitall. Can you help me?

BOATMAN: Thanks be to God! You will be the one who finally will tell me how to get out of this boat. For twenty years I have been condemned to pass people from one shore to the next. Only Old Man Knowitall knows how I can stop. I will take you across and show you the way. But you must promise to get the secret from Old Man Knowitall.

ONDIN: Of course. But first get me across and show me the way.

NARRATOR: Ondin continued on his route until he came to a man sitting beneath a dead looking tree.

ONDIN: Hello. I'm looking for Old Man Knowitall. I need three golden hairs from his head.

MAN: Thanks be to God. You are the one who can find out how to bring my tree back to life. It is a magic apple tree. And whoever eats the apples will not grow old. But twenty years ago it ceased to bear fruit and has been barren ever since. Only Old Man Knowitall knows how to bring it back to life. Can you help me?

ONDIN: Yes, of course. But show me the way to the palace of Old Man Knowitall.

NARRATOR: Ondin continued his journey until he came to a man who was sitting next to a well with an empty bucket.

ONDIN: Hello friend. I am looking for the Old Man Knowitall to get three golden hairs from his head.

MAN: Thanks be to God. For twenty years my well has run dry. It was a magic well. Whoever drank the water would be cured from whatever disease aided him. Now it is dry. Only Old Man Knowitall knows how to make it fill up again. Will you help me if I show you the way?

ONDIN: Sure, just show me the way to Old Man Knowitall's palace.

NARRATOR: Ondin finally arrived at the glorious palace of Old Man Knowitall. He was not there, but his wife was. She was a kind and good woman.

ONDIN: I have come to get three golden hairs from the head of Old Man Knowitall.

KNOWITALL'S WIFE: Young man, I will help you, but it is not as easy as that. My husband is the sun. He starts each day as a child, and ends each day as an old man with golden hair. He does not give his hair up easily. Not only that, no human can look upon him and survive. You will be burned up if you do not hide. Get in this chest and I will try my best to get you three hairs.

ONDIN: I have also promised to get the answers to three questions to help my friends.

KNOWITALL'S WIFE: What are these three questions?

ONDIN: What must the boatman do to stop having to pass people from one shore to the next? How can the tree with the apples of youth be made to bear fruit again? And what must be done so that water will flow into the well with the healing waters?

KNOWITALL'S WIFE: I will try and ask. But please, hurry into this chest and hide yourself before my husband gets here.

NARRATOR: The brilliant, but tired sun arrives after a hard day. His wife makes him comfortable and he falls asleep. While he is sleeping, his wife pulls out a golden hair. He wakes suddenly.

THE SUN: Ouch! You've pulled out a hair.

HIS WIFE: Yes. I had a dream of a boatman who was condemned to cross a lake forever until the spell is broken. The dream bothered me greatly and I woke with a start.

THE SUN: Nothing easier. He only has to pass his oars to someone else and jump to the shore. (*The SUN falls asleep.*)

NARRATOR: His wife pulls out a second hair.

THE SUN: Ouch! Are you crazy?

HIS WIFE: No, my love. I just had another bad dream about a tree with magical apples that no longer gives fruit and it bothered me greatly.

THE SUN: Oh, that. There is a serpent that has a nest in the roots and sucks out the sap. All they have to do is transplant the tree and kill the serpent.

NARRATOR: The sun sleeps again, and for the last time, his wife pulls out a golden hair.

THE SUN: Good grief woman! I'll be bald before the night is up. What is it?

THE WIFE: I dreamed of a well with magical water that is dry. It used to heal the sick but does so no longer.

THE SUN: Oh, that. Nothing easier. A giant toad sits in the well and blocks the water. They must kill the toad and the water will flow again. Now let me sleep.

NARRATOR: So the night went by and the sun got up to start a new day as a shining youth. When he had left, Ondin got out of the chest to thank Knowitall's wife and take the golden hairs.

ONDIN: Thank you good woman. I have heard everything and will tell the others what they must do. You have been very kind and generous with me. (*Leaves.*)

NARRATOR: Ondin returned on his way, and each time he shared the secrets he learned with each of the men. And each time he was richly rewarded.

ONDIN: (*Greeting the MAN by the well.*) Hello friend. Your well will fill with magic water after you kill the great toad that is sitting in the hole in the bottom.

THE MAN: Thank you so much. Here, take this bag of gold and jewels in reward. It is the least I can do.

ONDIN: (*Greeting the MAN by the dried up tree.*) Hello friend. To make your tree bear fruit again, you must dig it up and kill the serpent which lives at the root and sucks out the sap. Then it will bear apples again.

THE MAN: Oh thank you. Here, take these bags of gold and silver. It is the least I can do for you.

ONDIN: (*Arrives at the BOATMAN.*) Boatman, take me across and I shall tell you the secret to end your service on the lake.

(*The BOATMAN takes ONDIN across. ONDIN jumps on the shore with his bags of riches.*)

ONDIN: When the next man comes to cross the lake, you hand him the oars and jump out onto the shore. Then he will have to take people across until he learns the secret.

BOATMAN: Thank you so much. I can hardly wait.

NARRATOR: Ondin finally arrived at the palace. His wife and mother in law were glad to meet him, but the King was not. Ondin presented the King with the three golden hairs from Old Man Knowitall and the bags full of gold and jewels.

ONDIN: Your Majesty, here are the three golden hairs. Plus, I have caused the apple tree with the magic fruit to bloom again. Whoever eats those apples will have eternal youth. And I have caused the well with the magic water to fill again. Whoever drinks that water will be cured of all disease.

KING: I would like to eat those apples and drink that water. Tell me the way to go now.

ONDIN: First you must go to the great lake. There will be a man in a boat. You must ask him to take you across. From there it is easy to continue on to the magic tree, the magic well and the palace of Old Man Knowitall.

(The KING rushes offstage.)

NARRATOR: So Ondin and his bride lived happily every after. When the King never came back, Ondin was declared the new king. He ruled his kingdom long and well. And his father-in-law is probably still rowing people from one side of the great lake to the other to this day.

THE END

KENT HOUSE 1812

CAST OF CHARACTERS

LOUISE BAILLO: Daughter of the owners of Kent House. She speaks with a very slight French accent.

DESIREE LACOUR: Daughter of the LaCour family of Cane River, a light skinned mulatto, *gens de couleur libre* (free people of color.) She speaks with a pronounced French accent.

ALEXANDRA FULTON: Daughter of a local Alexandria merchant. She has an American accent, not British.

PATRICIA (PATTI) GOUDEAU: Louise Baillo's slave. She does not speak with a French accent, but more with a Southern rural accent.

SETTING

Garden party at the Kent House Plantation, circa 1812. The girls are dressed in period costumes. There is a table with plates, glasses, food and whatever evokes a young ladies' birthday party.

The four principal characters will be associated with up to 20 young girls who have come for Louise's birthday party. They play in the courtyard of the large house. The other girls can be a mixture of white, Creole or black and should reflect the diversity of the population at that time. The moment is a happy one, but the children are aware of the great changes which have occurred since the Louisiana Purchase and the menace of an impending war with Great Britain. One or several girls can share the four principle characters depending on the number of speaking parts required. The dances may be shortened or edited if necessary.

LOUISE: I would like to thank you all for coming to my birthday party. Mama told me to be a perfect hostess since I am all grown up

362

and to lead you all in games in the garden. (*Looks around the group*.) Now I think we should start by dividing up in groups to play a game. What do you think?

ALEXANDRA: (*Haughtily*.) I think all of the city girls should come with my group. We can be the real Americans.

DESIREE: What does that mean?

ALEXANDRA: I mean you and Louise are really French, so it stands to reason that the other girls need to come with me.

DESIREE: *Françaises*? Are we French? Why do you say that? My papa says that Napoleon sold us to the Americans. So we are not French, any more than you are. We are all Americans here, *n'est-ce pas* Louise?

LOUISE: *Bien sûr*. I mean, of course. We are as American as you and the others. We may speak with an accent, but we all belong to *la Louisiane* and *la Louisiane* belongs to the United States.

ALEXANDRA: Oh, you know what I mean. You still speak French with your parents at home and with each other. That makes you different. My father says we English speakers are the future and you are the past.

LOUISE: Very interesting. And what if my papa says you are the invaders and have come to bring exploitation and misery to this beautiful land. What of that?

ALEXANDRA: Exploitation? No, papa says we bring progress. How can you say we bring exploitation when you have Patricia here and she is your slave? This is real exploitation, isn't it?

LOUISE: She is not my slave. She is my friend. (*Takes PATRICIA's hand*.) We were both born on this very land. Patricia's parents have always had this plantation as their only home and they are treated with much kindness.

DESIREE: It is true! I have seen it. And my family's slaves are not so well treated as here at the Kent House. Our slave children cannot even play with me like Patricia plays with Louise. (*Takes PATRICIA's hand.*) Tell Alex that it is so. You are just like us.

PATRICIA: I am treated right nice and so are my parents.

ALEXANDRA: So you live in the big house, is that it?

PATRICA: Of course not, Miss Alexandra! That would not be right. We are still slaves and we know our place.

LOUISE: Patti knows how to read and write, just like me. Mama says that even *les noirs* can be educated and act like anyone else. Isn't that right, Patti?

PATRICIA: It's true. We go to mass and I can read the Bible in English to my parents and the other black folks in the cabins.

ALEXANDRA: You're not supposed to be able to read. I know that's the law. Louise Baillo, you are breaking the law and I should report you to the sheriff.

DESIREE: I read, too, in French and in English. I have a good education and I can even play on the piano. Is that against the law? After all, we are *les gens de couleur libres.*

ALEXANDRA: No, I don't suppose it's illegal for you. But you're free. You have always been free with those other people up in Cane River. Those are special black folks, with slaves and everything. Papa says some are even rich. And you're not really black anyway, you're all mixed up.

DESIREE: We are rich, richer than many poor white folks on either side of the Red River. So it's not the color, I suppose. It's probably just the money. If you're rich, you can read and if you're poor, you can't. (*Pauses.*) And besides, we were not always free. *Grandpère* and *Grandmère* bought my mother father and made us free when we were very little children.

LOUISE: Stop this bickering. That is all old history. This is supposed to be my day and I don't want any fighting. Everyone just make a circle and listen up. I'll teach you a French song. Repeat after me, *Sur le pont d'Avignon, on y danse, on y danse. Sur le pont d'Avignon, on y danse tous en rond.* Good. Now let's all walk to the left eight steps and back to the right eight steps while we sing together.

ALL THE GIRLS:

> *Sur le pont d'Avignon, on y danse, on y danse.*
> *Sur le pont d'Avignon, on y danse tous en rond.*

DESIREE: I know this one! Now, follow me! *(Sings.) Les beaux messieurs font comme ça. (Bows very low.) Et puis encore comme ça. (Bows very low.) Les belles dames font comme ça. (She curtsies). Et puis encore comme ça.* Now, everyone.

ALL THE GIRLS: *Les beaux messieurs font comme ça. (All bow very low.) Et puis encore comme ça. (All bow very low) Les belles dames font comme ça. (All curtsy.) Et puis encore comme ça. (All curtsy.)*

DESIREE: Good! Now everyone together from the beginning! To the right.

ALL THE GIRLS:

> *Sur le pont, d'Avignon, on y danse, on y danse.*
> *Sur le pont d'Avignon, on y danse tous en rond.*
>   *(Stop and face the center.)*
> *Les beaux messieurs font comme ça. (All bow.)*
> *Et puis encore comme ça. (All bow.)*
> *Les belles dames font comme ça. (All curtsy.)*
> *Et puis encore comme ça. (All curtsy. Then set off to the right*
>   *walking briskly).*
> *Sur le pont d'Avignon, on y danse, on y danse.*
> *Sur le pont d'Avignon, on y danse tous en rond. (All stop and*
>   *clap with pleasure.)*

ALEXANDRA: That was fun. What does it mean, anyway?

LOUISE: It's about a bridge in France at Avignon.

ALEXANDRA: Where's that?

DESIREE: France? Or Avignon?

ALEXANDRA: I know where France is, silly. That's were Napoleon lives. I mean Avignon, where is that?

LOUISE: Somewhere in the south of France. Papa says there's a broken bridge there and a palace for the popes when they lived in France.

ALEXANDRA: My father says the pope lives in Rome in Italy, not in France. And that you can't be American and follow the pope at the same time.

LOUISE and DESIREE: That's silly. We are just as American as you.

ALEXANDRA: Okay. Let's not talk about that anymore. My mother says real ladies don't discuss politics or religion. Anyway, let's do an American dance now.

LOUISE and DESIREE: We are American!

ALEXANDRA: Okay, okay. I mean in English. I think everyone knows this one, The Mulberry Bush.

ALL: (*Everyone nods. Form one large or several small circles and start off to the left eight skipping steps and return to right with eight skipping steps.*)

> Here we go round The Mulberry Bush, the Mulberry Bush,
>   the Mulberry Bush,
> Here we go round The Mulberry Bush so early in the morning.

This is the way we scrub our clothes, we scrub our clothes, we scrub our clothes,
This is the way we scrub our clothes, so early in the morning. (*All make exaggerated scrubbing gestures to accompany the song.*)

This is the way we hang our clothes, we hang our clothes, we hang our clothes,
This is the way we hang our clothes so early in the morning. (*All make exaggerated clothes hanging gestures.*)

This is the way we iron our clothes, iron our clothes, iron our clothes,
This is the way we iron our clothes, so early in the morning. (*All make exaggerated ironing gestures.*)

(*Repeat the refrain and the first figure.*)
Here we go round The Mulberry Bush, the Mulberry Bush, the Mulberry Bush,
Here we go round The Mulberry Bush so early in the morning.

PATRICIA: It's my turn now! I know a song that field slaves sing. Wanna learn?

ALEXANDRA: How do you know a song like that? You don't have to do that sort of work. Do you?

PATRICIA: No, of course not. My mama works in the big house and my papa works in the blacksmith shop. We're not field slaves, we're do-mes-tics. (*Pauses.*) But I do hear 'em singin' out there in the cotton fields beyond the bayou and in the cabins on Sunday. Wanna learn? It's fun.

(*ALEXANDRA, DESIREE AND LOUISE look skeptical.*)

DESIREE: I don't know if Mama would want us to learn field slave songs. Ours slaves up in Cane River can barely speak English or French. It doesn't seem right to me. It's not dignified.

LOUISE: (*To PATRICIA.*) Does your mama know you are learning songs like this? It might not be right.

PATRICIA: (*Looks around to make sure no adults are around.*) Ain't no adults around here that I sees, black or white. If I can learn to read, than you learnin' a song is not goin' to kill you. Here's how it goes. First, put your hands on your hips. When you say "jump," you jump in place. And when you say "turn around," you make a half turn around in two steps. And when you say "pick a bale of cotton," you stoop down like you were pickin' cotton. It's not hard. (*Sings and demonstrates.*)

> Gonna jump down, turn around, Pick a Bale of Cotton,
> Gonna jump down, turn around, Pick a Bale of Cotton,
> Gonna jump down, turn around, Pick a Bale of Cotton,
> Pick a bale a day.

See! That's not hard. Now everyone try.

ALL: Gonna jump down, turn around, Pick a Bale of Cotton,
Gonna jump down, turn around, Pick a Bale of Cotton,
Gonna jump down, turn around, Pick a Bale of Cotton,
Pick a bale a day.

PATRICIA: Good! But it's a lot harder than that to pick cotton. The field slaves have to fill them bags up and if they don't do a good job, it's not a pretty sight. That overseer is not nice like your folks, Miss Louise. He will use that whip like nobody's business. I seen it happen. (*Pauses.*) Anyway, now comes the chorus. You holds your hands up and shakes them while you turn half around in two steps when you says "Oh Lawdy." And then you acts like you're picking cotton when you says "Pick a bale a day." Got it?

ALEXANDRA: I don't know if I should be learning this sort of song. Papa says we should try and be as separate as possible from colored folks because God make us that way.

LOUISE: Oh, come on. We aren't that different at all. We just live in the big house and everyone else lives out here in back.

DESIREE: We are all in the same church and listen to the same mass, how different can we be?

ALEXANDRA: That's for Catholics, not us! We have one church for the whites and a different one for the blacks and the preacher says that's the way it should be. God made black and white people to be separate.

DESIREE: I'm not white or black but Créole. Do I have to stay separate, too? Which side do I go on? And to which one of your churches?

LOUISE: Well, we're not in anyone's church here, and it's my birthday party and if Patti's going to teach us this new song and dance, I think we ought to just go ahead and learn it. What do you all think about it?

ALL: (*Some hesitation, then girls nod and agree.*)

ALEXANDRA: All right. But don't tell my father or I'll have a spanking for sure. Okay.

ALL: (*Nod in agreement.*)

ALEXANDRA: Cross your hearts?

ALL: (*Some cross their hearts in an "X" and other use the Catholic sign of the cross.*)

PATRICIA: Ready?

ALL: Yes!

> Gonna jump down, turn around, Pick a Bale of Cotton,
> Gonna jump down, turn around, Pick a Bale of Cotton,
> Gonna jump down, turn around, Pick a Bale of Cotton,
> Pick a bale a day.

Oh Lawdy, Pick a Bale of Cotton,
Oh Lawdy, Pick a Bale of Cotton,
Oh Lawdy, Pick a Bale of Cotton,
Pick a bale a day.

(*The song and chorus and become increasingly wild, unrestrained and loud. Everyone laughs and enjoys themselves.*)

OFF STAGE VOICE: You girls quiet down out there! *Vous faites trop de bruit!*

ALL: (*Repeat once more, but very quietly, and then stop.*)

Gonna jump down, turn around, Pick a Bale of Cotton,
Gonna jump down, turn around, Pick a Bale of Cotton,
Gonna jump down, turn around, Pick a Bale of Cotton,
Pick a bale a day.

Oh Lawdy, Pick a Bale of Cotton,
Oh Lawdy, Pick a Bale of Cotton,
Oh Lawdy, Pick a Bale of Cotton,
Pick a bale a day.
(*All make a shushing sound with a finger pointed to their lips.*)

ALL: (*Sit down in a circle and fan themselves.*)

ALEXANDRA: You want to hear a secret?

ALL: (*Nod.*)

ALEXANDRA: I was listening to my father and he was talking about a war.

ALL: (*Look concerned and whisper.*)

LOUISE: War, with who? The French?

DESIREE: *Non, bien sûr que non.* We are friends with Napoleon. He sold Louisiana to President Jefferson. So why would he want to go to war with America?

ALEXANDRA: The British!

LOUISE: The red coats? We already fought them a long time ago. Why would they want to fight us again?

ALEXANDRA: My father says the British are just sore losers. They are attacking American ships and taking sailors. And he says that they really want to take America back because we are becoming too strong.

DESIREE: Maybe Napoleon can take us back and protect us?

ALEXANDRA: No, silly. He's off fighting in Europe. He doesn't have time for Louisiana anymore. Besides, he lost a whole army in Saint Domingue, at least that's what my papa said. And lots of French people came to New Orleans after that.

LOUISE: *Dommage.* I think it would be nice to be part of France again. (*Pauses.*) But we are Americans now.

ALEXANDRA: My father says it's just a matter of time before the British send a big army here to take Louisiana back. The British have been mad every since Napoleon sold Louisiana and it slipped right between their fingers.

PATRICIA: Do the British have slaves?

ALEXANDRA: I don't know. I don't think so.

PATRICIA: Maybe it would be all right if they took over Louisiana. Then the slaves would be free.

LOUISE: British have slaves! Monsieur McFarland visited our house last summer and talked about his plantations in the West Indies,

Jamaica or some place like that. (*To PATRICIA.*) I don't think it would be any better with the British or the French. Everyone has slaves. It's just the natural order of things.

DESIREE: Señor Castillo from Nagodoches visited my parents and said they did not have slaves in Mexico now, at least not very many.

PATRICIA: It doesn't seem that natural to me. Maybe Mexico will take over Louisiana.

DESIREE: The Spanish already had Louisiana for many years and the Mexicans are too weak and foolish to take us over. At least that's what papa told me.

LOUISE: Spain did rule us before for a long time. My grandfather got this land grant from Spain.

ALEXANDRA: That's old history and way too complicated. Who's afraid of the British, anyway?

ALL: (*Many girls raise their hands and speak at the same time.*) Me! Me! Moi!

LOUISE: Okay, enough talk of war. We're children. We don't have to worry about war.

DESIREE: It is scary.

LOUISE: Yes. But so are Yellow Fever and Malaria and smallpox and measles and all those terrible diseases. Look! We have all survived up until now and all those dangers are always around us. Too much talk about sickness. Let's dance and get our minds off these depressing thoughts. Okay. (*Claps.*) Line up with a partner in front of you and form two lines. Everyone knows "Skip to My Lou."

ALL: Yes, yes. (*They form two lines, parallel to the audience.*)

LOUISE: Okay, first skip forward in four steps, then skip back, then skip forward again and circle around with your right elbows. Ready?

(CHORUS)
Lou, Lou, skip to my Lou; (*four skipping steps forward and bow.*)
Lou, Lou, skip to My Lou; (*four skipping steps back and bow.*)
Lou, Lou, skip to my Lou; (*four skipping steps forward.*)
Skip to My Lou, my darling. (*Four skipping steps turning around with right elbow hold.*)

(*End couple on the right forms an arch and the other couples skip through and add to the arch. Eventually all the couple will go through and the partners separate and begin again.*)

Lost my partner, what'll I do? (*First couple skips through, forms arch.*)
Lost my partner, what'll I do? (*Second couple skips through, forms arch.*)
Lost my partner, what'll I do? (*Third couple skips through, forms arch.*)
Skip to My Lou, my darling. (*Fourth couple skips through, forms arch.*)

(CHORUS)
Lou, Lou, skip to My Lou; (*Fifth couple skips through, forms arch.*)
Lou, Lou, skip to My Lou; (*Sixth couple skips through, forms arch.*)
Lou, Lou, skip to My Lou; (*Seventh couple skips through, forms arch.*)
Skip to my Lou, my darling. (*Eighth couple skips through, forms arch.*)

(*Dancers separate and repeat the first back and forth figure.*)
I'll get another one, prettier than you;
I'll get another one, prettier than you;
I'll get another one, prettier than you;
Skip to My Lou, my darling.

(End couple does a polka step down the line of couples from right to left while the others clap in place. When the first couple reaches the end, they separate and clap in place.)

(CHORUS)
Lou, Lou, skip to My Lou; *(First couple polkas down.)*
Lou, Lou, skip to My Lou; *(Second couple polkas down.)*
Lou, Lou, skip to My Lou; *(Third couple polkas down.)*
Skip to My Lou, my darling. *(Fourth couple polkas down.)*

Gone again, skip to My Lou; *(Fifth couple polkas down.)*
Gone again, skip to My Lou; *(Sixth couple polkas down.)*
Gone again, skip to My Lou; *(Seventh couple polkas down.)*
Skip to My Lou, my darling. *(Eighth couple polkas down.)*

(Repeat the first figure to end the dance.)

Lou, Lou, skip to My Lou;
Lou, Lou, skip to My Lou;
Lou, Lou, skip to My Lou;
Skip to My Lou my darling.

ALL: *(Laugh and fall exhausted to the ground.)*

LOUISE: That was such fun, but I'm dead tired now.

DESIREE: Dead, dead, dead! Dead from fatigue. Dead from having babies. Dead for no reason at all. It gives me the creeps. Antoinette LeBrun died from the Yellow Fever, *la Fièvre Jaune,* just last month. She was a young girl, not much older than me. Then her two sisters died just after. We do not have to fear the British a thousand miles away. We need to be afraid of the Yellow Fever right here.

ALEXANDRA: Yellow Jack, they call it in New Orleans. When Yellow Jack is back, the rich folks come up river. That's what my papa says.

PATRICIA: No safety up here. That fever kills you if you be white, yellow, brown or black. No keeping folks apart in the grave.

ALEXANDRA: That's not true. They got separate places in the cemetery, just like in the church, at least in our cemetery.

DESIREE: Mama taught me a sad song and dance about someone who's died.

LOUISE: Can you teach us?

DESIREE: *Bien sûr.* Everyone take a partner. The words are in French, but it's the French from the Cajun folk down further South. Swing your arms forward and back, then turn around yourself. Come back together and repeat the swings, then turn around on yourself again and bow to your partner at the end. It's easy, *très facile. (Demonstrates the dance with PATRICIA. They join inside hands. It is a slow waltz step.)*

> *J'ai passé devant ta porte, (Swing arms forward and back and forward.)*
> *J'ai crié "Bye bye chérie," (Separate and turn on yourself in a circle.)*
> *Tu ne m'a pas répondu, (Swing arms forward and back and forward.)*
> *Oyyaie, mon coeur est malade. (Separate and turn on yourself and end by bowing to your partner.)*

DESIREE: Okay, now everyone try. Be real sad because Chérie is dead from the fever.

> *J'ai passé devant ta porte, (Swing arms forward and back and forward.)*
> *J'ai crié "Bye bye chérie," (Separate and turn on yourself in a circle.)*
> *Tu ne m'as pas répondu, (Swing arms forward and back and forward.)*
> *Oyyaie, mon coeur est malade. (Separate and turn on yourself and end by bowing to your partner.)*

ALEXANDRA: This is too sad. We need something happy, something American.

LOUISE, DESIREE and PATRICIA: We are Americans! All Americans!

ALEXANDRA: Okay, okay. We are all Americans.

DESIREE: Even the free people of color, us Creoles from Cane River?

ALEXANDRA: Yes.

PATRICIA: Even us slaves?

ALEXANDRA: (*Hesitates.*) Yes.

LOUISE: Even us French-speaking folks, the ones that were here before *les américains*?

ALEXANDRA: (*Hesitates.*) Yes, everyone. Now, no more sad songs, in French or English.

PATRICIA: I got a great song. Line up in a big line and take a partner.

ALL: (*Line up facing the audience.*)

PATRICIA: Everyone knows this one. It's a march and it comes from New Orleans.

> (*The couples form a line perpendicular to the audience. The couples march forward toward the audience. When they reach the front, they split in two and form two lines that march back away from the audience in a semi-circle. When the first couple meets up, they form an arch and each couple goes through and forms a new arch. When all the couples have gone through, the first couple grabs one hand and goes through the arched couples. Each couple follows. All the dancers form a circle and walk around clockwise. On the last couplet, the dancers form couples and dance a polka. When they stop, all bow toward the audience.*)

Oh, when the saints go marching in
Oh, when the saints go marching in
Lord, how I want to be in that number
When the saints go marching in

And when the sun refuse to shine
And when the sun refuse to shine
Lord, how I want to be in that number
When the sun refuse to shine

And when the moon turns red with blood
And when the moon turns red with blood
Lord, how I want to be in that number
When the moon turns red with blood

Oh, when the trumpet sounds its call
Oh, when the trumpet sounds its call
Lord, how I want to be in that number
When the trumpet sounds its call

Oh, when the new world is revealed
Oh, when the new world is revealed
Lord, how I want to be in that number
When the new world is revealed

Oh, when the saints go marching in
Oh, when the saints go marching in
Lord, how I want to be in that number
When the saints go marching in

THE END

ABOUT THE AUTHOR

Dr. David J. Holcombe was born in San Francisco and raised in the East Bay Area in the shadow of Mount Diablo (in Contra Costa County). He received a BSA from the University of California in 1971 and a MSA from the Institute of Food and Agricultural Sciences at the University of Florida in Gainesville in 1975. He subsequently graduated with an MD from the Catholic University of Louvain in Brussels, Belgium in 1981 and completed his residency in internal medicine at Johns-Hopkins University in 1986. After twenty years of work as an internist with a large multi-specialty group in Alexandria, Louisiana, Dr. Holcombe changed professional orientation and continued in public health.

During his academic training and subsequent professional career, Dr. Holcombe has continued to write, paint and folk dance. His self published works included *"Like Honored and Trusted Colleagues,"* *"Cappuccino at Podgorica,"* and *"Beauty and the Botox."* Eight of his short plays have been produced in the context of the Spectral Sisters Productions Ten Minute Play Festival in Alexandria. He and his wife, Nicole, live in Central Louisiana, where they contribute to the cultural life of the city and state. Dr. Holcombe regularly submits medical articles to local publications and serves as the volunteer Vice President and Medical Director for the Community Health Worx, a local free working people's clinic.